TIME AND REALITY

Studies in Contemporary Fiction

TIME
AND
REALITY

Studies
in Contemporary Fiction

by
MARGARET CHURCH

Chapel Hill
The University of North Carolina Press

PRINTED BY THE SEEMAN PRINTERY, DURHAM, N.C.
Manufactured in the United States of America

PREFACE

I wish to express my gratitude to the Purdue Research Foundation for two XL Grants that assisted me in the completion of this work and also for a publication subsidy for the book itself. I should like to thank the Ford Foundation for a grant extended through its program for assisting American university presses in the publication of works in the humanities and the social sciences. To the Carnegie Foundation for the Advancement of Teaching I am indebted for two grants that enabled this project to get underway in the summers of 1948 and 1949.

I am particularly indebted to the following people for help and for encouragement: at Purdue University to Professor Harold H. Watts; to Professor Barriss Mills; to Professor Robert L. Lowe; to Professor Dean B. Doner; to Professor Maurice Beebe; to Professor Helmut Gerber; to Professor and Mrs. Robert S. Hunting; to Professor Edith Weisskopf-Joelson.

At Duke University to the late Professor Newman I. White; to Professor William M. Blackburn; to Professor Charles Richard Sanders; to Professor Esther Schwerman; to Professor Grover Smith. At Ohio University to Professor Edward Stone. At The University of North Carolina at Chapel Hill to Professor Lucie Jessner.

Professor Heinz Politzer of the Department of German at the University of California has been of special help with suggestions for the chapter on Kafka.

My gratitude goes also to the Purdue University Library and its staff; to the Duke University Library and its staff, particularly Miss Florence Blakely; to the Harvard University Library, and to the Library of the University of Illinois. For assistance with typing I am indebted to Mrs. George L. Shaffer.

Portions of the following chapters appeared earlier in somewhat different form in journals: Chapters 1 and 6 in *The Bucknell Review*, Chapter 5 in *The Hopkins Review*, Chapters 3 and 4 in *Modern Fiction Studies*, Chapter 7 in *PMLA*, and Chapter 6 in *Twentieth Century Literature*. Permission to reproduce material in Chapters 4 and 5 that appeared originally in *College English* and material in Chapters 2 and 6 that appeared in *The Explicator* has been granted by the editors of these journals.

Lafayette, Indiana
January, 1963

CONTENTS

PART I

FRANCE

CHAPTER ONE

THE BIRTH OF AN IDEA:

BERGSON AND PROUST

The purpose of this book is to indicate how an author's concept of time influences the value and meaning of his novels. Therefore, the authors in this study have been selected not only for their significance and for their contribution to the subject of time but also for their contrasting qualities. Intentionally, English and American authors have been chosen who have been influenced by Bergson or by Proust or by both.* *La durée réelle* of Bergson and *la mémoire involontaire* of Proust act, as it were, as motifs in the book. Partly because of the influence of Bergson, the question of existentialist integration of subject and object may also be seen at the core of some of the discussions. For the German authors the source of this integration was not Bergson but Schopenhauer, Nietzsche, and Kierkegaard, who have provided a fertile source of contrasts. The section dealing with the German writers has been inserted between those sections dealing with English and American writers to emphasize these contrasts. And finally the work of

---

*Since the axis of this book is English and American literature, I have in quoting from French and German authors used translations when they have been available. When they have not been available, I have usually paraphrased in English or translated into English.

Sartre represents an important breaking away from the Bergsonian rationale and thus provides a fit conclusion. Two
authors, Joseph Conrad and Henry James, who both were
deeply concerned with the question of time, have been omitted
as outside the nucleus of those involved with Bergsonism.

The understanding of the form, content, thought, and motif
of fiction depends on the understanding of an author's attitude
toward time and space. Jean-Paul Sartre has stated that "the
critic's task is to bring out the author's metaphysic before
evaluating his technique."[1] And Georges Poulet in *Studies in
Human Time* sees "the essential effort of the critic to be that
of discerning the total meaning of a writer's work by paying
attention to his sense of man's temporality and place."[2] In turn,
an attitude toward time and space is conditioned by matters of
personal adjustment which this study will not explore, leaving
them rather to the social sciences. Let it suffice to say here that
a self-styled 'extravert' like the early Aldous Huxley finds a
reliance on the outer world of objects and events a necessity
whereas a man like Kafka retreats to an inner world where he
finds refuge from the very objects and events sought out by the
extravert. Time, therefore, for the early Huxley is clock time;
time for Kafka is the time of the dream where past, present,
and future have no meaning.

The novel as a whole reflects thus the author's attitude toward time. *Antic Hay* deals with the mores of London in the
twenties, contains a plot developed chronologically, satirizes
the unreason of the times, and has as a motif Gumbril's
patented trousers because for Huxley time is spatialized, whereas Kafka's *The Trial*, where time is seen as an inner affair, deals
with no particular time or place, describes a world where past,
present, and future are meaningless, explores the unreason of
life in general, and uses motifs from the dream world of the
author: courts, advocates, the room with the skylight. The basic

1. Jean-Paul Sartre, "Time in Faulkner: *The Sound and the Fury*," in
William Faulkner: Two Decades of Criticism, ed. Frederick J. Hoffman and
Olga W. Vickery (East Lansing, Michigan, 1951), p. 180.
2. Georges Poulet, *Studies in Human Time*, trans. Elliott Coleman (Baltimore, 1956), Translator's Preface.

difference here is that Huxley sees the outer world as separate from the observer whereas Kafka sees the outer world as meaningful only in terms of the observer.

Rarely does an author follow with any consistency the dictates of a particular philosophy, nor should he, for art is more than the expounding of an aesthetics or a metaphysics. A philosophy appeals to an author because latently he has already adjusted to it; thus he takes from it what he is ready to take. Joyce, for instance, did not interpret Vico's divisions of history literally but psychologically.[3] Nor can Proust be classed as a Bergsonian although, despite his statements to the contrary, he has much in common with Bergson.

This book begins with a discussion of Bergson and Proust because of their profound influence on other writers in their own culture and in other cultures. Contemporary literature is saturated with a sense of Bergson's *durée* and of Proust's *mémoire involontaire*. There is a whole European literature on the subject of Bergson, Proust, and their relation to each other which it cannot be the purpose of this chapter to review. Nevertheless, some indication of the positions of these two men on the question of time, of their differences and similarities, is necessary in understanding the authors who came after them. A bibliography of works on the relation between Bergson and Proust appears in Kurt Jäckel's *Bergson und Proust* (1934). Since 1934 there have been a number of increments to this list. One of the most important of the more recent studies is that of Floris Delattre which will be discussed later.

Bergson's fame and influence are due not to the originality of his theories, but to the fact that he made an extensive study of the question of time at a moment when philosophy and psychology were clearing the ground for his metaphysics and when science was about to give support to his work. Wyndham Lewis in the process of debunking Bergsonism wrote, "Bergson was supposed by all of us to be dead, but Relativity, oddly enough, at first sight, has recently resuscitated him."[4]

3. Richard Ellmann, *James Joyce* (New York, 1959), p. 565.
4. Wyndham Lewis, *Time and Western Man* (New York, 1928), p. 50.

The details of Bergson's philosophy of time are too complex to be included in an introductory chapter. However, an account of his principal theories on the subject will be helpful. In *Time and Free Will* (1889) he states that the general conception of time is that of a medium in which our feelings, impressions, emotions are arranged in the same kind of order that we find in space, that is, one after the other. But, he asks, "Does the multiplicity of our conscious states bear the slightest resemblance to the multiplicity of the units of a number?"[5] It is doubtful. The kind of time in which we enumerate things is only space. Pure duration, or *durée* as he calls it, is something different.

Proof that we confuse time and space appears if we consider that the sort of time in which states of consciousness can be counted would have to exist all at once. And thus time would take on the same characteristics as space, as a plank of wood, a plot of earth, a cubic foot of gas. In considering material objects we find that they stem from a medium that allows spaces and order.

This kind of medium is quite different, says Bergson, from the medium in which the consciousness exists. One state of consciousness does not necessarily preclude another. Furthermore, even when states of consciousness are successive they are interdependent and often pervade each other.

"Therefore," he concludes, "time under a homogenous medium is a false concept and trespasses on the idea of space."[6]

Durée, or duration, untouched by the conception of space, is a state in which we do not part the present from the past or from the future; "our ego lets itself *live*."[7] We do not set up time in any order; rather all states melt into one. Bergson illustrates his point by comparing pure duration with the rhythm in a piece of music. If, he says, we interrupt the rhythm in music by remaining too long on one note, it is not the inordinate length of the note which calls our attention to the error, but rather the "qualitative change caused in the whole

5. Henri Bergson, *Time and Free Will*, trans. F. L. Pogson (London, 1928), p. 90.
6. *Ibid.*, p. 98.   7. *Ibid.*, p. 100.

of the musical phrase."[8] Therefore, he calls succession "a mutual penetration."[9] Space does not have this quality of "mutual penetration"; rather in it objects exist *per se*. Order and number imply space. Pure duration, then, the opposite of succession that occurs only in space, is qualitative and has no relation to number. It consists of states that do not separate themselves from one another. As in a piece of music each note becomes part of and changes the entire composition, so each moment of time changes the whole.

Furthermore, Bergson argues that the time of the physicist or chemist seems quantitative but is actually qualitative. This appears when we see that simultaneity stands at the intersection of time and space. There is space in which objects may be enumerated, and there is duration in which one state of consciousness flows into the next. We confuse these two states because of simultaneity that makes an action occur apparently at the same time as our consciousness takes note of that action. For instance, if the hand of the clock points to four and we observe this fact, what we observe is space. Our several states of consciousness at four o'clock are quite different. They penetrate one another. Because the fact of four o'clock and our states of consciousness at four o'clock are simultaneous, we are likely to believe that states of consciousness may be enumerated. Actually, however, in both cases there is interpenetration. By the time that we think 'four o'clock,' the clock no longer says four; furthermore, the flow of consciousness constantly moves, incorporating into it states from all of existence. Bergson concludes, "Consciousness makes a qualitative discrimination without any further thought of counting the qualities or even of distinguishing them as *several*."[10]

In *Matter and Memory*, which was published seven years later, Bergson extended his idea of duration; now he saw it as a principle that existed independent of the body. In the world, he says, we are aware that "millions of phenomena succeed each other."[11] In nature there are successions like those of our

8. *Ibid.*   9. *Ibid.*, p. 101.   10. *Ibid.*, p. 121.
11. Henri Bergson, *Matter and Memory*, trans. Nancy M. Paul and W. Scott Palmer (London, n.d.), p. 274.

own consciousness, even more rapid sometimes. This is not, he continues, an impersonal duration, for there is no one rhythm that duration follows. Instead there are many rhythms. These different tensions, as he calls them, of duration would enable one to fix things and living organisms in their places on a kind of scale of being. It is our duty, Bergson writes, to place ourselves within this pure duration "of which the flow is continuous and in which we pass insensibly from one state to another."[12]

It is in *Matter and Memory* that Bergson makes his famous distinction between two forms of memory: the first is a memory of habit, the memory that enables us to recall a lesson by heart; the second is true memory that records every moment of duration and takes place continuously in our lives. However, we tend to set the memory of habit in the foreground because it is more useful. Normally a person remembers that which applies in some way to the present situation, but there is also a spontaneous recollection, a memory-image, which may appear at intervals, an involuntary memory. This memory-image, according to Bergson, is not the product of associationism which causes a discontinuous multiplicity of elements. Bergson would have seen Proust's *madeleine* as something that distracted us from the continuity of being because it contained something of what preceded it and something of what followed. It forms a mixed state rather than a simple, pure state like that of the atom. "To *picture* is not to *remember*,"[13] writes Bergson. On the other hand, if an image were not in the past, we would never know it for a memory.

Bergson saw, however, as Proust did also, that life consists in orientation toward the future and, therefore, that we experience it chiefly in its practical aspects and do not reach the essence of experience. Beside utility, for Proust, selfish desires, imagination, or passion, cloud the vision, and only in reliving experiences of the past detached from these forces can we touch real existence.

Creative Evolution, appearing in 1907, goes further than

12. *Ibid.*, p. 243.   13. *Ibid.*, p. 173.

Matter and Memory in seeing duration as synonymous with life. "Duration is the continuous progress of the past which gnaws into the future and which swells as it advances."[14] Furthermore, duration is irreversible; we could not relive an experience, for we would have to erase all that had followed that experience. It is important to notice that for Bergson, the past, although it exists in the present as part of a great snowball, is always clearly past as it is for those who follow him. In this Bergson diverges from the Neoplatonist who sees past, present, and future as distinctions with no validity whatsoever. Also for the mystic these distinctions are a mirage. In general, Bergson's influence on the contemporary writer has been to indicate for him a sense of time which was humanly meaningful in terms of man's inmost existence, to free him from the artificial distinctions of clock time as well as to show that the inner time of man is not a kind of inferior adjunct to a Christian, Hindu, or Buddhist eternity. It is clear then why T. S. Eliot and Aldous Huxley in their search for an eternity outside time reject Bergson and why Joyce, after he had adopted the time of Vico, a system exterior to man, calls Bergson Bitchson.

Like all the young intellectuals in France in the 1890's, Proust read Bergson. Furthermore, Proust was related on the maternal side to the Neuburger family, and when Mlle Louise Neuburger married Henri Bergson, Proust was one of the "garçons d'honneur de sa cousine."[15] *Remembrance of Things Past* (a translation that Proust quite rightly felt destroyed his title, which emphasizes the searching out of lost time) must be surveyed as a whole if one is to understand Proust.

There are three basic sources for Proust's aesthetic doctrine: the last chapter of *The Past Recaptured (Le temps retrouvé)*, a letter of early November, 1913, to René Blum, and an interview accorded to Élie-Joseph Bois, an account of which appeared in *Le Temps* in November, 1913. Proust makes it clear that only literature dominated by involuntary memory is realistic, for it

14. Henri Bergson, *Creative Evolution*, trans. Arthur Mitchell (New York, 1944), p. 7.
15. Floris Delattre, *Bergson et Proust: Accords et dissonances* (Paris, 1948), p. 39.

is the only device that enables us to experience a sensation simultaneously in past and present. He was aware, as can be seen in *The Past Recaptured,* that Chateaubriand in *Mémoires d'outre-tombe,* Gérard de Nerval in *Sylvie,* and Baudelaire had already employed the device of spontaneous memory. He is, in a sense, their heir. Justin O'Brien has pointed out that Taine in *De l'intelligence,* the work of Th. Ribot in 1896 and of Frédéric Paulhan in 1904 in psychology, and of Mauxion in 1901 in philosophy had explored involuntary memory and that Rousseau, Vittorio Alfieri, Flaubert, and J.-K. Huysmans among others had used it long before Proust.[16] O'Brien cites as a curiosity an obscure American writer, Henry Harland, who wrote in 1895 a piece called "Tirala–Tirala." The similarity to Proust is striking: "I shut my eyes for a moment and the flavour of that far-away afternoon comes back fresher in my memory than yesterday's."[17]

A detailed discussion of the philosophical and psychological antecedents of Proust's involuntary memory is contained in the work of Elisabeth Czoniczer. "The revolution which the epoch accomplished in the domain of psychology exercised a profound influence on literature, a long and slow inoculation of ideas which ended by exploding the corpse of realism." Proust only repeated what psychology and philosophy had been saying on "subjectivism and the unconscious."[18]

Throughout all the volumes of Proust's novel the central theme is that of rediscovering the past, leading us constantly to consider the question of time. In the "Overture" the problem is posed and is not to be answered fully until the final volume, *The Past Recaptured.* Proust, while accepting Bergson's theory of qualitative time, was primarily interested in the opportunities that existed (since time was of this nature) of recalling the past.

16. Justin O'Brien, "La mémoire involontaire avant Marcel Proust," *Revue de littérature comparée,* XIX (1936), 19-36.

17. *Ibid.,* p. 33.

18. Elisabeth Czoniczer, *Quelques antécédents de "À la recherche du temps perdu"* (Genève, 1957), pp. 160-61.

As well as Bergson's influence, that of Marie-Alphonse Darlu must be considered. Dr. Robert Proust[19] puts Bergson's influence as second to that of Darlu, who set in motion Proust's "long-drawn-out meditation on the unreality of the sensible world, on memory, and on the problem of time"[20] during the year that Proust sat under Darlu at the Lycée Condorcet (1888-89).

It is important too to keep in mind that Proust was enthusiastic in his admiration of Ruskin. George Painter has shown that Proust knew *Praeterita* well and that both the title and the theme of his novel owe something to this work. Painter discusses a passage in *Praeterita* in which Ruskin as he draws a tree finds that the tree itself contains meaning beyond human apprehension of it. An experience of this sort, Painter considers, is a prelude to Proust's regaining of time lost.[21] Jean Autret in his book on Ruskin and Proust has indicated the following influences of Ruskin: Ruskin like Proust deplored the effect of habit on our sensations; on the other hand, both saw that habit could endear us to a familiar object. Ruskin and Proust both demanded that one see with the freshness of an infant; for both, imagination could play fully upon an object only when it was absent; for both, the business of the artist was to represent appearances. Literature and painting may be pure impression, erroneous perception, but it is the vision of the artist that counts.[22] In late 1909 or early 1910 Proust wrote to Robert de Billy that no literature had more hold on him than English and American literature, and he cites George Eliot, Hardy, Stevenson, Emerson, Ruskin, and James Barrie "in the Pantheon of my admiration."[23] Proust, as these studies will indicate, has

19. "Marcel Proust intime," *La nouvelle revue française*, XXIII (January, 1923), 25.

20. André Maurois, *Proust: Portrait of a Genius*, trans. Gerard Hopkins (New York, 1950), p. 28.

21. George Painter, *Proust: The Early Years* (Boston, 1959), pp. 346-47.

22. Jean Autret, *L'Influence de Ruskin sur la vie, les idées et l'oeuvre de Marcel Proust* (Genève, 1955), pp. 89-92. See also Henri Lemaître, "Proust et Ruskin" in *Pyrénnées*, No. 16 (January-February, 1944), pp. 311-97.

23. Robert de Billy, *Marcel Proust lettres et conversations* (Paris, 1930), pp. 180-81. Consulted for the dating of the letters was Philip Kolb, *La Correspondance de Marcel Proust* (Urbana, Illinois), 1949.

repaid his debt to English and American literature in full measure.

Proust first touches the theory of duration in his analysis of sleep at the beginning of *Swann's Way*. If, he says, a man changes his position as he sleeps, at once the succession of years and days about him is broken. Then when he awakens he will have lost all idea of time. Furthermore, if a man falls asleep in a chair or in an unaccustomed place he will often have no idea when he awakes of the month or hour, but he will imagine "that he went to sleep months earlier."[24] These assertions of Proust's illustrate Bergson's point that real time is not that which is imposed upon us by space but that which lives within us. Any slight shift of our spatial surroundings frees us from space and lets us experience duration.

This theme is further developed in the last part of the "Overture" in the well-known incident of the hero's tasting the *madeleine*. Many years after the writer's childhood in Combray he comes home at tea time one day in Paris. His mother offers him a *madeleine* and some tea, and although he does not usually drink tea, he does so today. The effect is extraordinary and exquisite. For a moment he cannot distinguish the origin of his sensation. The second mouthful and the third bring less poignant feelings. After some effort the memory returns; it is that of a *madeleine* soaked in tea which his aunt Leonie had offered him many years before in Combray.[25]

And from this incident Proust deduces the entire plot of his long novel. The stage is now set and the actors are about to appear. In the last part of the "Overture" we feel the hush before a curtain rises. Proust indicates that his books are to be about lost events that the tea and the *madeleine* have re-created or about lost events that have been re-created by similar experiences, particularly with the senses of smell or taste, but not exclusively with these two senses.

As he himself writes: "The past is hidden somewhere out-

24. Marcel Proust, *Swann's Way*, trans. C. K. Scott Moncrieff (New York, 1928), p. 4.
25. *Ibid.*, p. 54.

side the realm, beyond the reach of intellect, in some material object (in the sensation which the material object will give us) which we do not suspect. And as for that object it depends on chance whether we come upon it or not before we ourselves must die."[26]

Our senses, he says, wait for us to recognize by association past experiences with which they are connected. And then in the "tiniest drop of their essence [we may observe] the vast structure of recollection."[27] Proust's recollections *were* vast; they led through the mazes of the human personality and eventually to the clarifying in the final volume of the Proustian thesis.

It is easy to see how Proust's time is superficially the kind of which Bergson speaks. It is time in which past and present exist simultaneously, every moment containing both. Of course, each moment changes, but it is a qualitative and not a quantitative change.

Other church spires and steeples bring back to the hero the spire in Combray, as if he were "trying to remember, feeling deep within myself a tract of soil reclaimed from the waters of Lethe, slowly drying until the buildings rise on it again."[28] The spire itself re-creates for him thus both time and space. Benjamin Crémieux and Kurt Jäckel have indicated the relation between the later episode concerning the spires of Martinville and Bergson's intuitive approach to reality.[29] These sources show that underneath appearances there is for both Bergson and Proust a reality discovered only with great effort. After Combray there come the memories of Swann, of Gilberte. Then the Guermantes, their pompous attitudes and lofty social position heightened in the boy's mind by his awe-struck memories of Geneviève de Brabant on the slides of the magic lantern that he had owned as a child. Albertine in *The Captive* and then the "sweet cheat gone." And finally in the last volume the invitation from the Guermantes which in his own words

26. *Ibid.*   27. *Ibid.*, p. 58.   28. *Ibid.*, p. 82.
   29. Benjamin Crémieux, *XXe siecle* (Paris, 1924), p. 22, and Kurt Jäckel, *Bergson und Proust* (Breslau, 1934), pp. 27-34.

"kindled a spark of attention, brought up from the depth of my memory a cross section of the past associated with that name."[30]

There is a premonition in the hero's mind that this reception will mean something more than the usual one. He has been for many years in a sanatorium away from Paris, but now he has come back for a few weeks to attend to some affairs. The invitation arrives; it "would surely carry me back toward my childhood, and the depths of my memory where I saw it mirrored."[31]

He is not to be disappointed. The walk toward the Guermantes' residence forms the prelude for the evening ahead. Melancholy pervades his spirit. Then as he nears the house a carriage forces him to step quickly back. That sensation of stepping backward suddenly onto a stone a little lower than the one on which he stands immediately banishes his melancholy. Complete happiness invades him. It was the same happiness that he had felt at the sight of certain church spires in Martinville or in seeing some trees near Balbec. This time he determines to trace the sensation to its source. The motivations that are only hinted at in the "Overture" are here in *The Past Recaptured* completely revealed.

He places his feet in the same position, one lower than the other. Instantly "the dazzling, elusive vision brushed me with its wings. . . ."[32] And then suddenly he knows that his experience is the counterpart of one in Venice many years ago. In exactly the same way that the *madeleine* had recalled Combray to him so this posture recalls Venice.

On the same evening other like experiences crowd upon him. A servant strikes a spoon against a plate bringing back to him an incident in a railroad carriage and the sound of a hammer used in repairing a wheel. A napkin with which he wipes his mouth recalls Balbec and its blue sea, the starched towel with which he had dried himself on his first day at Balbec.

From these experiences, the uneven flagstones, the sound of the spoon against the plate, the starched napkin, he con-

30. Marcel Proust, *The Past Recaptured*, trans. F. A. Blossom (New York, 1932), p. 179.
31. *Ibid.*   32. *Ibid.*, p. 192.

cludes that: "The most insignificant gesture, the simplest act remain enclosed, as it were, in a thousand sealed jars, each filled with things of an absolutely different colour, odour and temperature. Furthermore, these jars, ranged along the topmost levels of our bygone years . . . stand at very different altitudes and give us the impression of strangely varied atmospheres."[33]

Because we have the ability to forget, there is no link between a past sensation and the present until a chance recurrence of the experience suddenly reanimates the sensation, that sensation which he says, "poets have vainly tried to establish in Paradise."[34] When such a recurrence comes, Proust feels as if he were living simultaneously in two times; he is uncertain in which period he is. Thus he discovers that in such moments he is entirely outside of time. It is not memory or his brain which arouse the exquisite emotion in him. It is rather some part of his inmost self, one of the sealed jars of the past, which has suddenly been opened, thus bringing to him not just a single moment from the past, but, what is much more, the union of past and present. Proust writes that it was now possible "for the being within me to seize, isolate, immobilise for the duration of a lightning flash what it never apprehends, namely, a fragment of time in its pure state."[35]

The writer reasons that his inmost being does not flourish in a present, devoid of a true time sense, in an intellectual perusal of the past, or in a future "which the will constructs out of fragments of the past and present."[36] And as he ponders, the noise of hot-water pipes recalls for him the whistles of boats on summer evenings in Balbec. It is not merely that he remembers the sound, that the experiences are similar; the actual sensation recurs.

The importance of his discussion of sleep in his first volume becomes evident as he compares the bewilderment felt by the individual experiencing duration to the bewilderment of a person falling asleep or awakening. Fleeting as the joyous

33. *Ibid.*, p. 195. 34. *Ibid.*
35. *Ibid.*, p. 198. 36. *Ibid.*

sensation of eternity is, the author feels that it is the only "fecund and real"[37] experience in his life. And thus he determines to spend his days in the study and pursuit of it, in the composition of *Remembrance of Things Past.*

For Proust, literature which is content to describe objects and events is unreal. Even friendship is for him a waste of one's inner self. The restoration of being caused by recurring sensation is a reality, and art that deals with this will takes on its reality. Thus Proust's literature is to be that which deals with this search for identity. Maurice Muller has indicated the necessity of distinguishing in Proust between psychological analysis and an almost Cartesian search for an absolute quality in the *moi.* These two kinds of investigation are united in Proust, representing two characteristic currents in French literature and philosophy, the first stemming from Racine and the moralists, the second from Descartes, who was a forerunner of the Bergsonian revolution.[38] Hans Jauss, on the other hand, sees Proust's novel as a study of successive states achieved by the *moi.* The "way of Marcel" lies, according to Jauss, in the plurality of his *moi successifs* and in his search for the world of others.[39]

Proust makes it clear in his letter of early November, 1913, to René Blum that his novels are not Bergsonian novels, for he says that the distinction between voluntary and involuntary memory does not figure in Bergson's philosophy.[40] Involuntary memories are, he feels, the primary subject matter of a work of art, the only means of creating a sense of reality in the novel. Nine years later in a letter to Camille Vettard, Proust concedes that he concurs with Bergson in attempting to reveal to the conscious mind phenomena that, completely forgotten, sometimes lie very far back in the past. Nevertheless, he insists that

37. *Ibid.,* p. 201.

38. Maurice Muller, *De Descartes à Marcel Proust* (Neuchâtel, 1947), pp. 55-56.

39. Hans Robert Jauss, *Zeit und Erinnerung in Marcel Prousts "À la recherche du temps perdu"* (Heidelberg, 1955), Chapter IV.

40. Léon Pierre-Quint, *Comment parut "Du côté de chez Swann"* (Paris, 1930), pp. 57-63.

there has not been, "insofar as I am aware, any direct influence."[41] Letters to Robert Dreyfus in 1920[42] and to Jacques Boulenger in 1921[43] make essentially the same point. Georges Poulet in his excellent chapter on Proust writes: "Nothing is more false than to compare Proustian duration of Bergsonian duration. . . . Far from being as Bergson wished it, a 'continuité mélodique,' human duration in Proust's eyes is a simple plurality of isolated moments, remote from each other."[44]

Nevertheless, Fernand Vial has pointed out the opportunities Proust had to become acquainted with Bergson's work and has concluded that it is necessary to admit a relationship although it is perhaps not a conscious one. Bergson's influence is, according to Vial, the result of a progressive penetration, a slow maturation. In his effort to express the profound homogeneity of our psychological life, Proust is like Bergson. According to Vial, under the influence of Schopenhauer, Hartmann, the symbolist poets, and Bergson, Proust created a new means of psychological investigation.[45]

Floris Delattre, on the other hand, discusses the differences as well as the similarities between Bergson and Proust. Both used introspection in exploring duration (Proust's style with its sinuous sentences is the style that Bergson declared indispensable in revealing the secrets of our consciousness); both focused attention not on facts but on what is retained in the depths of the soul. However, Delattre sees that Proust's "psychological impressionism continued to have recourse to procedure, method, and to cold constructions of the intelligence."[46] Proust sometimes affirms that different parts of time are mutually exclusive and thus spatialize time. Whereas Bergson speaks of being plunged into the river of time, Proust sometimes observes the river from the banks. Delattre con-

41. Marcel Proust, *Correspondance générale* (Paris, 1932), III, 194-95.
42. Robert Dreyfus, *Souvenirs sur Marcel Proust* (Paris, 1926), p. 289.
43. Proust, *Correspondance générale*, III, 236.
44. Poulet, *Human Time*, p. 316.
45. Fernand Vial, "Le symbolisme bergsonien de temps dans l'oeuvre de Proust," *PMLA*, LV (December, 1940), 1191-1212.
46. Delattre, *Bergson et Proust*, p. 56.

cludes that Proust is an intermittent Bergsonian or a Bergsonian despite himself.[47]

In the matter of memory, too, there were agreements but also differences. Delattre points out that both saw memory as a key to spiritual life, but that with Proust this led chiefly to individual fulfillment. In the final volume of his novel, memory becomes for Proust a kind of refuge, an almost mystical experience. Proust's chief contribution to the theory of spontaneous memory is in the intensity that he confers on the past. Although his novel is apparently only the concrete application of two Bergsonian themes, *la durée* and spontaneous memory, actually "the wind of Bergsonian thought, like that which passes on a high plateau, only ruffled without actually animating Proust's subtle and cold heart."[48]

The central difference between Bergson and Proust seems to be then that Bergson saw duration as a continuous process. Proust saw it in terms of successive states of being. Furthermore, the use of the catalyst to evoke the past reinforced a sense of discontinuity found in Proust but not in Bergson. These distinctions are of importance and reveal why a book may be Bergsonian without being Proustian, like *Finnegans Wake*, for instance, which with its stream-of-consciousness method comes closer to Bergson's *durée réelle* than Proust's novel. Few writers exposed to them have escaped without bearing in their work the mark of either Bergson or Proust or both as the studies that follow indicate. Joyce was acquainted with the work of both Bergson and Proust; involuntary memory and a sense of duration both appear in his work. Virginia Woolf's novels are clearly indebted to Bergson as well as to Proust. Aldous Huxley, although he claimed that he detested both Bergson and Proust, employed involuntary memory as well as a technique he calls a technique of "multiplicity." Thomas Wolfe read Proust and speaks of Proust's influence on his work. William Faulkner acknowledges his debt to Bergson and states that he wishes he had written Proust's book himself. Thomas Mann read Proust after the writing of *The Magic Mountain*, but is in-

47. *Ibid.*, p. 60. 48. *Ibid.*, p. 124.

debted neither to Bergson nor Proust. And Sartre as a professional philosopher is, of course, well acquainted with Bergson
although in disagreement with him and with Proust.

Of the authors discussed here only Kafka and Mann were
not exposed significantly to these influences. The contrasts
arising in subject matter and technique as a result of disparate
philosophical heritages become the theme of this book. Kafka's
sense of universals and his reliance on the inner dream world of
man sprang from an interest in Plato, in the existentialist
Kierkegaard, and particularly from the Austrian-German literary heritage to which he was heir. Although time is an inner
affair for Kafka, it is *man* rather than *men* with whom he deals.
He succeeds thus in combining in a unique fashion two tradi-
tions that are usually seen as distinct in Anglo-American literature. That they are seen as distinct is partly owing to the
influence of Bergson with his emphasis on a duration of
different rhythms for individual beings and to Proust with his
emphasis on the recall of the personal past of the hero of his
novel, a novel that explores all the intricacies, sinuosities, and
secret depths of an individual human soul.

In conclusion, it should be explained that the focus of this
book is directed more toward values and meaning than toward
structure and technique. Excellent studies exist and more remains to be done on the question of time and technique in the
novel. Günther Müller in his provocative work in this field suggests the importance of exploring the relationship between
what he calls "Erzählzeit und erzählte Zeit."[49] Two treatments
of the Joseph story, that by Thomas Mann and that in the Old
Testament, illustrate what Müller means by these two times.
Both the tone and the whole character of a work are changed
by the time of the telling of a tale. It is impossible to tell life
as it originally happened. Thus what the author selects to

49. The following works by Günther Müller should be noted in particular:
(1) *Die Bedeutung der Zeit in der Erzählkunst* (Bonn, 1947); (2) "Erzählzeit
und erzählte Zeit," *Festschrift Paul Kluckhohn und Hermann Schneider
gewidmet zu ihrem 60. Geburtstag* (Tübingen, 1948); (3) "Über das Zeitgerust des Erzählens," *Deutsche Vierteljahrsschrift für Literaturwissenschaft und
Geistesgeschichte*, XXIV (1950), 1-31; and (4) "Zeiterlebnis und Zeitgerust in
der Dichtung," *Studium Generale*, VIII (November, 1955), 594-601.

"gather up" from the original events determines the nature of his work. Another way of stating this is that all imaginative work is a matter of omission. In Mann's *Joseph* books time, through the mediation of the novelist, loses its boundaries because many generations are involved, and events appear often vague or distant because of the immense gaps between the materials chosen for discussion. In *Genesis* the same tale is told with less awareness of the immense periods of time, thereby giving more compactness, a sense of proximity to the characters, an individuality. In this interplay of the time of the original event and the time allotted it in the novel, varied effects may be produced. But to explore fully these relationships in the works to be discussed here would require another book.

PART II

THE

BRITISH ISLES

INTRODUCTION

Although Bergson has been used as a starting point for these discussions of time, it is obvious that the authors to be dealt with often go far beyond Bergson or modify his theory in practice. Through Bergson's *durée,* or mind time as some have called it, subject and object are fused. In translating the sense of *durée* into literature the difficulty is to obviate the cold constructions of abstract thought and at the same time to retain a sense of form. Pure *durée* is, one suspects, incapable of becoming the sole basis of a work of art. The Proustian catalyst, a sense of the observer, or form break in on the stream of mind time.

Thus in James Joyce's work we often find a sense of the observer or the omniscient author breaking up the identification of subject and object, destroying the pure sense of *durée.* This is true of *A Portrait* and of parts of *Ulysses.* A more formal means of containment is that of the Viconian cycles employed in *Finnegans Wake* to bring order to the chaos of the dream. On the other hand, a close approach to pure duration comes, for example, in the monologue of Molly Bloom or in the emphasis on the dream as a subjective expression of the dreamer in *Finnegans Wake*. But duration cannot successfully compose the whole novel, for in the words of W. H. Auden, "Art is not life."

His use of involuntary memory links Joyce with his French contemporary Proust. In *A Portrait* involuntary memory acts creatively to free Stephen from a clock-centered existence, but later it is superseded by Stephen's recognition of a temporal continuum of which he is a part. Joyce does not feel, with Proust, that involuntary memory is the only means of creating reality in the novel.

Although it is not involuntary memory that is a chief tool for Joyce, he sees that the past must be integrated with the present if redemption is to be achieved. Proust's feeling that the *moi* could be "identified" through involuntary memory is perhaps another way of saying this. To dwell on the past as irrevocable leads in *Dubliners* to the Reverend James Flynn's insanity and in *Ulysses* to Stephen's anxiety about his mother's death.

As a means of contrast to Joyce and Virginia Woolf, who also is indebted to Bergson and Proust as well as to Joyce himself, Aldous Huxley has been selected as the third author in this section. Huxley, who professes an aversion to Bergson, employs a technique of multiplicity in a number of his novels. This technique proposes a juxtaposition of various experiences in dealing with events. It is a construction imposed by the author on the experiences of his characters and has no relation to their flow of mind time, for it is an arrangement external to the inner being, a kind of intellectual experimentation with events. By rearranging events certain curious effects may be obtained, but it is a rearrangement dependent upon the intellectual virtuosity of the author rather than on the mind time of a character.

Huxley's tendency to abstraction carries over also into his treatment of mystical doctrine. Huxley, like Joyce, has been concerned with Eastern mysticism, but it is interesting to notice that Huxley never incorporates its thesis of reincarnation into the structure of his novels as Joyce does. The reason is that Huxley does not see recurrence in terms of this life alone but in connection with another timeless world of the spirit. For Joyce eternity could be achieved within time.

Huxley's divine Ground, of all the concepts discussed here, is the one farthest removed from the time experience itself. Huxley's concept of eternity moves us into an unknown realm, a realm that is the opposite of the animal realm. There is an element of such abstraction about Huxley's divine Ground that the characters who attain it are unable to communicate effectively with other characters or with the reader although Huxley can write *about* it.

Another theory of time which must be mentioned here is that of Vico. Joyce saw Vico's cycles in terms of the various inner stages of individual man and of mankind. In the psychological life of each of us there is the Divine Age (the age of the parents), the Heroic Age (the age of the sons), the Human Age (the age of the people), and the Recorso. This pattern may be repeated many times in a single life span. Any traumatic experience may act as a recorso and initiate a new age of the parents from which it is necessary to progress once again through the other stages. Furthermore, there are cycles within cycles, which may be seen in *Finnegans Wake* in its complexity of themes and structure. While an individual may be living in a new age of the parents emotionally, he may simultaneously be involved in an age of the sons religiously.

Joyce's patterns objectify the central development of life—the reliance on parental-like authority in the early stages of any undertaking changing into a reliance on self and on one's contemporaries, in turn developing into the ability to merge interest in self with the good of the whole. Once this final stage is achieved there must be disintegration of this particular cycle in the interest of progress. Life then is composed of millions of cycles within cycles continually breaking up and reforming for the purpose of furthering life itself. For change and death, which seem, viewed by themselves, as senseless phenomena,

Joyce's cycles propose a definite role in the development of man. Although individual death cannot be abrogated, whatever has been is not lost and will be reincarnated in yet a finer form with each turn of the wheel. Joyce was aware of parallel doctrines in Eastern mystical philosophies to which he refers in his books.

Thus we find that whereas a sense of return as an intuitive principal is a focal one in both the work of Joyce and of Virginia Woolf (although in Mrs. Woolf's work it loses its Viconian identity, for she was principally influenced in the matter of 'return' by *Ulysses* where the Viconian ages do not appear overtly), the return of the past in Huxley's novels is chiefly an intellectual exercise. Even the mystical moment of Mrs. Woolf is closely connected with the inner life of the individual character involved. Huxley's abstractions lead him away from the flow of life into the realm of theory, so that his novels are often more truly essays through which he may expound his ideas.

A sense of *durée* has led Joyce and Virginia Woolf to write in terms of the inner consciousness of being; a rejection of *durée* has led Huxley to write in terms of the intellect in the early novels and of non-being in the later ones.

CHAPTER TWO

JAMES JOYCE:

TIME AND TIME AGAIN

1

Joyce's ballast office clock, which for Stephen in *Stephen Hero* is capable of an epiphany, a sudden spiritual manifestation, symbolizes a polarity that underlies all of Joyce's work. This polarity is that of the firmness and yet mutability of human experience, ballast giving stability in contrast to the ineluctable movement of the hands of the clock. The ballast that Joyce sought in order to counteract time passing came in the Viconian philosophy of his later works. Even in *Dubliners,* however, one senses a developing concern with the counteracting of linear time. In the *Portrait* Joyce takes on as ballast his art and a sense of the persistence of the past whereby man defeats mutability. In *Ulysses* this ballast is supplemented by a sense of recurrence, a sense fully expressed in *Finnegans Wake.*

Dubliners shows the pathos and tragedy of everyday lives caught in meshes often not of their own making. One of these meshes is the mesh of clock time of which an industrialized and mechanized society has become increasingly conscious. Clock time moves forward relentlessly, leaving the past to the past and the dead to the dead. The stories illustrate how a reliance on clock time obscures the basic time sense of the inner being, a being in which at every moment past and future mingle. Thus the tragedy of the broken chalice in "The Sisters" need not have been a tragedy had the Reverend James Flynn seen that the past is redeemable, for it exists in the present as well as in the past. By indicating in *Dubliners* the narrow confines of linear time in which many of his characters are imprisoned, Joyce proposes a sense of time whereby man may be freed for the future by redemption of the past in the present.

In many of the stories in *Dubliners,* characters are doomed to failure and to defeat because linear time, which Bergson called space, is more meaningful to them than their own inner sense of duration. In "Araby" the boy is too young for Mangan's sister. Several years separate them. Further frustration comes to the boy when his uncle arrives home too late for the boy to reach the bazaar in time to buy his gift. The boy feels victimized by his youth and by his uncle's late arrival, by the time of calendar and of clock, instead of recognizing that the "Arabys" in life are not achieved through time and place but through an inner attitude toward time and place. Oriented toward the future, as youth generally is, the boy sees the demarcations of the clock as a barrier holding him back from the promise of what lies ahead. This sense of time brings for him only "anguish and anger."

Eveline's understanding of time and space is likewise an outer one. Fearing change, she cannot see that the distinction between her "old home" and her "new home" need not be divisive. She clings to the familiar objects in her room, to the emblems of the past, as if they in themselves, apart from her, had significance. She is unable to follow Frank beyond "the barrier" at the dock because space and time lie outside of her. An inner sense of duration would have freed her from her fear of leaving the past and enabled her to see that the past within her persisted and would persist even in the distant "Buenos Ayres."

Further conflicts are caused by a reliance on the time of the clock in *Dubliners* because of the artificial distinction it makes between "fast" and "slow." Thus Little Chandler in "A Little Cloud" feels that he is a failure and Gallaher a success because Gallaher's motto is: "Press life. Always hurry and scurry."[1] Thinking of Gallaher, Little Chandler quickens his pace. The same sense of failure arises in Farrington in "Counterparts" because of a mechanical concept of time by which he is forced to judge himself day after day in an office ruled by Mr. Alleyne. Alleyne bullies Farrington because Farrington is slow, has not finished his copy, spends too much time at lunch, hesitates before leaving the office. In a minor counterpart to this relationship, the typist, Miss Parker, is urged to work faster by the chief clerk. Mr. Alleyne and Farrington "had never pulled together from the first" (p. 114). Farrington's desire to ignore, to be rid of this mechanical time, is symbolized when he pawns his watch. It is not that Farrington wants more time but less time, less time in the office, less time in life. Working slowly, hoping thereby that time itself will stop, he paradoxically lengthens time. Only in the achievement of a sense of time in which "fast" and "slow" are meaningless could Farrington have been released from his tortured life, but he is able to acquire no perspective toward the clock. Reliance on the mechanical time of the outer world causes misunderstanding, defeat, and failure in *Dubliners*. Only in the final story, "The Dead," does a sense of inner time bring the resolution of a conflict. With Gretta's confession at the end, the past takes its rightful place in the present. "That the dead do not stay buried is, in fact, a theme of Joyce from the beginning to the end of his work; Finnegan is not the only corpse to be resurrected."[2]

Counteracting time passing and time past, there is in *Dubliners* a tale presaging Joyce's later sense of cyclical recurrence. At the beginning of "After the Race" the cars came "scudding in"; almost imperceptibly the story slows down until it halts with the "dark stupor" of the central figure. Then comes the thunderclap as the young men cheer, shaking the cabin.

1. James Joyce, *Dubliners* (New York, 1926), p. 91. Subsequent references to this volume appear in the text.
2. Richard Ellmann, *James Joyce* (New York, 1959), p. 253.

The story ends with the words of the Hungarian, "Daybreak, gentlemen!" And thus another cycle begins. "After the Race" is, of course, Viconian only by accident. It does not represent Joyce's conclusions about time at this period, for the book ends with "The Dead" in which Joyce moves towards the position on time he was to elaborate in the *Portrait*.

In "The Dead" the past is for Gretta and becomes for Gabriel a living part of the present. In acknowledging the persistence of the past through her confession to her husband, Gretta achieves some measure of peace in sleep, and Gabriel is reconciled to life as he reflects that a blanket of snow is covering all of Ireland and Michael Furey's grave. In contrast, the Reverend James Flynn in "The Sisters" confesses only to himself and is found mad, sitting in the dark in his confession box. The past for him, the past of the broken chalice, is never integrated with the present. Gretta's confession, even though perhaps a partial confession, has in a sense laid the ghost of her lover. A mature understanding of time is one in which acknowledgment of the ghosts of the past frees us for our "journey westward," a journey that Gabriel now feels he can undertake unlike the Reverend James Flynn whose life is described as "crossed." In *Dubliners* we see, then, an understanding of time, which stresses the need for a creative integration of past and present, of subject and object.

The problem of time in *A Portrait of the Artist as a Young Man*, where this integration is made, is far more complex. Time in the *Portrait* includes a sense of the individual time of the hero, a sense of the persistence of the racial past, a sense of cyclical recurrence, a Jesuitical sense of eternity as opposed to time, and a transcendence of time achieved by the artist. The development of Stephen's sense of time and the contrasting time sense of other people with whom he comes in contact form the subject matter of the book.

Stephen Hero, preceding the *Portrait*, is much less involved in its treatment of the time problem. Joyce in *Stephen Hero* emphasizes to a lesser degree the polarities between time and eternity, mind time and clock time. The episodic framework of

Stephen Hero stands in sharp contrast to the sense of duration in the *Portrait*. There are, however, interesting parallels with the *Portrait* which can be traced. Stephen Hero is aware of the persistence of his past in the present. Like Proust's hero he sometimes evokes this past so that it becomes a living reality. Memories of Clongowes are several times re-created. A group under a colonnade about to return to their convent reminds Stephen of his own life as a seminarist as does his walk toward Clonliffe College with Wells. As Stephen and Emma Clery ride home together on the Rathmines tram, both are magnetized in an instant that brings back a day from childhood when they had ridden together on a tram. The odor of peasants in the carriage on the way to Mullingar re-creates for Stephen his first communion in the chapel at Clongowes.

An inherent sense of the past of his race is also apparent in *Stephen Hero* as, for instance, when he considers the past of the arts and seems "almost to hear the simple cries of fear and joy and wonder which are antecedent to all song ... to see the rude scrawls."[3]

Linear time, which Stephen Hero rejects as a reality, is a cornerstone for Cranly, whom Stephen ridicules for his compulsive attention to time. Stephen goes with Cranly twice to the station where Cranly looks at timetables. The failure of Stephen and Cranly to communicate is partly owing to their different attitudes toward time. For Stephen the clock itself cannot be separated from the experience of the viewer. Thus the clock on the ballast office is capable of an epiphany through which time is transcended. "Imagine my glimpses at that clock as the gropings of the spiritual eye which seeks to adjust its vision to an exact focus. The moment the focus is reached the object is epiphanised" (p. 211). In this epiphany Stephen finds Aquinas' third quality of beauty, radiance. For Cranly, as for the boy in "Araby," time is a force against which he contends whereas for Stephen Hero, time is not perceived by itself but only in the relation of its "whatness" to his own. In the *Portrait* these

3. James Joyce, *Stephen Hero*, ed. Theodore Spencer (New York, 1944), p. 33. Subsequent references to this volume appear in text.

approaches to time, which in *Stephen Hero* are fragmentations, are reconciled and molded into a unified work culminating in the transcendence of time by the artist through his art. This transcendence is only vaguely suggested in *Stephen Hero* in the epiphany that Stephen tries in vain to explain to the clock-centered Cranly, who responds by wondering if "that bloody boat, the *Sea Queen*" ever got underway.

But Joyce himself, as Hugh Kenner says, saw that *Stephen Hero* never had a theme.[4] The *Portrait*, on the other hand, develops its rationale of time in terms of its theme. From one point of view, time in the *Portrait* is relative to the individual who experiences it. In other words, the whole book is about "the encounter of baby tuckoo with the moocow: the Gripes with the mookse."[5] Time with space. "Eins Einstein within a space."

For the boy Stephen, however, time threatens in much the same way as it threatened the child in "Araby." Time to Christmas vacation, to the day when he will be grown up seems like an insuperable barrier. Soon, however, he begins to observe that re-creation of time is possible, that the present is the sum of the whole past and of the future, and that clock time has no real relation to his own existence. Visions of past and future mingle with the present. In the castle at Clongowes Wood he *sees* the "old servants in old dress."[6] Later he sees the "image of himself grown older, standing in the garden with Mercedes" (p. 68). Memories of his childhood return on the train to Cork with his father. And the word *foetus* cut into the desk shows him in imagination "the broad shouldered youth" who had carved it (p. 100).

There are two versions of time implied in these early experiences of Stephen. The first and the more important is seen in the heavy shadow the past casts on all that Stephen does and thinks. Like those of Proust's hero, Stephen's memories carry him back into his childhood. The color of his tea brings back

4. Hugh Kenner, *Dublin's Joyce* (Bloomington, Indiana, 1956), p. 111.
5. *Ibid.*, p. 114.
6. James Joyce, *A Portrait of the Artist As a Young Man* (New York, 1928), p. 16. Subsequent references to this volume appear in the text.

for him "the dark turf-colored water of the bath at Clongowes" (p. 202) as Proust's *madeleine* had re-created another world for his hero. Nevertheless, the underlying sense of time in the *Portrait* is more Bergsonian that Proustian. For Stephen the emphasis is not on these discontinuous instants of recall so much as on the coalescence of past and present, in a rejection of clock time whereby we distort reality and become objects that can be located in this place or that. He is able thereby to transcend space within his own life. Sometimes he foreknows the future. For Bergson, as for later existentialists, becoming is the essence of time. The theme of the *Portrait* points toward the future, toward the role which the young man will later fill. In Stephen's own words: "The past is consumed in the present and the present is living only because it brings forth the future" p. 296).

Although the similarity to Bergson is marked,[7] there is also a Jungian sense of time apparent in the *Portrait*. Stephen's vision of the castle and of the death of its master on the battle-field of Prague shows that the racial past is also implicit in each individual existence. Memories of his personal past sometimes lead to a sense of the historical past. For instance, he remembers sitting at the piano striking chords, and from this scene arise visions of Agincourt and Greensleeves (p. 257). Stephen also is able to visualize the old Irish Parliament as he and his father stand in the building, now a bank, which once housed it. The school days of his father in Cork seem to be a part of him. "His mind shines on their strifes like a moon on a younger earth" (p. 107).

These views of time as related to the viewer are sharpened by the contrasting opinion of the priest in his sermon of damnation. For the church, time itself, duration, has no importance, for it is transient. For Stephen, all time exists in the present, but for the priest only doomsday will bring eternity. Memory for the church is one of the torments of conscience whereas for Stephen its function as re-creator of the past is a desirable one.

7. See Shiv K. Kumar, "Bergson and Stephen Dedalus' Aesthetic Theory," *Journal of Aesthetics and Art Criticism*, XVI (September, 1957), 124-27.

The church separates past and present: "Time is, time was, but time shall be no more" (p. 129). In his illustration of eternity by means of the mountain of sand from which every million years a bird carries away a grain, the priest dramatically opposes time and eternity.

Stephen, who has until now found a measure of eternity in time, is forced after the sermon to separate the two. But in this separation he finds only momentary peace. Memories of Clongowes arm him against acquiescing in becoming a priest. He feels it would end his freedom in time. As he walks seaward at Dollymount he hears within him "a confused music . . . as of memories and names . . . then the music seemed to recede . . . A voice from the world was calling" (p. 194). Returned now to a concept of the importance of time as it relates to his own being, Stephen realizes that the name "Stephanos Dedalos" carries powerful significance. It is at once a legacy and a prophecy; it is the past and the future met in the present, a synthesis of the Bergsonian and Jungian attitudes toward time.

Stephen transcends time at the end of the *Portrait* not by getting outside of it, but by finding within time the elements of eternity. And it is the myth of Daedalus that provides the background for his solution. Daedalus, like Stephen, imprisoned in his own labyrinth, supplies wings by which he escapes. The moment when Stephen hears his classmates call the name "Stephanos Dedalos" is a moment that dilates for Stephen. Rudd Fleming in his article on Husserl and Joyce[8] has pointed out that the feeling of Husserl for the capacity of a single moment of existence to expand itself into endless perspectives of reality is like that of Stephen Dedalus, and one might add of Joyce himself. Joyce like Blake was able to see a world in a grain of sand.

Although Stephen has now recognized his role as fabulous artificer, his work to create life from real life, the transcendence he has achieved is not static or timeless in the sense that it is divorced from experience in this world. Stephen knows that he

---

8. Rudd Fleming, "Dramatic Involution: Tate, Husserl, and Joyce," *Sewanee Review*, LX (Summer, 1952), 445-64.

will live, err, fall, and triumph (p. 200). Although his vision of Daedalus is described as a mystical experience, it leads to a recognition of his own position in relation to the past and to the future, "a prophecy of the end he had been born to serve" (p. 196). His thoughts of the early Danes bring him a sense of timelessness within time, a sense of the relation of the past to the present. Stephen's epiphany is, therefore, existential rather than transcendental in character.

Existentialism recognizes the *Augenblick,* as Kierkegaard calls it, "the pregnant moment." For this moment Paul Tillich has developed the concept of *Kairos,* "time fulfilled." This moment contains more than simply a glimpse into another world, for it always presents the necessity of a personal decision, a new orientation.[9] Having rejected the eternity offered by the church, Stephen chose to find within his own being the elements of another eternity. His epiphany is a moment of heightened awareness in which time rather than being rejected is seen subjectively in terms of his own relation to it. Bergson, in *Time and Free Will,* saw that time must be dealt with in terms of the individual. Later for Bergson duration was not a feeble imitation of eternity but constituted life itself.

Symbolism in the *Portrait* is designed to point up Stephen's discovery of eternity within time. In all Joyce's works imagery of clocks, of watches, is never far to be sought. These symbols of clock time were for Joyce a foil against which other attitudes toward time could be clearly seen. The importance of Farrington's watch and of the ballast office clock has already been noticed. In the final chapter of the *Portrait,* Stephen as he walks sees a dairy clock that tells him it is five minutes of five, but then another clock strikes eleven strokes. When he had left home that morning the battered alarm clock had been an hour and twenty-five minutes fast. The "right time" was twenty minutes past ten. But the term "right time" has meaning for Stephen only in a certain context—that of his mother and of the

9. Rollo May, "Contributions of Existential Therapy," in *Existence,* ed. Rollo May, Ernest Angel, Henri F. Ellenberger (New York, 1958), p. 71.

schedule of lectures at the university. These episodes occurring immediately after the epiphany scene at the end of Chapter IV emphasize the conflict between subjective and objective time with which Stephen contends.

It is significant that the epiphany scene takes place near water, the sea, another time image, one which reconciles rather than separates time and eternity. The sea with its periodic tides is capable of telling us the "right time." On the other hand, on the sea, apart from the shore, one experiences a sense of eternity. That Stephen is standing on the shore observing the relation of sea to land symbolizes that he is at the point where eternity meets time, the point that he achieves in his consecration to his art.

In addition, the water in this scene may be a symbol of time with its constant flux in relation to the shore, which is space. In the rivulet the relation of water to land is even closer. As Stephen wades in the rivulet, the tide is running out because, like the salmon,[10] he must swim both in and against the tide of life in order to spawn his art. The split between subject and object, between time, which is Stephen or the water, and space, which is the world about Stephen or the banks of the rivulet, disappears in his symbolic immersion. It is a baptism from which emerges at the end of the book Stephen's "Welcome, O life!" In other words, the encounter between time and space, which Hugh Kenner has seen as the theme of this book, is dramatized in this episode.

The third image of importance to the time question is that of birds. Stephen observing birds on the library steps is reminded of Swedenborg, who had said that birds know their times and seasons because unlike man they have not perverted that order by reason. The bird accepts instinctively his relation to the nature around him; his time and space are one. Thus the girl who acts as catalyst for Stephen's epiphany is seen in terms of bird imagery—her long legs like those of a crane, the fringes of her clothes like soft, white down, her bosom like "the breast

10. Note the salmon imagery discussed later in this chapter in the section on *Finnegans Wake*.

of some dark-plumaged dove" (page 199). And Stephen, who bears the name of a bird-man, like Daedalus would become bird and soar above the world while at the same time remaining in relation to it, uniting subject and object, time and space, time and eternity.

These syntheses show us that the time orientation in the *Portrait* is chiefly like that of Bergson and Jung although it is not implied that these influences were necessarily conscious ones. Stephen rejects the division of the church of time and eternity. Time in the *Portrait* is never transcendent in the sense of Aldous Huxley's "perennial philosophy." The Bergsonian and Jungian rationales allow for a transcendence within time, symbolized by the flight imagery and seen in the experience of the epiphany and consecration and in the sense of recurrence implied in the use of myth. Also in the imagery of circles and of cycles in the *Portrait*, we see an embryonic sense of the Viconian pattern that was to unite time and eternity for Joyce in his later works. The train at Dalkey (the key) where Vico Road is located roars and stops, roars and stops like Vico's cycles. Vacation and term alternate for Stephen in the same way. Stephen practices on a circular race track, the moon circles, Stephen's soul fluctuates cyclically.

At the end of the *Portrait*, Stephen has grasped that eternity may be discovered within time as he goes "to encounter for the millionth time the reality of experience." In this phrase he is able to recognize himself both as a recurrent figure and as one immersed in present experience. But Stephen has not learned "what the heart is and what it feels" (p. 299) as his mother recognizes. It is this failure to involve himself which causes his later defeat. His high hopes of communion with life and with art are never to be realized, for *Ulysses* shows us this Stephen's weaknesses and for Stephen's art substitutes Bloom's humanity.

Exiles, coming between the *Portrait* and *Ulysses*, reveals why the Stephen figure as Richard Rowan becomes the Stephen we find at the beginning of *Ulysses*. David Aitken sees the characters in *Exiles* as archetypes: Richard as spirit, Beatrice as intellect, Bertha as fecundity, Robert as body. The play is, says Aitken, about the failure of spirit and body to work together.[11] This split was an inherent danger in the position toward time as centered in himself which Stephen had adopted at the end of the *Portrait* and shows us why Joyce adopted, in addition to Jung and Bergson, Vico, who provided a point of reference outside of the life experience.

The scenes at the beginning of Chapter V in the *Portrait*, in which Stephen is unable to assimilate the times of the inner and the outer worlds, indicate an incipient failure to reconcile subject and object. To ignore time as it appears in the *Umwelt* and to accept only the time of the *Eigenwelt* is Richard Rowan's dilemma. Richard sees physical relations as "the death of the spirit." According to him nature is subject to change, Bertha's beauty will fade, but the world of art, the life of the spirit is eternal. Thus he adopts a position of indifference toward what is occurring between Bertha and Robert. His position is more than indifferent, for it assumes the irrelevancy of the life of the body. This is an escape from time more extreme than any proposed by Dedalus whose wings at least related him to the earth. Richard's exile, one which can lead only to sterility, Robert's exile of the opposite kind, exile from spirit, and Beatrice's exile in intellect occur to characters with no *Mitwelt*, no sense of communion; and it is just at this point that we find Stephen in the opening scenes of *Ulysses*. As Bernard Bandler points out, to Richard the contemplation that is the artist's is an end in itself, and thus all life which comes into contact with the artist must be sacrificed to his art.[12] In Richard's world of doubt at the end of the play, there lies, however, some hope that reconciliation with the Robert within him will be possible. That he has been wounded at all is indication that his exile from time is not complete. *Exiles* through the negative attitudes of its characters toward time implies Joyce's ideal attitude.

11. D. J. F. Aitken, "Dramatic Archetypes in Joyce's *Exiles*," *Modern Fiction Studies*, IV (Spring, 1958), 42-52.

12. Bernard Bandler, "Joyce's *Exiles*," *Hound and Horn*, VI (January-March, 1933), 266-85.

2

A Jungian sense of the persistence of the legendary past is the most obvious of the approaches to time in *Ulysses*. However, Joyce never admitted his debt to Jung or to Freud; once he stated that Vico stimulated his imagination as Jung and Freud never could. Only the least sensitive reader could fail to be aware of the influence of both these men on Joyce's work. Mary Colum once challenged him to admit his indebtedness to them. "Isn't it better to be indebted to great originators like that than to . . . ?"[13] She was referring to Dujardin, whom Joyce saw as the source of his *monologue intérieur*.

In *Ulysses*, Stephen Dedalus and Richard Rowan become Telemachus. In the Telemachus figure we find a man who no longer has in him the potentiality of the father, of Daedalus, who could plan his own escape. Instead, he is now the son, the seeker of the father, the Icarus who has fallen from his flight. Like Telemachus', his immaturity prevents him from protecting either himself or his mother from the usurper, Mulligan, and like Telemachus he lives in a hostile atmosphere, lacks community with those about him.

Ulysses rejects the ideals of the *Portrait*, for Daedalus of the myth carried within him the seeds of his son's failure. For Bloom, the figure who emerges to replace Stephen, there are no images of escape or of wings. Instead of forsaking home, Bloom like Odysseus is returning home. Instead of centering on flight, *Ulysses* centers on the land, on Dublin, a labyrinth where Bloom is content to remain. Through the emergence of Bloom and the rejection of Stephen, Joyce is saying that art is the art of living with oneself and with one's fellow men. To separate art as a vocation from life is to become sterile. Stephen has imposed exile from life upon himself; Bloom, however, has learned to live with whatever exile life brings, exile as a Jew, exile as a husband, exile as a father. Thus for the artist Joyce advocates the same synthesis he would advocate for the advertising man or for the tavern keeper. The pride of the artist is

13. Ellmann, *James Joyce*, p. 647.

Stephen's in assuming that flight is possible, that his own vocation is a dedicated one, above that of the "ordinary man." Molly's affirmation at the end of *Ulysses* is no affirmation for Stephen, not even indirectly. He is doomed to failure to participate, and his fate is his final ridicule in the figure of Shem in *Finnegans Wake*.

Parallels with *The Odyssey*, like the parallel between Stephen and Telemachus, keep the reader aware of a distant time as well as providing a commentary on both the present and the past. Whereas the parallel between Daedalus and Stephen in the *Portrait* was a fairly simple one, confining itself chiefly to the flight theme, Stephen's interaction with Telemachus is more intricate. The purpose of what follows is to show how through the plot of *Ulysses* Joyce has worked out the Stephen-Telemachus relation and then the Bloom-Ulysses relation as the book progresses.

As *Ulysses* opens Stephen is Telemachus insofar as he is now the son, insofar as he is powerless against Mulligan, insofar as he seeks (albeit not very strenuously) for the father, insofar as he chafes against his position and is offended by Buck Mulligan's insult to his mother. Stephen's mother stands in the background of the scene evoking a sense of guilt in Stephen, who feels that he has failed her as Telemachus at the opening of the *Odyssey* feels that he has failed Penelope.

Since the *Odyssey* concerns chiefly the *Umwelt* of the characters, Joyce has a good deal of freedom in manipulating the *Mitwelt* and the *Eigenwelt* of his characters. Thus Telemachus' despair can easily be translated into Stephen's guilt. And thus in the second episode Stephen's relationship to Mr. Deasy is a blown-up version of what is implied by the simple fact that Nestor cannot give Telemachus news of his father. Mr. Deasy, like his shells, is empty as is his approach to history. Nestor's news of the past had likewise been empty for Telemachus. Mr. Deasy is Nestor by virtue of his interest in horses and his inability to help Stephen. The boy Sargent is Peisistratus, who accompanies Telemachus as Sargent accompanies Stephen, who sees in him a kindred spirit. Nestor does, however, send

Telemachus on to Menelaus as Mr. Deasy foresees that Stephen is a learner, not a teacher, and that he will not long remain in the school. *Ulysses* is, in a sense, the *Odyssey* retold in terms of *Mitwelt* and *Eigenwelt*.

In the fourth book of the *Odyssey*, we find Telemachus at the home of Menelaus. In his search for news of his father, Telemachus listens to Menelaus tell of how he tamed Proteus, the sea god, who changed into many forms in attempting to escape. To learn of Odysseus it was necessary to conquer form, to pin it down, to perceive its "ineluctable modality." Thus Stephen in the opening of the third section of *Ulysses* expresses a sense of the form of things and of their signatures. Then he shuts his eyes and is aware of the "ineluctable modality" of sound as his feet crush the shells (Mr. Deasy's shells). As Telemachus may have identified himself with Menelaus as Menelaus tells his tale, so Stephen in this episode is Menelaus seeking to conquer Protean change, which appears to him as evil.

The irony of the Telemachus-Stephen correspondence in *Ulysses* is that having conquered Protean change and having expressed in the library scene his scorn of the "life esoteric," Stephen is, even then, unable in the *Nostos* to assist Bloom as Telemachus assists Odysseus. His attitude toward Bloom is one of indifference and passivity. Telemachus, like Stephen, does not find the father; it is the father who at the last finds him. But having found him, Odysseus with Telemachus' active assistance proceeds to destroy the suitors and to re-establish order in his household. Stephen offers no assistance to Bloom; in fact, some of his remarks in the Ithaca episode may be interpreted as hostile. It is this failure to participate in life which marks his difference from Telemachus. Telemachus is thus a commentary on Stephen Dedalus as well as a parallel figure, and it is this double relation that the myth serves.

In Jungian terms Stephen is out of touch because he never becomes aware of his role as Telemachus as he had been aware of Daedalus as his earlier prototype. Stephen's intellectual abstractions, his superior sophistication, are seen as shoddy in

the light of Telemachus' superior humanity. The parallel
between Bloom and Odysseus shows us, however, that the
sword is doubled edged and that although the figure of
Telemachus implies criticism of Stephen, Bloom and Odysseus
serve as commentaries on each other with Bloom eventually
evidencing human qualities superior to those of Odysseus. As
Richard Ellmann puts it, "Joyce's version of the epic story is a
pacifist version."[14] Bloom is aware of his prototype, and this
enables him to transcend both prototype and himself.

We first meet Bloom as we meet Odysseus held captive on
the island of Calypso. Whereas Odysseus will escape Calypso,
Bloom is caught by the static round of everyday duties on
Calypso's isle. Although like Odysseus he thinks of return to
the east and imagines his lost homeland after seeing the pro-
spectus on the orange groves of Jaffa, a cloud covers the sky,
his thoughts turn to the Dead Sea and to "Poor Dignam!" His
sympathy for Dignam is perhaps self-directed, for it reflects
Bloom's own imprisonment or living death in the haunts of
Calypso. But it is a living death that he accepts with equanimity.

Bloom in the *Umwelt* always fails where Odysseus succeeds.
Thus in the episode of the lotus eaters, Bloom is content to be a
passive observer of a drugged society whereas Odysseus uses
force to drag his men back to the ships. Bloom lolls in his bath
at the end of the episode, languid and oblivious to action,
whereas Odysseus and his men push off, striking the white surf
with their oars. Bloom unlike Odysseus does not come from
Hades with directives and knowledge of the future. Rather
Bloom is "chapfallen" as a result of Menton's (Mentor's) snub.
Teiresias has not pointed the way for Bloom. "Menton" is aloof,
no friend in disguise like Athene. When Odysseus fails in the
Umwelt, Bloom fails too. Thus Aeolus' rejection of Odysseus is
paralleled by Bloom's rejection by Myles Crawford. Odysseus'
failure has been the result of the distrust of his men; no one
actively distrusts Bloom—he is ignored as Stephen and his
friends leave the newspaper office for a drink.

14. *Ibid.*, p. 370.

The Lestrygonians, represented as Blazes Boylan, pose a threat to Bloom from which he escapes as Odysseus escapes, but Bloom's escape is only a temporary one, inside the museum. As Bloom passes between Scylla and Charybdis, Mulligan and Stephen, he is seen by Mulligan as a pervert. Thus he loses face as Odysseus in losing six of his men had lost face. Odysseus listens to the song of the sirens tied to the mast whereas Bloom listens tied not to a mast but to a domestic situation that is anything but satisfactory. In these scenes Bloom appears as ineffectual and slightly ridiculous. His "weakness" is made apparent in the implied comparison with Odysseus' strength and resourcefulness.

The episode which, however, brings the Bloom figure into focus is that of the Cyclops. It is here that we see clearly that Bloom has virtues in the last analysis superior to those of Odysseus, and the episode enables us to re-evaluate the Bloom of the earlier episodes. Here the Citizen, Polyphemus, baits Bloom in the Citizen's lair. Bloom, a Jew, is a "foreigner" like Odysseus. His "knockmedown cigar" is his stick that unlike Odysseus he does not use to blind the Cyclops. The Citizen throws a biscuit box after Bloom as Polyphemus had thrown rocks at the vanishing Odysseus. But Bloom responds by preaching love, reconciliation, and moderation. Unlike Odysseus he is not brash; he does not shout back at the Cyclops; he invents no clever scheme to maim him. On the surface he comes out rather badly, a laughing stock to all who are present. Nevertheless, his weapon, love, may at last be superior to Odysseus' charred stick. And his philosophy that it is "a mistake to hit back" may be superior to Odysseus' thirst for revenge.

In the maternity hospital, Bloom exceeds Odysseus by accepting the responsibility of Stephen. He does not go to sleep as Odysseus does on the island of Thrinacia. Like Odysseus, Bloom saves his man from the clutches of Circe, but he does not do it by overpowering Circe. Circe (Bello) overpowers Bloom, who is humiliated in every possible way and yet achieves his end without losing even Elpenor. At this point we see the apotheosis of Bloom effected by parallels with Christ as well as by parallels with Odysseus. Bloom "saves" Stephen while undergoing terrible humiliation both from outside forces and from his own conscience which causes him in his trial and demagogue fantasies to be terribly punished. Bloom, unlike Odysseus, is transformed by Bello's fan into an animal. But it is through humility that Odysseus lacks that Bloom triumphs. In the *Nostos* Bloom offers hospitality and love to Stephen, expecting and receiving nothing in return.

It is Bloom's humility, his inability to think of himself as "son of God," his tolerance of his fellow man, his rejection of force, his equanimity in the face of fate which the parallels with Odysseus show us in stark relief. Here is an Odysseus who has overcome more than giants and suitors; he has overcome himself. Joyce's book argues, then, against a romantic idealization of the past, for "heroes" are to be found also in the present. Bloom's treatment by Molly is the final humiliation that Bloom rises above by realizing that "he is neither first nor last nor only, nor alone in a series originating in and repeated to infinity."[15] It can be seen only as deeply ironic that Bloom is first and last in Molly's thoughts as she falls to sleep.

We find in Bloom's realization a Viconian echo. If Odysseus is representative of the heroic age and Bloom is representative of the human age, neither one acts as commentary on the other, for each is sufficient to his own age. To have treated the Cyclops with a sermon on love would have led to Odysseus' certain death. But Bloom's virtues are made possible by the nature of his age. For Vico each cycle progressed upwards from divine age (Polyphemus) to heroic age (Odysseus) to human age (Bloom). Then with the next cycle man had another chance to improve himself in the light of history. Some critics feel that Joyce has distorted Vico's theory, that retrogression rather than progress is Joyce's conclusion.[16] But Odysseus overcomes Polyphemus through force whereas Bloom overcomes the Odysseus within him through abnegation of self.

15. James Joyce, *Ulysses* (New York, 1934), p. 716. Subsequent references to this volume appear in the text.
16. Thomas J. Fitzmorris, "Vico Adamant and Some Pillars of Salt," *Catholic World*, CLVI (February, 1943), 568-77.

Joyce's human age is corrupt, but it is perhaps less corrupt than Homer's heroic age, an age in which slavery, piracy, sacking of cities, wasting of a neighbor's goods, and bloody revenge were generally condoned. The corruption in Bloom's time is the result of the crumbling that will lead to the recorso of Vico. We see Bloom struggling against this disintegration. Joyce, it appears to this writer, agrees with Vico in seeing the cycle of history as a progressive one. Joyce's use of mythological archetypes in *Ulysses* provides us with a sense of recurrence in history as well as with a sense of history's variations. If Vico is right Bloom will be destroyed to be replaced by a Cyclops, and later by another Odysseus, and still later by another Bloom, who although not the same Bloom will possess at least the example of the earlier Bloom by which to improve himself. Bloom and Odysseus are to be seen as individuals but also as representatives of the ideals of their own ages. However, everyone in the human age is not Bloom, as the discussion of Stephen Dedalus has shown. Stephen in the human age with his superior understanding is incapable even of the warmth that Telemachus displays for his father in Book XVI of the *Odyssey*. "And now they both broke down and sobbed aloud without a pause like birds bereaved."[17]

The language of the Ithaca episode, scientific, catechistic, impersonal, in itself prevents any expression of warmth or empathy. What comforts Bloom is that he himself "had proceeded energetically from the unknown to the known" (p. 682). And after Stephen leaves, Bloom feels "the cold of interstellar space, thousands of degrees below freezing point" (p. 689), a reaction not likely to be felt by a man who has at last established communion with his son. The indifference of Stephen is still another of the burdens that Bloom must accept and bear. In the light of the relation worked out by Joyce between Odysseus and Bloom, Stephen's failure to measure up even to Telemachus seems more complete.

In the same way Molly fails to measure up to Penelope (or

17. Homer, *The Odyssey*, trans. E. V. Rieu (Harmondsworth, England, 1946), p. 259.

even to Gaea-Tellus), thereby causing Bloom his ultimate
humiliation. Molly's monologue is Bloom's "indispensable passport to eternity" in the sense that the person who should know
him best, knows him and knows how to value him least well.
To accept her attitude toward him and her infidelity with
equanimity would provide any man with a passport to eternity.
It is this woman whose bottom he kisses. Bloom, however,
knows how to accept Molly for what she is, and he would see
her final "yes" as definitely something in her favor. Joyce concludes the book with Molly's soliloquy to prevent us from feeling that Bloom's newly gained equanimity and abnegation will
not be put to the test. "Pathetic as her Ulysses is because of her
treatment of him, she does not even deserve him."[18]

Her chief role in *Ulysses* is as another obstacle against
which Bloom must contend.[19] Unlike her prototype Penelope,
she accepts suitors in the absence of her husband. Bloom's
ability to see beyond even the infidelity of his wife is his final
triumph over Odysseus and over the suitors of Molly. With his
sense of recurrence, of man's role, Bloom is able to put events
and people into focus, even Molly. For Bloom some of the
individual significance of Blazes Boylan becomes absorbed in
his symbolic significance. The title of the book, *Ulysses*, indicates at its deepest level this absorption of the individual in
his role.

The preceding discussion should point up Joyce's immense
skill in manipulating the mythical level in its relation to the
present. But Joyce also has his two central characters express a
sense of recurrence on which the book is based and thus he
reiterates its theme. In the views of both Stephen and Bloom
we find echoes of Vico. The difference is that whereas for Stephen the concepts he expresses are often merely concepts,
abstractions, for Bloom they have been evolved from experience.

Stephen expresses his ideas on time in the Nestor and
Proteus episodes and in the library scene. A. M. Klein has

18. Erwin Steinberg, "A Book with Molly in It," *James Joyce Review*, II
(Spring-Summer, 1958), 61.
19. For a contrasting view, see Ellmann, *James Joyce*, p. 388.

elaborated on Vico's influence in the Nestor episode. Vico Road, Dalkey, is indeed Vico, the Key. Klein quotes from a letter of Joyce's: "I would not pay overmuch attention to Vico theories beyond using them for all they are worth."[20] Stephen, teaching history at Mr. Deasy's school, finds his work distasteful, sees history as a nightmare because such teaching involves separating past from present, seeing history as a group of facts and dates with no relation to the present. For Stephen the battle at Asculum is actually re-created. He *sees* a corpse-strewn plain, a general speaking to his officers because he defines time as recurrent. But ironically the student Armstrong, who lives on Vico Road, Dalkey, does not even know who Pyrrhus was. Stephen reflects that for Haines and Mulligan, "For them too history was a tale like any other too often heard" (p. 26). Possibilities, he decides with Aristotle, are not possibilities unless they carry within them the potentiality of becoming actual. The Viconian theory could not rest on any other theory of possibilities since certain patterns must reappear. The Viconian theory is essentially one in which Stephen is able to find support in an order imposed from outside and in escape from death in a sense of recurrent being.

Three times he has been in Mr. Deasy's study and each time it has been "the same room and hour, the same wisdom, and I the same. Three times now. Three nooses around me here" (p. 31). In the pattern of Viconian cycles, history repeated itself in the same way. It is Stephen who visualizes the races evoked by Mr. Deasy's pictures of horses. Mr. Deasy's view of history is symbolized by his shells and by his pictures of horses. Stephen sees these horses in action on a race track, not as photographs. Races and race tracks are repeatedly used by Joyce as symbols of cyclical recurrence, the race of life run on a circular track. "As it was in the beginning is now and ever shall be" (p. 30). Mr. Deasy's academic approach to history is for Stephen empty, and for this reason he abandons his work at the school.

20. A. M. Klein, "A Shout in the Street," *New Directions*, XIII (1951), 327.

In the Proteus episode Viconian theory finds further expression. Stephen rejects Protean change that stands in direct opposition to Viconian cyclical recurrence. He stresses the "ineluctable modality" of form and of sound and prefers the Aristotelian view of matter to the Platonic. "See now. There all the time without you: and ever shall be world without end" (p. 38). The umbilical cord that plays such a large role in Stephen's fantasy world is for him important because through it he is linked to Edenville and through it the cycles of the Viconian theory are related. The esoteric doctrine of *Manvantara* occurs to Stephen because like Vico's doctrine it is cyclical; "the tidewave of humanity approaches its shore, runs through the evolution of its seven races, and ebbs away again."[21] Turning from the sea, leaving the soggy sandflats, Stephen symbolically overcomes Proteus and Protean flux as he reaches firmer sand.

The sea in this scene plays an entirely different role from the sea in the scene of consecration in the *Portrait*. There, it will be remembered, it represented the synthesis between time and eternity which Stephen hoped to effect through his art. Here in the Proteus episode we find Stephen, having patterned eternity by means of Viconian cycles, rejecting the flux represented by the sea. He fears water, wants land under his feet. His thoughts turn to drowning, to death, to a drowning man Stephen could not rescue, to the death of his mother, to the death of the father. At the end of the episode a three-master appears, homing, signifying the theme of "return" so necessary to Stephen's well-being.

Stephen's almost compulsive hold on the "ineluctable modality" of the present, his fear of change and of that which is without form finds further expression in his reference to Akasic records, a reminder of the esoteric belief in the indestructibility of words and thoughts, in the Aeolus episode, and in his defense of Aristotle in his discussion with A. E. in the library scene. "Space: what you damn well have to see.... Hold

21. A. P. Sinnett, *Esoteric Buddhism*, p. 171, quoted in Stuart Gilbert, *James Joyce's "Ulysses"* (New York, 1952), p. 125.

to the now, the here, through which all the future plunges to the past" (p. 184).

Both parallel to and divergent from Stephen's ideas of time are Bloom's ideas that go beyond "time is the time the movement takes" of the Nausicaa episode. They are symbolized by the word *metempsychosis* that Bloom is called on to define in his opening scene. Metempsychosis, or reincarnation, has implications parallel to those of Viconian recurrence although for Vico the same soul was not actually reborn. But it is significant that the word *metempsychosis* comes first from Molly, who suspects some sexual significance. From the sexual act implied in Molly's "met him pike-hoses" springs the possibility of recurrence, the umbilical cord connecting us with Edenville. Bloom's Edenville is his early married life, and his thoughts in *Ulysses* continually return to this time. This illustrates the difference between Stephen and Bloom: for Stephen Edenville is an idea; for Bloom it is an experience. Bloom's sense of recurrence is a natural one that he does not have to justify with wordy arguments. Also he accepts flux as a part of life. Thus he acquiesces in the two complementary principles found in *Ulysses*, "the mutation and the continuity of experience."[22]

We see Bloom reflecting on the flux of life in the Lestrygonian episode as he walks by the River Liffey. "How can you own water really? It's always flowing in a stream, never the same, which in the stream of life we trace. Because life is a stream" (p. 151). The stress on watches and clocks throughout Bloom's day is symbolical of his concern with time passing. In this episode he notices by the timeball on the ballast office that it is after one. Bloom, made uneasy by the coming rendezvous between Blazes Boylan and his wife, thinks of the passing of time. You can't hold time back, he reflects. The ballast office timeball is worked by an electric wire from Dunsink. Time flies. "Like holding water in your hand" (p. 165). Bloom accepts this fact whereas Stephen in the Proteus episode had feared it. As Bloom enters Davy Byrne's pub, time is still going

22. Richard M. Kain, *Fabulous Voyager* (New York, 1959), p. 48.

on. It is two o'clock. The regularity of clock time serves to
magnify Bloom's tensions.

However, several references in this episode operate to
counteract the effect of time passing. Through memory Bloom
returns to Howth Hill to a time when he and Molly had been
in love. Furthermore, the timeball itself, connected as it is with
the ballast office, gives a sense of stability and continuity. The
timeball brings to Bloom's mind Sir Robert Ball and parallax,
also Molly's "met him pike-hoses." Both parallax and "met him
pike-hoses" are means of reconciling the flux and continuity of
experience.

But as four o'clock nears, Bloom's thoughts turn more and
more often to the clock. In the Sirens episode he thinks, "Not
yet. At four, she said. Time ever passing. Clock hands turning."
A sense of the flowing of time becomes paramount. The Siren
episode is full of taps, snaps ("Sonnez la cloche"), ticks, and
crepitations. As well as supplying the musical pattern, these
sounds emphasize the passing of time which for Bloom is agony
at present. He would like to hold time back, but this is impossible. Wherever he turns, he is reminded of the moment when
Boylan and Molly will meet. "Big Benaben. . . . Big Benben.
Big Benben." As Boylan nears Molly the tempo of the scene
increases for Bloom until the climax is reached, "Pprrpffrrppfff.
Done." It is at this point that Bloom's watch stops.

But he does not realize that it has stopped until the
Nausicaa episode when Cissy Caffrey asks him for the time. The
stopped watch symbolizes "death" as achieved in the sex act.
In a different way Bloom is "dead" to his wife, impotent.
Furthermore, he is a wanderer, a foreigner, apart from the time
of the world, unable to give people the "right time." Also in
Viconian terms in the fourth cycle (at half past four) came the
thunderclap, the end of one series and the beginning of
another.

Thus Bloom realizes in this episode that every death implies
a rebirth. History repeats itself. The experience with Gerty
MacDowell has brought back to him his wooing of Molly. "June
that was too I wooed. The year returns . . . Names change:

that's all" (p. 370). Bloom is reconciled to his fate in this cyclical world that combines the principles of change and stability. Although he laments that returning is never quite the same, he realizes that repetition is a good idea and thinks of using it in his advertisements. The episode ends with the ironical sounding of a cuckoo clock. A bell chimes. Bloom is once more in the stream of life, but it is a "cuckoo" clock that brings him back to it.

A complete synthesis between flux and immobility is eventually established by Bloom in the Ithaca episode, which is filled with images of "return." The Viconian cycles provide both a fixed pattern and yet a mobility within that pattern. And it is in adopting this understanding of time that he is able to accept the infidelity of Molly, for he recognizes that no one stands alone, that we are all only parts of a series, that we (although not individually) return as parts of another series. Although the Connemara marble clock in Bloom's house has stopped, that is, although Bloom's and Molly's marriage is dead, there will be other Blooms and other Mollys. He sees himself in fantasy reborn "an estranged avenger, a wreaker of justice on malefactors, a dark crusader," thus recognizing his kinship with Odysseus (p. 712).

The solution to the whole problem of alienation in *Ulysses* rests on a correct understanding of time. One is not alienated if one recognizes one's role in the cycle of life. With the striking of St. George's clock, Stephen's thoughts turn to a prayer he always associates with his mother's death, and we see that Stephen has reached no solutions in the book; he is still centered in himself at the point in the present where we find him in the *Telemachia*. Guilt for his mother's death still haunts him. Bloom hears, however, in the striking of the clock, "*Heigho* (the bracelet-bells of the Hours) four times repeated."[23] Bloom's equanimity in the face of fate is achieved through his recognition of the "four times repeated" cycles of Vico. For Joyce as for Bloom the Viconian philosophy provided permanence to counteract the flux Stephen so feared. But the flux of life must

23. Gilbert, *Joyce's "Ulysses,"* p. 365.

be accepted as well as one's recurrent role in it, and Stephen fails to accept either of these. We find him at the end still fixated in reminiscences of his past and in thoughts of his mother. The ideas of recurrence enunciated by Stephen in the Proteus episode will have no meaning for him until he is able to achieve like Bloom abnegation of self.

In Joyce's stream-of-consciousness technique and in the evocation of the past of his characters, there is evidence of a sense of *la durée*. Bergson saw no fixed patterns of recurrence as Vico did. Stephen's thoughts return at random to Clongowes, to his early life at home, to Brother Michael in the infirmary, to Father Nolan with the pandybat, to an apple roasting on the hob. And Bloom's memories carry him back to his childhood, to thoughts of his father in Vienna, to his dead son, to his early life with Molly. In the Circe episode Bloom actually becomes the "pigeon-breasted, bottleshouldered" youth he had been. Scenes from his childhood, climbing a tree with Lotty Clarke, are re-created. Often, as in Proust, a catalyst is present to effect the transition between past and present. Thus Bloom lighting the fire in the Ithaca episode brings back to Stephen Father Butt lighting the fire in the physics theatre.

Both the persistence of the past and the *monologue intérieur* should be related to Freud as well as to Bergson, although Joyce's attitude toward Freud was consistently negative. To Djuna Barnes Joyce once said, "In *Ulysses* I have recorded, simultaneously, what a man says, sees, thinks, and what such seeing, thinking, saying does, to what you Freudians call the subconscious."[24] This was the closest Joyce ever came to acknowledging his debt to psychoanalysis.

The stream-of-consciousness technique is based on a sense of duration. Robert Humphrey writes of this technique in the Penelope episode.[25] Through free association Joyce does away with distinctions in time. The montage technique used in the Wandering Rocks episode also produces a sense of simultaneity

24. Ellmann, *James Joyce*, p. 538.
25. Robert Humphrey, *Stream of Consciousness in the Modern Novel* (Berkeley, California, 1954), pp. 46 ff.

obtained by superimposing scenes upon each other and then by connecting the characters at the end by means of the viceregal (Vicoregal) progression. In the Aeolus episode the same sense is achieved by moving from formal Victorian headlines to vulgar modern ones thus showing the essential unity in diversity of time since all the action of the episode is in the present. In the same way a sense of the persistence of the past is produced in the Oxen of the Sun episode by changes in style from a classical invocation to a passage of American evangelistic oratory. In the Cyclops episode the interpolations unite past and present in achieving a mock effect. And the dramatic technique of the Circe episode, with its emphasis on making the fantasy world concrete, is another means of circumventing the barriers erected by time.

In conclusion, the persistence of the personal past seen in the *Portrait* and a sense of the racial past discovered also in the *Portrait* are both present in *Ulysses.* Now added to these is a sense of Viconian recurrence. Joyce saw in Viconian cycles a corrective to the uncontrolled flux of life. In the *Portrait* he had tried to overcome the flux by means of a sense of duration and myth. But Stephen, as Richard Rowan shows us, fails. In *Ulysses* Stephen has become one more test and trial for Bloom. Stephen fears flux and would like to see a recurrent pattern in history. Bloom accepts the flux of life while evolving from it a pattern of cyclical recurrence within which he finds security and through which he overcomes more trials than even Odysseus. Like Odysseus he in the end reaches home, but it is not home as a place providing only roof and physical sustenance, but home as a firm philosophical position from which he can again like Odysseus set forth in his progress from the unknown to the known, "through the incertitude of the void" (p. 716).

3

Finnegans Wake, in Joycean "fermented words" is "one continuous present tense integument slowly unfolded all marryvoising moodmoulded cyclewheeling history."[26] Joyce's interest

26. James Joyce, *Finnegans Wake* (New York, 1955), p. 186. Subsequent references to this volume appear in the text.

in dreams and dream interpretation is evident as early as 1916
when he kept a dream book to record Nora's dreams and his
interpretations. Two years later Frank Budgen noted the keen
interest Joyce took in a notebook in which Budgen had
recorded his dreams and that Joyce's interpretations were
nearly always Freudian.[27] In spite of his outspoken antagonism
for Freud, Freud's influence on Joyce cannot be overlooked.
Finnegans Wake is the dream of Everyman, of HCE (Here
Comes Everybody). The dream reveals the unconscious mind
of the human race, and the man H. C. Earwicker, who awakens
at the end, is but one manifestation of this unconscious that
continues to express itself in this dream. In other words, the
dreamer, Everyman, never awakens although he dreams of a
man who does. In this conception of his central figure Joyce is
again influenced by Vico as well as by Jung. Vico had said that
characters of the heroic age are not to be understood as real
persons but as representatives of a class, drawing to themselves
the sum of attributes of that class.[28] Thus he sees Homer not as
one bard but as the bardic type. Joyce sees HCE not as a man,
but as *man*. We have seen Joyce moving toward this interpretation in the figure of Bloom.

The title of the grasshopper's book, "Ho, Time Timeagan,
Wake!" (p. 415) gives us a clue to the theme of *Finnegans
Wake*. The title addresses time, tells time to awaken. "Time and
time again" is another way of describing the central character
of Joyce's book. H. C. Earwicker, with his wife Anna Livia, his
boys Shem and Shaun, his girl Izzy, is but the latest exemplar of
the larger figure, HCE or Everyman. HCE has existed down
through the ages in all four of Vico's cycles. His accomplish-
ments have ranged from "wegschicking" the Duke of Wellington at Waterloo to braving "Brien Berueme" (p. 541). He
declares that it is idle to ask about his birth, for it was
spontaneous (p. 546). He is mated with a river, a constant
source of fertility and of flux. HCE is Leopold Bloom magnified
to gigantic proportions. Stephen Dedalus has become in *Fin-*

27. Ellmann, *James Joyce*, p. 450.
28. Fitzmorris, "Vico Adamant," *Catholic World*, p. 574.

negans Wake a polarity that has no function apart from its opposite. Stephen (Shem) twinned with Shaun is one aspect of HCE. Molly Bloom's infidelities and limited capacities are submerged in Anna Livia, the river, which suggests the principles of birth and rebirth. And daughter Milly is given scope in the figure of Iseult. *Finnegans Wake* moves further away from the *Umwelt* than even *Ulysses*. In *Finnegans Wake* we find Joyce recording the unconscious world of mankind whereas in *Ulysses* he had recorded the conscious actions and thoughts as well as the unconscious lives of his characters.

The number *four*, representing Vico's four cycles, is basic to *Finnegans Wake*, written in four books. The first book, Book of the Parents,[29] is divided into eight sections, the first four dealing with the father image, the last four with the mother image and its projections. Wherever there are groupings of four, one can find parallels with Vico's four cycles, the divine, the heroic, the human, the recorso. Joyce refers to this system as a "vicociclometer" ("eggburst, eggblend, eggburial and hatch-as-hatch can") (p. 614), implying that Vico's pattern works with the regularity of an instrument. It is this regularity and predictability that drew Joyce to Vico and counteracted for him the insecurity found in uncontrolled flux. In conjunction with Vico, we find Jung, Bergson, Bruno, and J. W. Dunne all playing parts in Joyce's interpretation of time in *Finnegans Wake*.

Richard Ellmann's interpretation of Vico's influence on Joyce is significant. Ellmann writes, "Joyce did not share Vico's interest in these [cycles] as literal chronological divisions of 'eternal ideal history,' but as psychological ones, ingredients which kept combining and recombining in ways which seemed always to be *déjà vus*."[30]

In terms of Vico, here is what Joyce is saying in his first four chapters. "Finnegan's Fall" represents the prehistoric age of giants, the dawn of history. The uncouth giant, Finnegan, has

29. Titles of books and chapters used here are those of Joseph Campbell and Henry Morton Robinson, *A Skeleton Key to "Finnegans Wake"* (New York, 1944).

30. Ellmann, *James Joyce*, p. 565.

fallen and lies stretched out over the landscape about to be replaced by his successor in the Heroic Age. In Phoenix Park war wages like that of the Roman twilight. Chaos reigns. The images center upon present-day means of preserving the distant past, for the progress of the "vicociclometer" depends on the lessons learned from previous ages. Thus we visit a museum where we find mementos of famous brother conflicts and famous betrayals in history.

The legend is another means of preserving the past, the legend of Isis (Mistress Kathe) gathering the scattered fragments of Osiris. She gathers what she can of the past "so as to will make us all lordy heirs and ladymaidesses of a pretty nice kettle of fruit" (p. 11). This is also one of ALP's roles in relation to HCE. Ancient annals, anthropology, archeology, early books are additional means of preserving the past to sustain future generations. The creation of the two cave men, Jute and Mutt, shows us that in prehistoric times polarities existed such as those we find in the present, and the Prankquean legend emphasizes the theme of recirculation. Finnegan may lie back on his bier comfortable in the assurance that he will not be forgotten.

At the end of the chapter, Finnegan's replacement, HCE, arrives. He is referred to as a big "hooky salmon" whom a lad (presumably Shaun) is all ready to land. HCE himself will eventually be replaced. The salmon imagery is significant here and reminds one of the scene in the *Portrait* where Stephen wades upstream. Man is seen through this imagery in conflict with tremendous forces that he must overcome in order to perpetuate the life principle. When Shaun actually takes over in Book III, HCE is a salmon that is in the process of being landed. "They'll land him yet, slithery scales on liffey-bank, times and times and halve a time" (p. 526). His cycle is over and Shaun's begins.

Chapter 2 describes HCE's role in the Heroic Age of Vico as he contends with the current against which he swims. We see him in a position of trust, as bailiff, as bearer of the keys for the king. Then come the slanders against the hero, started by the tramp in the park who had asked him for the time.

The Age of the People is represented in Chapter 3 when the populace, difficult to identify ("cloudyphiz"), actually take over and try to imprison HCE. The opinion of the man on the street becomes law, and HCE is abused as Bloom had been. Like Bloom in the Cyclops episode, HCE does not reply; he preaches passive resistance and becomes thus a kind of Christ figure in this phase of his existence.

His demise and resurrection in the recorso chapter of this opening series reinforce the Christ parallel. He "prayed as he sat on anxious seat . . . during that three and a hell of hours' agony of silence" (p. 75). His resurrection and escape from his grave lead to the election of his successor.

Each group of four books could be outlined in this fashion. For instance, ALP, as prehistoric mother of the world in Chapter 5, gives way to hero Shaun in Chapter 6, to Shem crucified by the populace on his "cross of cruel-fiction" in Chapter 7, to the washerwomen translated into stone and elm, transmigration and recirculation, in Chapter 8. Without Vico, *Finnegans Wake* would be meaningless. Vico is present, however, not only in macrocosm but in the microcosm of the book.

In *Ulysses* Bloom has given Stephen cocoa. Cocoa appears in the imagery of the *Nostos* seven times. In the Eumaeus episode Dr. Tibble's "Vi-Cocoa" is mentioned, and we read in Chapter 1 of *Finnegans Wake* of Dr. Tipple's "Vi-Cocoa." Cocoa is for Joyce the drink of recirculation, the fuel for his "vicociclometer" since the word *cocoa* contains repeated twice, the last two letters of Vico's name. Add *Vi* (life) to *cocoa*, and we have, life in the circular pattern of Vico. Thus in Chapter 1 Finnegan is reassured by being told that Dr. Tipple's "Vi-Cocoa" is still on the market, that everything is going on the same.

References to the time of day in *Finnegans Wake* are often based on Viconian theory as was the 4:32 P.M. of Leopold Bloom's watch. 4:32 P.M. is referred to as "old time" (p. 290) in *Finnegans Wake* (the old time of *Ulysses*). When the tramp in the park asks the time in Book I, Chapter 2, it is twelve o'clock, the hour of recorso. The striking of the clock represents the Viconian thunderclap that introduces a new age as the tramp's question will do. In Chapter 4 it is twenty-four o'clock, two ages have passed, and the recorso is indicated by the thunder (p. 90). In Book II, Chapter 3, twelve o'clock is associated with the "abnihilisation of the etym" (p. 353), a prediction of the new cycle that will emerge from the destruction caused by the atom bomb.

The seasonal cycle itself is a restatement for Joyce of Viconian cycles: "the clad pursue the bare, the bare the green, the green the frore, the frore the cladagain, as their convoy wheeled encirculingly abound the gigantig's lifetree" (p. 55). Night and morning are used in the same way. Thus the conclusion of Book I takes place at the end of the day, of the cycle, as the washerwomen merge into stone and elm, into evening. Book II ends with night falling, the children in bed, and the four old men asleep in their berths. Since *Finnegans Wake* is a dream, the imagery usually emphasizes night and night falling rather than dawn, but in the recorso we find the cock crowing, "a shaft of shivery" (p. 597), to announce the new day, the new cycle, the "cockee-doodle aubens Aurore" (p. 244).

Other important Viconian imagery may be found. The four chroniclers, the Four Zoas of Blake, in Book I, become the four old men (Matthew, Mark, Luke, and John) who conduct the trial of HCE. These four old men may be equated with Vico's four cycles. Their mansions are described as thunderclap, marriage, disintegration, and return (p. 367). References to the phoenix, to Phoenix Park imply Viconian rise and fall. The circus is another frequent Viconian image played on in the phrases "wringlings upon wronglings" (p. 367) and "Raggeant Circos" (p. 132). HCE is said to be "coowner of a hengster's circus" (p. 529).[31] Trams and races are Viconian in character. In The Study Period mention is made of an exarchon who

31. The reader will recall Bloom's attendance at a circus where a clown had declared that Bloom was his, the clown's, papa.

pedals around the park, "apparently in the lead but at the same time pursuing."[32] In the story of the Norwegian captain, who himself in his reappearances is Viconian, there is Kersse, who figured as Persse O'Reilly in Book I, re-entering from the races. The tram travels on the "four-fold loop line of regeneration,"[33] the Lucas-Dublin line (p. 482).

Clothes and the washing of clothes may be seen to be circular in character since clothes wear out and must be replaced or renewed, "habit reburns" (p. 614). Thus the washerwomen in Book I are busy with the work of recirculation as is the tailor in Book II. The tailor theme suggests Carlyle's *Sartor Resartus*, the different material sheaths that will change from age to Viconian age, but which cover essentially the same core of being. Stephen Hero's ballast office clock is seen in Viconian terms in Book III, Chapter 3. The Four Old Men have asked Shaun at what time Box and Cox fought. Attempting to evade the question he asks, "By which of your chronos ... ?" They reply: "Dunsink, rugby, ballast and ball," in other words, all four (p. 517). Dunsink is the place of origin of the time, the divine age; rugby is the game that develops heroes; ballast is the counteraction of the Age of the People; and the ball rotates, spins, like the recorso connecting all three ages. That is, Dunsink time is told in Dublin by means of a timeball, rugby is played with a ball, and the timeball is located on the ballast office. Still another Viconian image is Humpty Dumpty, who continually falls in *Finnegans Wake* and whose pieces ALP assiduously picks up and reassembles. "The seim renew" (p. 226).

The rainbow dance of the hours (p. 227) like the dance of the hours in *Ulysses* signifies recurrence and return. By "vicere-versing" the clock, the dancers return to the present that they had left as the clock revolved forward, revealing them as they would be decades later. The circles of history revolve with certain great men representing certain states. "One world burrowing on another" (p. 275). ALP is clothed in "burrowed circus clothes" (p. 375).

32. Campbell and Robinson, *Key to "Finnegans Wake,"* p. 179.
33. *Ibid.*, p. 294.

Ship images abound in *Finnegans Wake,* vessels which leave their harbors to return to their berths (births). The tavern becomes in Book II a ship; HCE arrives on a ship from Denmark. River images provide the circulatory system of *Finnegans Wake.* Rivers, the means by which ships and men come and go, are also in themselves circular in that the water they carry to the sea is drawn up by the sun and falls as rain and dew again over the land and into the rivers. Anna Livia represents this particular cycle.

In the recorso, where the polarities of Asia and Europe are finally joined, Hindu and Buddhist cycles appear to reinforce the Viconian cycle. The jambutree, in Sanskrit the tree of life, is linked with Vico through the name "Jambudvispa Vipra." *Manvantara,* which Stephen had mentioned in *Ulysses,* is referred to in *Finnegans Wake.* The scenery of the circular road reveals new times, old customs, as ALP in her final monologue returns to the sea, her father. Return, reincarnation, metempsychosis, "The untirities of livesliving being one substance of a streams becoming" (p. 597).

These images represent only a small portion of the references to Vico in *Finnegans Wake,* but they are some of the central ones. There should be no question at all of Vico's importance to Joyce; in fact, to mention Vico in connection with Joyce is today almost a cliché. Most critics of Joyce have recognized his influence. Among the more interesting references to Vico are those of Fred H. Higginson[34] and Kristian Smidt.[35] Higginson sees Vico's as the most important of the concepts behind *Finnegans Wake* and suggests that the key to the book is to be found in the sentence, "From quiqui quinet to michemiche chelet and a jambebatiste to a brulobrulo!" (p. 117) in which Joyce points to Quinet, Vico, and Bruno as influences in *Finnegans Wake.* A passage from Quinet appears in Book II, Chapter 2 (p. 281), and fragments of this passage recur throughout the book. It is a passage suggesting that

34. Fred H. Higginson, "Homer: Vico: Joyce," *Kansas Magazine* (1956), pp. 83-88.

35. Kristian Smidt, *James Joyce and the Cultic Use of Fiction* (Oslo, 1955).

immortality is attained through natural recurrence. Michelet was a translator of Vico. It may be added that the name "jambebatiste" suggests, in addition to Vico, that Joyce is already connecting Eastern and Western systems of cyclical recurrence. "Brulobrulo" is, of course, Giordano Bruno of Nola whose theories of contraries influenced Joyce. Higginson also shows that Joyce links Vico with Bergson in the phrase "Elanio Vitale" (p. 221) that prompts the children's pantomime, "The Mime of Mick, Nick, and the Maggies." In the same way, Bergson's *élan vital*, Italianized in honor of Vico, prompts *Finnegans Wake*.

Kristian Smidt, on the other hand, feels that Vico's idea of cyclical recurrence is diametrically opposed to Joyce's desire to gain at least "imaginative and aesthetic mastery of time."[36] Vico's theory is the equivalent of a cultic doctrine, a kind of substitute religion. In this way Smidt points up a seeming paradox that underlies Joyce's approach to time. For Stephen Dedalus of the *Portrait* the adoption of Viconian theory would have been impossible, but it should be remembered that Bloom has replaced Stephen and that for Bloom the "vicociclometer" would have definite attractions. The "imaginative and aesthetic mastery of time" was an ideal that Joyce abandoned in favor of seeing life as the interaction of contraries, the flux of life and the permanence of Viconian recurrence. Bloom is able to accept both these principles. Stephen fails for the very reason that he believes in the power of the individual to remain above his creation, through his art to overcome time. Joyce, through Bloom, arrives at the position where he sees that the individual by himself is meaningless except as he achieves immortality through his place in a recurrent series, in an order outside of him. There is not so much a paradox here as a development from one attitude toward time to another.

The influence of Vico was supported in Joyce's works by Jung's theory of the collective unconscious. William Troy suggests that the idea of the collective unconscious may have come

36. *Ibid.*, p. 66.

from Yeats or from A. E. as well.[37] Through such a theory the individual transcends himself by reidentification with the symbols of myth and religion. In his article "Psychology and Poetry" in *Transition,* Jung defines the poet as "the collective *man,* the carrier and former of the unconsciously active soul of mankind."[38] Stanley Edgar Hyman writes that Jung's theory

is based on the concept of a 'collective unconscious' bearing the racial past, which generated mythic heroes for the primitive and still generates similar individual fantasies for the civilized man, and which finds its chief expression in a relatively familiar and timeless symbolism, endlessly recurring. (It should be obvious how close this idea is to cyclic theories of history like Vico's . . . and how captivating it would be to a writer like Joyce, already influenced by Vico, seeking a psychology he could use in creating H. C. Everybody.)[39]

It is in this sense that HCE supersedes Bloom as Bloom had superseded Stephen. The question remains, however, as to whether this collective figure of humanity is actually superior to the individual.

Among the myths that circulate through the collective unconscious of Joyce and of HCE are those of Oedipus, Tristram and Iseult, Finn Mac Cool, Isis and Osiris, and the Prankquean. In addition there is paradise lost and paradise regained and Christ crucified and Christ resurrected. The reader should refer to Marvin Magalaner's excellent discussions of myth in *Finnegans Wake* for a full explanation of the roles of particular myths.[40] Perhaps behind all of the myths in *Finnegans Wake* lies the Oedipus myth with its implications of guilt suffered at the death of the father. The action of *Finnegans Wake* opens at the wake when Finnegan is about to be replaced by his symbolic son. HCE's guilt is always hazy and undefined;

37. William Troy, "Notes on *Finnegans Wake,*" *Partisan Review,* VI (Summer, 1939), 105.
38. Stanley Edgar Hyman, "Maude Bodkin and Psychological Criticism," in *Art and Psychoanalysis,* ed. William Phillips (New York, 1957), p. 475.
39. *Ibid.*
40. Marvin Magalaner and Richard Kain, *Joyce the Man, the Work, the Reputation* (New York, 1956), pp. 216-55; Marvin Magalaner, "The Myth of Man: Joyce's *Finnegans Wake,*" *University of Kansas City Review,* XVI (Summer, 1950), 265-77; Marvin Magalaner, "James Joyce and the Myth of Man," *Arizona Quarterly,* IV (Winter, 1948), 300-9.

thus it is in a sense "the guilt he had taken upon himself in order to free his accusers."[41] It is also the guilt he may feel at the demise of Finnegan. Each of the two other central myths (Tristram and Finn Mac Cool) tie in to the Oedipal pattern in that the son (the younger man) replaces the father, loves the woman the father has chosen. The Oedipus pattern thus stands in somewhat the same relation to *Finnegans Wake* as the *Odyssey* stands to *Ulysses*. *Finnegans Wake* is in one sense a book about guilt and its resolution.

Joyce saw both Jung's and Vico's theories as means of defeating change. Vico's space-oriented pattern was the more effective of these means since it imposed an order on history from outside man. The third important influence on Joyce's attitude toward time, Bergson, was the least effective antidote to change, one he had found it necessary to supplement. In *Time and Free Will* Bergson stressed that the personal past of the individual persisted. But Bergson's influence is still apparent in *Finnegans Wake* in the stream-of-consciousness technique and in the recognition of the existence within the individual of his own past.

From the point of view of the space-oriented man, however, the man who sees time as a series of equal intervals ticked off by the clock, Bergson and Einstein become Bitchson and Winestain. It is from this negative point of view that Professor Jones presents these two "time men" in Book I. Professor Jones (probably Wyndham Lewis, "windy Nous," who in *Time and Western Man* had attacked Joyce for his Bergsonian affiliations) tells two fables to illustrate his lecture. The Mookse and the Gripes is a tale of time and space in conflict. The space man, realistic and extraverted, sits on a stone; whereas, the time man, indrawn, brooding on the past, and idealistic, hangs from a tree. The Gripes has to ask the Mookse the time because for the Gripes clock time is space. When these two figures come to blows and the Mookse overcomes the Gripes, it is their sister Nuvoletta who attempts a reconciliation. In the same way

41. Magalaner, "Joyce's *Finnegans Wake*," *Univ. of Kansas City Rev.*, p. 272.

Burrus (space) and Caseous (time) are united through the intervention of their sister, Margareen. Thus Professor Jones's tales, intended to prove the superiority of the space-oriented man, actually show the interdependence of space and time. Joyce completely demolishes Jones's theories of space by asking us to imagine a singer attempting to sing an *aria* minus the time element (p. 164). Thus Bergson and Einstein are justified and restored to their proper position. Geoffrey Wagner has pointed out that it was the resolutions Joyce made between time and space rather than the oppositions which angered Lewis.[42] In fact, Professor Jones in *Finnegans Wake* begs us to be "tolerant of antipathies" (p. 163).

Bergson and Einstein as representatives of the Pure River Society are always implicit in one member of each of Joyce's polarities. These figures, for example, Shem, Dolph, Chuff, Jerry, and Cain, represent time as the only determining factor in human experience. Shiv K. Kumar in his article on space-time polarity in *Finnegans Wake* has discussed in detail how Joyce's pairs represent the "contrapuntal nature of space and time"[43] and how Joyce was influenced by Bergson in making this opposition. For Bergson, however, *durée* was the only reality; Joyce, on the other hand, saw the necessity of both duration and space and of their interaction in *Finnegans Wake*. Bergson in this book represents only half of the truth for Joyce. Perhaps Wyndham Lewis had scored a point after all. The fate of Shem the Penman, time oriented, scribbling in his own excrement, is the fate of Stephen Dedalus of *Ulysses*, who had declared in the library scene that the writer setting forth to encounter experience meets only himself. Stephen and Shem see time only in relation to themselves. Joyce, however, acknowledges the role of Shem as a foil to Shaun, who is oriented in space. It is through the influence of Bruno of Nola (Nuvoletta), with his theory of the coincidence of all contraries, that Shem and Shaun are synthesized in HCE, who

42. Geoffrey Wagner, "Wyndham Lewis and James Joyce: A Study in Controversy," *South Atlantic Quarterly*, LVI (January, 1957), 64.
43. Shiv K. Kumar, "Space-Time Polarity in *Finnegans Wake*," *Modern Philology*, LIV (May, 1957), 230-33.

combines the principles of change and of resistance to change. Time-oriented Shem (Bergson) cannot stand by himself.

A minor influence, supporting that of Bergson and Einstein, is that of J. W. Dunne, whom Joyce refers to as "Promoter Dunne" (p. 210). Dunne's idea of a multi-dimensional reality explains references in *Finnegans Wake* to people in the future like W. H. Auden, whom Earwicker could not according to some critics possibly have been able to foresee. Dunne believed that the dream allows us insight into other dimensions than those of waking life and that in these other dimensions past and future exist as surely as the present exists for the man who is awake.

In a final evaluation of the influences on Joyce's sense of time, one may see, as the titles imply, *A Portrait of the Artist as a Young Man* as chiefly Bergsonian, *Ulysses* as chiefly Jungian, and *Finnegans Wake* as chiefly Viconian. Each of these philosophers presented progressively stronger defenses against change and against death toward which Joyce moved. Vico's philosophy appealed to Joyce as a synthesis between time and space, between that which changes and that which remains. Through it he transcended the fact of man's impermanence. But Bergson, Jung, and Vico should not be taken categorically as the only influences against change that Joyce relied on. A sense of the stream of consciousness was abroad in Europe. William James had defined it, and Freud was employing it in psychoanalysis. In physics Einstein had proposed a four-dimensional continuum. The collective unconscious may be found in A. E. and in Yeats, as well as in Jung. And a sense of recurrence, of return, is implicit in many myths and especially in those of the Celtic revival that Joyce had witnessed.

The two forces around which Joyce's work centered, time and space, flux and permanence, change and continuity, are forces that have shaped the course of Western philosophy in the conflict between the idealist and the realist, the Platonic rationale and the existential. Joyce attempts a synthesis of these two forces; time and eternity both are implied in Viconian recurrence. And thus from Anna Livia, the great river recirculating out into the ocean to merge with its source, comes the cry: "Carry me along, taddy, like you done through the toy fair" (p. 628).

The Viconian pattern is one that is inherent for Joyce in the natural order of the world and does not necessarily imply for him a god who imposes this pattern. On the other hand, one feels that Joyce never entirely abandoned the Catholicism of his early years, for he found substitute ways of expressing the very tenets he claimed to have rejected. Behind the scenes of *Finnegans Wake*, in essence a gigantic confessional, stand the figures of the Virgin Mary as the great river mother, Anna Livia, who generates life spontaneously, and of Christ in His crucifixion and resurrection.

CHAPTER THREE

THE MOMENT AND

VIRGINIA WOOLF

1

*"What sound hath made thy heart to fear? Seemed it
of rivers rushing forth from the grey deserts of the
north?"*

This question from Joyce's *Chamber Music* XXVI might
well have been addressed to Mrs. Woolf. "It is we who change
and perish," she writes. "But the river Wensum still flows."[1]
Like Joyce, Virginia Woolf saw that permanence must be
sought in change itself. The influence of Joyce is an undeniable
one on the work of Virginia Woolf. From her article on modern
fiction we know that she had read *A Portrait* and parts of *Ulysses* by April, 1919.

Her attitude toward Joyce was, however, an ambivalent
one: she felt that he was sincere, that he was concerned "with
the flickerings of that innermost flame,"[2] and yet that he was
centered on self to the exclusion of that which was outside him.
She read him with wonder and with discovery and yet with

1. Virginia Woolf, *The Captain's Death Bed* (New York, 1950), p. 27.
2. Virginia Woolf, *The Common Reader* (London, 1925), I, 190.

"long lapses of intense boredom."[3] Perhaps with the publication
of the complete diary we may one day learn more about why
she says, "I had my back up on purpose."[4] Part of her attitude
toward *Ulysses* seems to be a reaction to T. S. Eliot's praise of
the book. The very fact that Joyce's position was a controversial
one for her may have caused him to have more effect than a
neutral figure would have had. The influence of Joyce cannot be
discounted as James Hafley tends to do or, on the other hand,
overemphasized as some critics like J. Isaacs[5] have done. Both
Joyce and Virginia Woolf were heirs to Bergsonian philosophy.
Joyce's river and ocean imagery, his clock imagery, his sense of
flux in *A Portrait* and in *Ulysses* would have appealed to Virginia Woolf. Furthermore, Virginia Woolf, like Joyce, attempted to make something permanent of the moment. The
"moments of vision" at the end of many of her novels have
something in them of Stephen's consecration scene in the
Portrait. Leon Edel, who says that the influence of Joyce on
Mrs. Woolf is "more profound than is generally believed,"[6] sees
that the structure of *Mrs. Dalloway* (originally *The Hours*) is
related to that of *Ulysses* and that a "certain sense of oneness"[7]
in *Mrs. Dalloway* comes from Joyce. It should be added that
the influence of the *Portrait* is at least as profound as that of
Ulysses. Another critic, Floris Delattre, discusses a paradox
common to both authors. Both seek to establish a profound tie
between the small, incoherent universe of one man and the
immense unity of the great city representing the mysterious
whole. On the other hand, the city is in continual flux whereas
it is in a man's power, small as he is, to arrest this flux.[8] In both
Joyce and Virginia Woolf the contrast between man and the
city is double edged.

The change in Virginia Woolf's style between the writing

3. Virginia Woolf, *A Writer's Diary* (New York, 1954), p. 349.
4. *Ibid.*, p. 49.
5. J. Isaacs, *An Assessment of Twentieth-Century Literature* (London,
1951), p. 131.
6. Leon Edel, *The Psychological Novel* (New York, 1955), p. 190.
7. *Ibid.*, p. 195.
8. Floris Delattre, *Le roman psychologique de Virginia Woolf* (Paris, 1932),
p. 160.

of *Night and Day* and *Jacob's Room* could have been caused in part by Joyce of whom she wrote in 1920, "what I'm doing is probably being better done by Mr. Joyce."[9] It was also surely caused in part by a reawakening of her interest in Bergson during these years. Floris Delattre writes that Virginia Woolf had not failed to interest herself in the success of Bergsonian ideas in England from 1908 to 1914.[10] In 1908 Bergson had come to Manchester College, Oxford, to deliver a series of lectures. Bergson appealed to her, says Delattre, because he represented a position between the absolute idealism of T. H. Green and F. H. Bradley and the materialistic empiricism of Spencer and Huxley.[11] However, her contempt for lectures is a well-known part of her inheritance from her father. Bergson was brought to her attention again by Karin Stephen, her sister-in-law, who published in 1922 *The Misuse of the Mind: A Study of Bergson's Attack on Intellectualism.* Without a doubt Virginia Woolf knew of this work before it was published; even certain phrases seem to be echoed in her own work, says Delattre.[12] In the book Karin Stephen describes in detail the Bergsonian conception of reality and defends Bergson against the charge that he throws reason overboard. Delattre discusses Virginia Woolf's debt to Bergson which in his opinion is a large one.

Not until after Virginia Woolf finished the first draft of *Mrs. Dalloway* did she begin to read Proust in 1922. In 1923 she temporarily changed the title of *Mrs. Dalloway* to *The Hours,* and in her diary she describes how she tries to "dig out beautiful caves" behind her characters, caves that connect "and each comes to daylight at the present moment."[13] Caves remind one of Proust's concept of the past, Proust of whom she wrote in 1925, "he will, I suppose, both influence me and make me out of temper with every sentence of my own."[14] In her essay "Phases of Fiction" (1929) Virginia Woolf speaks of the accumulation of objects which surrounds any point in Proust.

9. Woolf, *A Writer's Diary,* p. 27.
10. Floris Delattre, "La durée bergsonienne dans le roman de Virginia Woolf," *Revue Anglo-Américaine,* IX (December, 1931), p. 105.
11. *Ibid.,* pp. 105-6.   12. *Ibid.,* p. 104.
13. Woolf, *A Writer's Diary,* p. 59.   14. *Ibid.,* p. 71.

Proust's characters, she says, rise from the depths of perception "like waves forming, then break and sink again into the moving sea of thought and comment and analysis which gave them birth."[15] A connection between her own book *The Waves* and Proust's work may thus be seen.

Delattre in commenting on this point sees that Virginia Woolf, like Proust, reserved a large place for critical reflection in her work. Her work was more than analyses of the inner life, for she also discovers truths. She tried to express a philosophy with emotion and beauty. Like Proust, in analyzing the individual she presents an aggregate of perceptions and emotions, a succession of infinitely variable states, and like Proust she was concerned with involuntary memory.[16] Maxime Chastaing, however, objects to the attempt to "Bergsonize" Virginia Woolf. She also sees Virginia Woolf's time sense as different from Proust's in that it stresses flux as well as it attempts to impose a still point in the midst of that flux.[17] Nevertheless, Virginia Woolf's preoccupation in much of her writing is with a search for the past, evoked often by the Proustian catalyst.

Other influences on Virginia Woolf's concept of time in her novels were De Quincey, Sterne, and Roger Fry. Of De Quincey's *Suspiria de Profundis* she had written in an article called "Impassioned Prose" (1926) that it contained passages that "are descriptions of states of mind in which, often, time is miraculously prolonged and space miraculously expanded."[18] Sterne also, who was often the subject of her criticism, subscribes to a concept of time based on the succession of our ideas as *Tristram Shandy*, which Mrs. Woolf admired, illustrates. "Like Sterne, Virginia Woolf distrusted factual knowledge, and used facts only as stepping-off places for imaginative perception of reality."[19] An influence that is often neglected is that of the post-impressionist Roger Fry. John Hawley Roberts has

15. Virginia Woolf, *Granite and Rainbow* (London, 1958), p. 125.
16. Delattre, *Le roman psychologique de Virginia Woolf*, pp. 147-52.
17. Maxime Chastaing, *La philosophie de Virginia Woolf* (Paris, 1951), pp. 147-50.
18. Woolf, *Granite and Rainbow*, p. 39.
19. James Hafley, *The Glass Roof* (Berkeley and Los Angeles, California, 1954), p. 99.

pointed out the effect of Fry's ideas on Virginia Woolf's style. Like Fry Mrs. Woolf "flung photographic representation to the winds."[20] True artists, said Fry, do not attempt to give a pale reflex of actual appearance but try to arouse the conviction of a new reality. In her *Diary* in 1923 Mrs. Woolf writes: "I insubstantise, wilfully to some extent, distrusting reality—its cheapness."[21]

Doubtless there were other influences, among them those of William James and of Thomas Hardy of whose "moments of vision" she speaks in her diary,[22] but as David Daiches asserts "these things obviously had their effect ... but only because she had already formulated her own aim."[23] "It is not," says Daiches, "that Virginia Woolf is concerned with timeless entities, but rather that her insights into experience depend on making patterns within time that do not depend on chronology."[24] This point is a cogent one and is at the basis of Virginia Woolf's time sense. Through a discussion of some of the central characters in the novels, the characters who have bearing upon the distinction between "actual" time and clock time, a discussion of some of her techniques in the novels, and a discussion of various critics' views of Virginia Woolf's sense of time, it should be possible to illuminate this theme in her writing.

"Turgenev did not see his books as a succession of events; he saw them as a succession of emotions radiating from some character at the centre," writes Virginia Woolf.[25] Leonard Woolf had suggested that she center her method on one or two characters after he had read *Jacob's Room*.[26] In each of her books, there is, in fact, one central figure whose understanding of time surpasses and throws into perspective the time concepts of the other characters. Employing Mrs. Woolf's own "tun-

20. John Hawley Roberts, " 'Vision and Design' in Virginia Woolf," *PMLA*, LXI (September, 1946), 835.
21. Woolf, *A Writer's Diary*, p. 56.
22. *Ibid.*, p. 97.
23. David Daiches, *Virginia Woolf* (Norfolk, Connecticut, 1942), p. 54.
24. *Ibid.*, p. 14.
25. Woolf, *The Captain's Death Bed*, p. 58.
26. *Ibid.*, p. 46.

nelling process," let us work back, starting with the figures in *Between the Acts.*

Mrs. Swithin is sitting reading *The Outline of History* when the maid enters. Mrs. Swithin stands at the opening of *Between the Acts,* and her appearance at the very first of the book is a key to the rest of the novel. In fact, her name, S- within, indicates that consciously or unconsciously Mrs. Woolf saw her as a person whose inner recognition of reality was paramount. We are told that Mrs. Swithin was "given to increasing the bounds of the moment by flights into the past or future; or sidelong down corridors and alleys."[27] She is a kind of symbol for the entire novel, which itself illuminates the present by means of Miss La Trobe's play and its insights into the past. Mrs. Swithin in this opening scene has difficulty in wresting herself from the past and the prehistoric monster who is about to destroy a tree. "It took her five seconds in actual time, in mind time ever so much longer" (p. 9).

Mrs. Swithin's whimsicality, her charm beckon the reader on and stand behind *Between the Acts,* giving it for the moments when Mrs. Swithin appears a "Puckish" quality. She does not believe that there ever were such people as Victorians, "only you and me and William dressed differently" (p. 175). When William Dodge makes her his confidante, he realizes that her age and his maladjustment give them a point in common, that there is no "retreating and advancing" for them, that "the future shadowed their present" (p. 114). Although several of the other characters in the book voice their awareness of the actual nature of time, it is Mrs. Swithin who is the central time figure. It is she who is the link between Miss La Trobe's play and the actual life of the village because she makes us realize with her *Outline of History* or her remark about Victorians that the message of the play operates in living. And the message of the play is that, as Mr. Streatfield puts it, "We act different parts; but are the same" (p. 192). Times passes, but patterns remain unchanged.

27. Virginia Woolf, *Between the Acts* (New York, 1941), p. 9. Subsequent references to this volume appear in the text.

Isa has a momentary realization of this truth as she muses that she wanders in a field where there is no change, "nor greetings nor partings" (p. 155). As she looks up, the stable clock is about to strike, its hands at two minutes to the hour. But Isa's realization is hardly a conscious one. The stable clock is to her an incongruous article in a field that is harvestless, where the sun never rises, where the rose is "unblowing, ungrowing," in the field born of her mind. As she looks up at the clock she compares its stroke, which will sound, to lightning. Her vision will be shattered by it; the world of possessions returns. Thus Isa has an understanding of the contrast between the two kinds of time. But that understanding is not her *raison d'être* as it is Mrs. Swithin's. Isa's passionate unspoken desire for one of the guests at the play is her center until the end when the curtain rises for her and her husband. But Mrs. Swithin, partly through her age, has already achieved the vision of time which Miss La Trobe and Virginia Woolf wish to impart. There is no retreating and advancing now.

Miss La Trobe herself cannot form the link between the play and life because she is part of the play. We know little of her outside of her capacities as coach and author. There are some dark hints concerning her past, and we know that she drinks alone in the village tavern, but her role is that of presenter of the play. She is aware of the experimental nature of her attempts. She worries ceaselessly that the audience is missing the message she wishes to convey. As she prepares to "douche them with present-time reality" (p. 174), the rain descends, nature has co-operated, and the experiment is successful. The audience see themselves in their various roles from Viking to Vice-Admiral, and Mr. Streatfield arises with his superfluous interpretations.

Various other members of the audience, stimulated by the theme of the play, express their awareness of time. The machine that ticks throughout the performance forces clock time upon them.

" 'Marking time,' said old Oliver.

'Which don't exist for us,' Lucy murmured. 'We've only the present.'

'Isn't that enough?' William asked himself . . .

'No, not for us, who've the future,' she [Isa] seemed to say. 'The future disturbing our present' " (p. 82).

The general reaction to the play is one of detachment. The audience feel detached from themselves, neither here nor there. Miss La Trobe has succeeded in "jerking the ball out of the cup" (p. 149). But to Mrs. Jones as the machine chuffs in the bushes, "Time went on and on like the hands of the kitchen clock . . . Change had to come, unless things were perfect; in which case she supposed they resisted Time. Heaven was changeless" (p. 174). To most of the audience the play has granted a single suspended moment of truth. But Mrs. Swithin, who has nailed up the placard for the pageant, recognizes its deepest significance: "you've made me feel I could have played Cleopatra" (p. 159), she says to Miss La Trobe. It is Mrs. Swithin who understands "on a circular tour of imagination" that "sheep, cows, grass, trees, ourselves—all are one" (p. 175). *Between the Acts* produces, then, both a sense of time and of timelessness. "Time which works as a distracting element in the interstices, is at the mercy of the illustration of timelessness which the artist evokes,"[28] writes Marilyn Zorn of the pageant.

In *The Years* a number of characters recognize the validity of mind time, but it is to Eleanor Pargiter that the vision of the moment comes at the end. Both Rose and Kitty observe the unity of past and present. Rose when she visits Maggie and Sara, and Kitty when she hears *Siegfried* or when she is on the train going to her country place; but it is Eleanor's understanding of time at the end of the reunion which rescues the book from its subject, years, years that at the beginning slowly wheel across the sky "like the rays of a searchlight."[29] On the way to the reunion, Peggy broaches the question to herself, "But what is this moment; and what are we?" (p. 334.) It

28. Marilyn Zorn, "The Pageant in *Between the Acts*," *Modern Fiction Studies*, II (February, 1956), 33.

29. Virginia Woolf, *The Years* (New York, 1937), p. 4. Subsequent references to this volume appear in the text.

is Eleanor who answers Peggy's question as the reunion, itself symbolic of the past become present, progresses. Her first insight comes as she talks to Nicholas. Suddenly it seems to her as if it had all happened before. She even knows what Nicholas is about to say because he had said it once before. "As she thought it, he said it. Does everything then come over again a little differently? she thought. If so, is there a pattern; a theme, recurring, like music; half remembered, half foreseen? . . . a gigantic pattern, momentarily perceptible" (p. 369).

The circular nature of reality which had been evident to Mrs. Swithin in terms of human history is evident to Eleanor in terms of her own immediate experience. She hollows her hands in her lap in order to enclose the present moment, to make it full of past, present, and future. It is her understanding of the present moment which supersedes and demolishes the artificial structure of the book with its years and seasons. This time it is summer instead of autumn, but that fact is superfluous for the experience is the same. The conclusion of *The Years* emphasizes "time and time again."

The young man and the girl in the tweed suit, whom Eleanor watches get out of the cab and enter the house two doors down, represent the theme of return, just as Eleanor herself is about to turn around into the room and as the guests are about to return to their homes. The returning couple are proof of Eleanor's theory of the circular nature of reality, as Eleanor indicates with her "There!" as the door shuts behind them. They also complete Delia's earlier experience of seeing the young man getting out of a cab. The novel ends with the rising of the sun in its eternal circular progress. The years then are belied by the dates we give them, for there comes a moment of vision in which the tubes and the omnibuses are stopped, a still center in the midst of flux, in which the moment may be held in the hollow of one's hands. Not until Eleanor opens her hands, does the sun proceed; "it was growing light" (p. 428).

It is clear that Bergson's conception of time does not explain sufficiently Mrs. Woolf's concept of the moment. Her sense of repetition in time in *The Years* differs from Bergson's idea that each moment is unique. The moments that she commands to stand still are closer to Joyce's epiphanies or to Eliot's "still centre" than they are to Bergson's *la durée*. John Graham sees Virginia Woolf as moving from a position in which linear time mattered to one in which time was absorbed in eternity, to one in which mind time became supreme.[30] But the last novels do not indicate the supremacy of mind time so much as they indicate a means of counteracting its flux. In the early novels this was done by recognition of a stationary moment; in the later novels by recognition of eternal recurrence within this moment. As James Hafley puts it, "*The Years* and *Between the Acts* emphasize public as well as personal values—'future becoming' as well as re-creation of time past in the present moment."[31] Neither clock time nor mind time, interesting as their conflicts and counterpoint were, sufficed for Virginia Woolf, even in the later novels where as in the earlier novels mind time is superseded by the arrested moment, that which Virginia Woolf was able to put between herself and death.

In *The Waves* it is Bernard to whom the vision is granted. Instead of the years it is the hours that formulate the book as well as the age of the characters which corresponds with the time of day. As counterpoint to this mechanism stand the dialogue and the "monologue intérieur," making reading the book not unlike experiencing the throbbing of the waves in its title. But beyond these externalities, as John Hawley Roberts has pointed out, there is the "deep inner substance" of the work which is the true meaning of its title, waves on the surface of the ocean.[32] Only the surfaces change; the symbolic significances of the characters remain constant. The waves come on and on despite individuals like Bernard, Neville, or Rhoda and without them.

Several of the characters express their convictions about time, but the ideas of Louis and Bernard are best formulated.

30. John Graham, "Time in the Novels of Virginia Woolf," *University of Toronto Quarterly*, XVIII (January, 1949), 186-201.
31. Hafley, *The Glass Roof*, p. 164.
32. John Hawley Roberts, "Towards Virginia Woolf," *Virginia Quarterly Review*, X (1934), 598.

As a young boy Louis becomes conscious of the question of time as he leaves school on a train. Louis realizes, as he sits in the third-class railway carriage, that he is a direct descendant in time of the Egyptians in the era of the Pharaohs and that if he shuts his eyes for even a moment he cheats human history of a moment of sight. "Its eye that would see through me, shuts—if I sleep now ... burying myself in the past, in the dark."[33] Thus he establishes the continuity of time and his relation to that continuity. A realization of his individuality in relation to history characterizes Louis. He continually, therefore, identifies himself with the heroic dead and with some sorrow and a dash of egotism feels himself set apart from his friends. As he enters a restaurant to dine with the other five, he says to himself: "I am not single and entire as you are. I have lived a thousand lives already" (p. 127). He sees himself listening to songs by the Nile and the chained beast stamping; he sees himself as an Arab prince, as a great poet in Elizabeth's reign, as a Duke at the court of Louis XIV. Louis understands the repetitious nature of time and the truth that each individual wears different guises.

Again in his office these thoughts assail him, and he says: "Yet a vast inheritance of experience is packed in me. I have lived thousands of years ... I, now a duke, now Plato, companion of Socrates; the tramp of dark men and yellow men migrating east, west, north and south; ... all the furled and close-packed leaves of my many-folded life are now summed in my name" (p. 167). When Percival dies Louis feels that "all deaths are one death" (p. 170), that Percival died in Egypt or in Greece or in England. And when experience ends, the experience of the whole race ends, not merely that of a living generation. It is their last meeting at Hampton Court, and great silence pervades the court and them. Louis sees that when "our separate drops dissolved" human history did not lose some part of its existence. Rather the world continues to move through infinite space though we as individuals are "lost in the abysses of time, in the darkness" (p. 225).

33. Virginia Woolf, *The Waves* (New York, 1931), p. 66. Subsequent references to this volume appear in the text.

Bernard eventually takes Louis' place as illuminator of the time problem in *The Waves*. But Bernard's viewpoint is different from Louis'. Whereas Louis is interested in the past, its re-creation and nature, Bernard thinks of the nature of the present. He pictures time as a drop of liquid. As it forms it is made up of habitual actions, then falling, it "is time tapering to a point" (p. 184). This seems to Bernard to be the cycle that comprises the present. He is unable to recover the past as Louis had recovered it. As they walk down a street in London, he knows that once "a King riding fell over a mole-hill here" (p. 227), but he cannot in any way reanimate the historical past. He says: "Our lives too stream away down the unlighted avenues, past the strip of time, unidentified" (p. 227).

But Bernard recognizes a truth about time which Louis did not grasp. In a conversation with a chance acquaintance at the end of the book, Bernard remarks: "But it is a mistake, this extreme precision, this orderly and military progress; a convenience, a lie. There is always deep below it, even when we arrive punctually at the appointed time . . . a rushing stream of broken dreams, nursery rhymes, street cries, half-finished sentences and sights . . . that rise and sink even as we hand a lady down to dinner" (p. 255). This passage is in a sense the theme of the entire book. It describes the kind of time which Virginia Woolf wishes to clarify in *The Waves*, the real time of the mind which underlies all of our habitual actions. Bernard knows that this time is alive and deep. He recalls being immersed in it and gazing at a vase with a red flower in it "while a reason struck me, a sudden revelation" (p. 256). Although Neville speaks little about time, Bernard attributes his own realization of its nature to Neville. Neville first "began to live by that other clock which marks the approach of a particular person" (p. 273).

As Bernard finishes speaking he compares the story he has been telling to a bunch of grapes he has broken off. He feels uncertain of his identity, of his location. "I begin now to forget. I begin to doubt the fixity of tables, the reality of here and now" (p. 288). And as he talks he wonders who he is, "Am I all of them? Am I one and distinct?" (p. 288.)

Bernard's sense of time is more closely connected to the present moment than Louis', which tends to reach out to figures in the remote past who are connected to Louis by intellectual processes rather than by intuitive ones. Bernard's sense of unity lies in his immediate surroundings; his identity becomes merged in the identities of his friends. His intuitive recognition of reality is Bergsonian, but in eternal recurrence, in "the incessant rise and fall and fall and rise again" (p. 297), he finds permanence in change. At the end of *The Waves* as in *The Years,* dawn begins to whiten the sky. Against death the human race sends rider after rider, like Percival himself. Each wave breaks on the shore, on death, but there is permanence in the "rise and fall," the eternal process itself; and when the wave sinks back into the sea, its particles will help to form new waves. Bernard's vision is then his awareness of his individual impermanence but also of the permanence of the process of which he is a part. It is the same recognition that comes to Mrs. Swithin in *Between the Acts* and to Eleanor in *The Years.* When Mrs. Woolf was working on *The Moths,* her first title for *The Waves,* she spoke of it as "an abstract mystical eyeless book." During the same time she speaks of her feeling about the moment as both fleeting and yet everlasting. Although we change, she says, "we are somehow successive and continuous we human beings."[34]

Bernard's question, "Am I all of them? Am I one and distinct?" is answered by Mrs. Woolf in *Orlando* by means of the technique of projection. Orlando *is* "all of them"; she is the projection of Mrs. Woolf's own inner time into history, as is made clear when she speaks of the sixty or seventy different times (different years) "which beat simultaneously in every human system."[35] *Orlando* is not a fantasy in time like the works of H. G. Wells or Edward Bellamy,[36] for Mrs. Woolf in-

34. Woolf, *A Writer's Diary,* pp. 134-38.
35. Virginia Woolf, *Orlando* (New York, 1928), p. 305. Subsequent references to this volume appear in the text.
36. See Dayton Kohler, "Time and the Modern Novel," *College English,* X (October, 1948), 21.

dicates an external world, like Kafka's external world, in itself grotesque but corresponding to an inner reality. In this way it is possible to demonstrate graphically that time, place, and even sex are not essential contours of our being. Mrs. Woolf discovers the same unity in time in *Orlando* which Bernard discovers in *The Waves*. The deeper being that is the ocean itself may find expression as Orlando does in any number of waves. Reality turned thus inside out comes, as it often does in Kafka's work, as a shock to the reader, for we are accustomed to viewing only its externals. It is interesting that Mrs. Woolf herself did not realize the full significance of what she was doing in *Orlando*, for she speaks in her diary of the "externality" of the book. It is the method alone which is "external," for her story is that of the inner life in projection. That she speaks of the book as being "extraordinarily unwilled"[37] is a clue to its source in the unconscious.

When Orlando reaches the age of thirty, time when he is thinking becomes long; time when he is doing, short. And as he lies alone under the oak tree on his estate, the seconds "began to round and fill until it seemed as if they would never fall" (p. 99). One remembers that time as a drop occurs to Bernard also. All of Orlando's past seems to fill this drop, to color it, and to swell it many times its natural size. Orlando feels that these hours of reflection under the oak tree add years to his life. He would "go out after breakfast a man of thirty and come home to dinner a man of fifty-five at least" (p. 99). He recognizes the nature of time and measures some weeks as centuries, others as only three seconds. "Altogether," he concludes, "the task of estimating the length of human life ... is beyond our capacity, for directly we say it is ages long, we are reminded that it is briefer than the fall of a rose leaf to the ground" (p. 99).

As he sits under the oak, he remembers the past—Queen Elizabeth on her tapestry couch, the stags at Richmond Park, snow and winter, and Russian women. He associates elements of the present with fragments of the past. It is in this state of

37. Woolf, A *Writer's Diary*, p. 118.

mind particularly that the true nature of time becomes apparent to him; weeks become either centuries or seconds and half an hour two years and a half.

Orlando changes sex, and the centuries for her come and go like months. She remains about thirty for hundreds of years. In the nineteenth century when she breaks her ankle, she looks out to sea and watches Nelson's fleet and the Armada. In the same century her poem "The Oak Tree" is finally published by Nick Greene, who once rudely refused it, but whom the centuries have transformed into Sir Nicholas.

Suddenly Orlando is transported into the present moment, ten o'clock, October 11, 1928. The significance of the book becomes clear in the last section. We realize that *Orlando* is a fuller expression of Louis' experience in *The Waves*. Louis feels that he has lived many thousands of years. In a person like Virginia Woolf the past lives as surely as if she had lived it herself. Thus Orlando is attached to and evolving from the portions of the past which concern her.

The present moment, when Orlando thinks of it, is startling. How could we survive, she wonders, without the past and the future to shelter us? The nature of the present is once again revealed to her, as it had been under the oak tree. This time, in the twentieth century, she picks up a handbag in a department store. A vision of the old bumboat woman frozen in the ice comes to her; she sees a pink candle and a girl in Russian trousers. Then when she steps out of doors, she tastes herbs, hears goat bells by the mountains of Turkey or India or Persia. These two experiences, that of the great freeze and that of becoming one of a band of gypsies in the East, have occurred to Orlando as surely as if she had lived them. To emphasize the unimportance of this "as if," Virginia Woolf has had them actually occur. The last two sentences are paradoxical but so is *Orlando*. It is the story of a person who lived centuries ago and yet lives today, and a clock cannot give one the explanation of the phenomenon.

Orlando distinguishes at the end of the book between "successful practitioners of life" (p. 305) and the rest. Those who "succeed," she feels, are the ones who "continue to synchronise the sixty or seventy different times which beat simultaneously in every normal human sytem" (p. 305). These people live the exact number of years allotted them on their grave stones. "Of the rest, some we know to be dead, though they walk among us; some are not yet born, though they go through all the forms of life; others are hundreds of years old though they call themselves thirty-six" (p. 305). Nothing brings about this disorder in time more quickly than contact with the arts.

But as she stands by her motor car, the clock strikes, and she is "violently assaulted" by the sound. The function of the clock in these last scenes is much the same as the function of the clock throughout *Mrs. Dalloway*. It contrasts clock time with the existence of past eras in us and emphasizes the variety of times that each of us possesses. "For if there are . . . seventy-six different times all ticking in the mind at once, how many different people are there not . . . all having lodgment at one time or another in the human spirit?" (P. 308.) Orlando herself represents this hypothesis about humanity, for past, present, and future exist in her. Thus the message of *Orlando* is similar to that of the other novels: time is subjective, time flows, and yet within the present moment lies the principle of repetition, a pattern that saves life, if not the individual, from death.

Mrs. Ramsay is to *To the Lighthouse* what Mrs. Swithin is to *Between the Acts*. It is she who represents the flow and stability of time, she who understands the suspended moment. Even after her death she remains in the minds of the others to dominate the book. We first realize her significance to the time theme when at dinner she remembers the Mannings, people whom she had known once but with whom she has lost contact. Suddenly into the present are injected memories of the past, and Mrs. Ramsay sees that life, even that around the table, is "sealed up, and lay, like a lake, placidly between its banks."[38]

The scene at the table is a significant one not only for the

38. Virginia Woolf, *To the Lighthouse* (London, 1932), p. 145. Subsequent references to this volume appear in the text.

development of the time theme but for the presentation of Mrs. Ramsay's character. In it we see her as the central force around which the others revolve. Each of the individual fates somehow comes to its resolution in her—Paul and Minta's marriage, Charles Tansley's uncouthness, Mr. Ramsay's ill temper. For Mrs. Ramsay sees beyond the contours of the dinner table, and she understands that, although the moment is fleeting, here before her is something that will never change. She thinks, "There is a coherence in things, a stability; something, she meant is immune from change, and shines out . . . in the face of the flowing, the fleeting" (p. 163). She sees her guests and family, she hears them, but "for the moment she hung suspended." Whatever they say or do has the quality of suspended action.

At the end of the meal the mood vanishes, and she knows that the dinner is past; its atmosphere has changed in nature. As she goes upstairs to see the younger children, she recognizes change acutely. Her world is changing; the world of her family and friends is not. "The event [dinner] had given her a sense of movement" (p. 174). She recaptures her earlier mood, however, with the though that "it [dinner] seemed always to have been, only was shown now, and so being shown struck everything into stability" (p. 176). Her final realization is that no matter how long they live they will "come back to this night; this moon; this wind; this house: and to her too" (p. 175). This proves prophetically true, for none of the persons about the table fails to reach for the truth that Mrs. Ramsay offers. It is she who draws together the frayed ends of the characters, she who represents the fleetingness and simultaneously the stability of time. And in spite of her death it is she who remains and dominates the final section of the book, while the other characters become projections of her character. This is particularly true of Lily Briscoe.

In the third part of *To the Lighthouse*, Mr. Ramsay, Cam, James, Nancy, Lily Briscoe, and Augustus Carmichael arrive on the island late one September. The house has been reopened. We are concerned with two separate lines of action here: Lily Briscoe with her painting and Mr. Ramsay, James, and Cam on their way to the lighthouse. Lily Briscoe stands before her easel, and she remembers Mrs. Ramsay saying, "Life stand still here" (p. 249). Lily understands that Mrs. Ramsay wished to make something permanent of time, for she herself sought to make of the moment something permanent. Throughout the scene the boat carrying James, Cam, and Mr. Ramsay to the lighthouse is moving nearer and nearer to its destination. The threads of the two scenes become entangled. Lily follows the boat to the lighthouse while thinking of the moment, frozen and still. One of the reasons for the great power of the scene is this contrast of motion through space, one kind of time, with Lily Briscoe's thoughts, another kind of time. James, in the boat, becomes the counterpart of Lily Briscoe. He steers the boat, is concerned primarily with that same motion through space that she is concerned with as she steers her brush, and he has a vision of the past. He remembers adults who "look down" (p. 260); he remembers their knitting, a flash of blue, somebody laughing. This picture is to persist in James's thoughts until his arrival at the island where he finds the solution to his problem.

As Lily Briscoe's memories continue, she seems "to be sitting beside Mrs. Ramsay on the beach" (p. 264). She remembers Mrs. Ramsay's nearsightedness and how that day she, Lily, had "rammed a little hole in the sand" (p. 265) in order to bury and to preserve the moment. She compares it to a "drop of silver in which one dipped and illumined the darkness of the past" (p. 265). And now as Lily dips into her blue paint she remembers that Mrs. Ramsay got up. Lily goes on "tunnelling her way into her picture, into the past" (p. 267). The picture leads her back, and through it because it represents the permanency of art, though it may be stored in an attic, the reader is led to the past. It is the *madeleine* of Proust, and it invokes for Lily the past in the present and Mrs. Ramsay.

We return to James, who remembers his father saying, "It will rain. You won't be able to go to the lighthouse" (p. 286). Another scene flashes through his mind—following his mother from room to room, at last a room where in a blue light she talked with someone.

Lily continues to muse. She has a curious feeling that everything this morning is happening for the first time, maybe the last. She sees Mr. Ramsay pacing in front of Mrs. Ramsay; she feels the strange shock that passed over Mrs. Ramsay. She imagines Mrs. Ramsay's decision to marry him. As she paints she realizes with a start that there is a figure in the window, that it is Mrs. Ramsay. She runs to the edge of the lawn, for she wants to share her experience with Mr. Ramsay. This vivid re-creation of the past is startling for the reader as well as for Lily Briscoe. Suddenly the character who has dominated the third section of the book through memory and mind appears for a moment. The scene is one of the most skillfully done in Virginia Woolf's novels. The fact that one knows that the vision of Mrs. Ramsay is caused by shadows and reflections does not in any way detract from the central meaning—that Lily Briscoe has succeeded in her task, she has re-created the past. She understands that through her art she has given to Mr. Ramsay the only act of sympathy she knew to be worthwhile.

Meanwhile Mr. Ramsay has reached a solution and the lighthouse. By coming he is no longer detached from life; he has found peace. James, too, has discovered inner tranquility. For his conflicts, which have continued through memory during the trip out, suddenly are resolved when his father praises his steering. He forgives his father for his early disappointment and his hatred leaves him. It is he who has steered his father to the lighthouse.

But the moment of revelation in *To the Lighthouse* lacks the sense of eternal renewal which Mrs. Woolf was to emphasize in the last four novels. Lily Briscoe has her vision, a vision that shows us for one thing the connection of the past with the line that must be drawn on her canvas, the connection between mind time and clock time. The lighthouse with its revolving beam is superficially like a clock; on another level, its light represents security for those tossed by the restless flux of the waves. The lighthouse is static in the midst of flux; it symbolizes the moment of eternity granted occasionally in the huge ocean of time. For James this moment of eternity is achieved when his father by praising his steering enables him to assume manhood; for Mr. Ramsay it is achieved when his foot touches the land, when his philosophical abstractions become related to the problems of humanity; for Lily Briscoe it is achieved through the completion of her painting, her re-creation of Mrs. Ramsay, the only kind of creation of which she is capable. Each of these characters reaches the lighthouse, the suspended moment, which Mrs. Ramsay had reached before her death. The whole book is a movement toward a synthesis of time in eternity. Eternity means for Virginia Woolf some kind of permanent recognition or creation within life, like Stephen's recognition of his role at the end of the *Portrait*. But each moment of recognition in *To the Lighthouse* is distinct from the others. None of the characters see, as Eleanor sees that her role is part of "a gigantic pattern." It is possible by tunneling back through the novels to observe how the tunnel narrows at the inner end.

The vision of Clarissa Dalloway is more limited than that of Mrs. Ramsay, limited by the symbolism of its containment in a room with drawn curtains. Clarissa Dalloway lacks Mrs. Ramsay's warmth and largeness of character. Clarissa is a descendant of the earlier Clarissa Dalloway in *The Voyage Out* whereas Mrs. Ramsay is a descendant of Mrs. Ambrose. Mrs. Dalloway expresses no conscious understanding of mind time; the memory of the past floods back upon her, but she does not analyze her sensations. She makes no voluntary attempt to organize reality. Immersed in Richard's world, she thinks with only vague longing of the way Peter might have led her, for Peter's understanding of time is a conscious understanding when he reflects that scenes, many years after they have taken place, "flower out" again. Clarissa was "suggested by the oddest things."[39]

Despite the fact that the structure of the book suggests *Ulysses*, the intuitive approach to time of Mrs. Dalloway comes

39. Virginia Woolf, *Mrs. Dalloway* (New York, 1925), p. 232. Subsequent references to this volume appear in the text.

closer to Bergson than to Joyce. Even Mrs. Dalloway's recognition of her double, Septimus Smith, does not lead her to intellectualize her experience. She has a momentary perception of death in the midst of life, but that is all. It is clearer to the reader than to her that she and Septimus are somehow opposite sides of the same coin. She feels like Septimus; his act of self-destruction intensifies her sense of beauty and of fun, but she does not perceive the unity in all experience which the author perceives. The revelation for Mrs. Dalloway is scarcely a revelation. Septimus has seen that there is a unifying reality in time, but he is destroyed because he cannot live with this reality.

For this reason the author turns in the last lines of the book to Peter, whose vision of Clarissa is the real revelation. His ecstasy, his excitement are caused by her return. "I shall come back," she had said (p. 275). Although his vision is not the larger vision of eternal recurrence found in the later books, it is a personal recognition of return which serves to heal his wound, for in the suspended moment, the flux is arrested and there Clarissa is as she always would be. Peter's way is the middle way which the wordly failure of Septimus and the worldly success of Clarissa serve to illuminate. It is to Peter that the understanding of the true nature of time is granted. Peter alone makes the synthesis between time and eternity, but in this novel Peter's vision of reality is a kind of by-product of the interplay of Clarissa and Septimus; it is not the central experience of the novel which is essentially the exploration of two complementary failures, Clarissa's failure to recognize and Septimus' failure to accept the nature of time. Lytton Strachey saw "some discrepancy" in Clarissa, and Virginia Woolf herself admitted an ambivalent attitude toward this heroine who was "in some way tinselly."[40] The novel is weakened by the fact that neither Clarissa nor Septimus can have the ultimate vision. Although Mrs. Woolf attempted to make a central figure of the Clarissa-Septimus duality, the attempt never quite succeeds.

In *Jacob's Room,* Julia Eliot, Betty Flanders, and Jacob are

40. Woolf, A *Writer's Diary,* p. 77.

the characters to voice an understanding of time. To Julia Eliot it brings a curious sadness as if the present formed an elegy for the past, for past youth and past years. She feels "as if time and eternity showed through skirts and waistcoats, and she saw people passing tragically to destruction."[41]

Jacob Flanders is an earlier edition of Peter Walsh. Both are sensitive; both approach life through preconceived notions of how it ought to be; and both become attached to women who are essentially indifferent to them as lovers. Jacob, like Peter, is keenly aware of the passage of time and of the past. At Cambridge he stands looking out over the court, "the sound of the clock conveying to him ... a sense of old buildings and time; and himself the inheritor" (p. 71). And again at Cambridge he realizes that "long ago great people lived here, and coming back from the Court past midnight stood, huddling their satin skirts, under the carved doorposts.... The bitter eighteenth-century rain rushed down the kennel" (p. 105).

Mrs. Flanders shares her son's sense of the past, for she often feels at night that the church at Scarborough is full of people who have died, whose "sharp-cut words" forever "slice asunder time and the broad-backed moors" (p. 226). As she reads the commemorative scroll in the church, her "measured voice goes on, as though it could impose itself upon time and the open air" (p. 226). Mrs. Flanders has the potentialities of a Mrs. Ramsay, but Virginia Woolf never develops these. Jacob remains the principle figure in the book. There is no vision for Jacob although one is perhaps implied in the fact that he had left his letters strewn about as if he were coming back. His room with its eighteenth-century adornments is one to which people had come back and would come back for many years. That the individual dies but man persists and goes on is indicated by the contrast between Jacob's old shoes that are empty and useless now and his room that must be cleared so that it may be reoccupied.

Bonamy and Mrs. Flanders are involved with this cycle of

41. Virginia Woolf, *Jacob's Room* (New York, 1923), p. 287. Subsequent references to this volume appear in the text.

reoccupation as the book ends, and Bonamy turns from the window to resume the process of clearing up which had been temporarily interrupted by his view of the traffic jam in the street below. There is a hint of an epiphany for Bonamy as the leaves seem to raise themselves and he cries out "Jacob! Jacob!" as if for a moment he had perceived his friend as Lily Briscoe had perceived Mrs. Ramsay and as Peter had perceived Clarissa. At the end of *The Years* the omnibuses are also stopped as Eleanor turns from the window in her recognition of recurrence. "What I'm doing is probably being better done by Mr. Joyce,"[42] Virginia Woolf had written while she was working on *Jacob's Room*. The battered statue of Ulysses, the strokes of Big Ben, the clogged omnibuses, the procession, permeate the final pages of this book, reminding us of Joyce's own work.

Virginia Woolf's conception of time was never entirely Bergsonian as some critics have insisted. Her re-creation of the past in the present and her use of catalysts to effect this re-creation do relate both to Bergson and Proust. Her sense of continuous duration is interrupted, however, by certain moments in the novels when life stands still. Reality is not always on the march for her as it was for Bergson. These moments of perception are almost mystic in character since they indicate, especially in the later novels, the unity in all experience. In the early novels they tend to indicate simply a sense of personal recurrence. Like most mystical experience these moments are connected with a natural phenomenon—the lifting of the leaves in *Jacob's Room*, the stir of wind in *To the Lighthouse*, the whitening of the sky in *The Waves* and in *The Years*. Each of these moments provides a creative insight for the character who experiences it, although only in the later novels does the character in this moment become aware of a larger repetition in time.

Although Virginia Woolf's sense of repetition is never formalized as Joyce's was by Vico, it sometimes has the ring of Joyce. For Bergson each moment was unique in the process of

42. See p. 69, above.

becoming; for Joyce and for Virginia Woolf beyond becoming lay a reality that could arrest the process and in which a pattern could be observed. But Mrs. Woolf was more of a mystic than Joyce. Of her "mystical side" she speaks in her diary: "and time shall be utterly obliterated; future shall somehow blossom out of the past. One incident—say the fall of a flower—might contain it. My theory being that the actual event practically does not exist—nor time either."[43]

2

The *madeleine* of Proust, the handbag of Orlando, and the painting of Lily Briscoe are catalysts that have brought to their observers vivid sense impressions of former times. Likewise the strains of *Siegfried* bring to Kitty in *The Years* memories of "a young man with shavings in his hair" (p. 183) whom she had met years before in Oxford, and the sparks "volleying up the chimney" at Maggie's remind Eleanor of "Morris, herself, and old Pippy" (p. 294). But Virginia Woolf also invests other kinds of objects with the past. Sometimes interiors seem to hold it within them. In *Between the Acts* the dining room, hung with pictures of an ancestor and of an unknown lady, seems like a shell "singing of what was before time was" (p. 36). The room is empty and still, and because of its stillness time seems contained there. Also Mrs. Hilbery's study in *Night and Day* contains the past. Quiet and undisturbed, the room seems to Katharine to enclose "a deep pool of past time"; she and her mother feel "bathed in the light of sixty years ago."[44]

The house in *To the Lighthouse* is filled with images of time, and after Mrs. Ramsay's death, time runs together in it, "night and day, month and year." The drawers of the bureaus full of odds and ends, Mrs. McNab and Mrs. Bast rescuing "now a basin, now a cupboard" (p. 215) bring to the reader a strong sense of the identity of objects with persons. Virginia Woolf seems to say with Proust that objects are invested with the past that only waits to be awakened in them.

43. Woolf, *A Writer's Diary*, p. 101.
44. Virginia Woolf, *Night and Day* (New York, 1920), p. 113. Subsequent references to this volume appear in the text.

Not only buildings but certain aspects of nature bring to Virginia Woolf flashes of past time. To Katharine Hilbery in *Night and Day*, the stars freeze all of human history, and she sees man once more "an ape-like, furry form, crouching amid the brushwood of a barbarous clod of mud" (p. 196). She herself is transported outside of time by the stars.

It is interesting to notice here the function of the stars in "The Searchlight," a short piece appearing in *A Haunted House*. As Mrs. Ivimey talks to her guests at a club in London, the stars come out. The stars seem permanent, and the roar of London sinks away. "A hundred years seemed nothing. They felt that the boy Mrs. Ivimey's great-grandfather was looking at the stars with them."[45] And they are with him in a tower, overlooking the moors. Mrs. Ivimey's memories of the tale of her great-grandfather seeing her great-grandmother through a telescope have been reanimated by the searchlight, which for a moment shines directly at the party. " 'You'll never guess,' she exclaims, 'what that made me see' " (p. 120). Thus the past that has been brought into being by the searchlight is brought into focus by the stars. Time and eternity have co-operated.

In "Life Itself," an essay in *The Captain's Deathbed*, the river replaces the stars for Virginia Woolf. Perhaps a river, even more than the sea, contrasts the two kinds of time, for a river always moves in one direction like a clock or a train, and it is possible to stand on its banks and to observe the difference between its time and one's own. Paradoxically the river in "Life Itself" represents permanency; the great towns fall, we change and perish, but "the river Wensum still flows."[46]

The sea in several of the novels gives the same kind of permanency. Although there is no exposition of the relation between time and the sea in *Jacob's Room*, *To the Lighthouse*, and *The Waves*, one knows that in the background it beats forever and that the lives set against it are those of puppets whom it will outlast and to some extent control. The stars, the river, and the sea give us a perspective on our lives which we would

45. Virginia Woolf, *A Haunted House and Other Short Stories* (New York, 1944), p. 122. Subsequent references to this volume appear in the text.
46. See p. 67, above.

not have without them. In Joyce's *Portrait,* Stephen Dedalus' scene of consecration was set near the sea for this reason.

In the midst of the sea stands the lighthouse, man's attempt to impose order and permanence amid the restless flux of the waves. Although its permanence compared with that of the sea is limited, to reach it is the best man is capable of. Its light is to the expanse of sea as the searchlight is to the stars. Its revolving beam grants insight to those on the shore as well as to those at sea, and the prophecy of Mrs. Ramsay is not fulfilled until the party has reached it. They would "come back to this night; this moon; this wind; this house: and to her too" (p. 175).

It is necessary to distinguish between the power of natural phenomena like the stars, the river, the sea and that of man-made objects in evoking a sense of time. One notices in the novels that the natural phenomena generally remind a character of the shortness of human history and the infinity of the universe. The man-made objects bring to a character his personal past and contain in them fragments of past time. The lighthouse stands between these two classes of symbols, containing in itself characteristics of both time and of eternity. It is, then, a fitting symbol for the synthesis that most of the characters make of permanence and change. It is, in fact, an objective correlative for what Mrs. Woolf is saying in all of her novels. Although she is deeply concerned with the processes of life and with the relation of one's present being to one's past beings and to the long past of the race which preceded it, she is also concerned with that which is permanent, which enables man to see in the flux a point of reference which "is immune from change, and shines out ... in the face of the flowing, the fleeting, the spectral, like a ruby. ... Of such moments, she thought, the thing is made that remains for ever after. This would remain."[47]

The structure of Mrs. Woolf's novels as well as the images serves to bring out the contrapuntal relation of time and of eternity. In the midst of flux there is the unifying device, like

47. Woolf, *To the Lighthouse,* p. 163.

the car in *Mrs. Dalloway* which as it winds through the streets relates all the characters who observe it. When the car disappears the aeroplane takes over its role as it shoots and soars above the people. For the seedy-looking man who hesitates on the steps of St. Paul's, it is like the cross "which has soared beyond seeking and questing" (p. 42). For Septimus it is a signal, and for Rezia and the nursemaid it spells out "Toffee." Punctuating the unity and the flux are the sounds of Big Ben, serving both as a means of unity and as a means of division. Other unifying devices are the clocks of Harley and Oxford streets, the clouds in the sky, and the ambulance.[48]

With the Proustian sense of the return of childhood and the past which pervades *Mrs. Dalloway* is mingled a Joycean sense of the circular nature of reality. The aeroplane flies out over Ludgate Circus, the sounds of Big Ben spread out in leaden circles, both Peter and Septimus come back to Regent's Park, an ancient spring issues opposite Regent's Park Tube station; and behind all of these cycles lies the larger cycle of life and of death, Septimus' death pervading Clarissa's party, life and death alternating with one another. Peter returns to England and in the last scene, in another sense, Clarissa returns to Peter.

This sense of cycles was to be a unifying technique in many of Mrs. Woolf's novels. It was a means of surmounting the Bergsonian rationale that although granting the coexistence of past and present saw time as flowing continuously on like a running river. Virginia Woolf attempted to see beyond individual death through a sense of return. In fact, Clarissa's horror of death had led her as a young girl to believe that perhaps "the unseen part of us which spreads wide, the unseen might survive" (p. 232). Mrs. Woolf's own sense of return does often verge on the mystical. This sense is implemented by the basic structure of each of her novels, the circle, or a series of convergent circles.

In *To the Lighthouse* the beams of the lighthouse revolve in circles like the hands of Big Ben in *Mrs. Dalloway*. The

48. Nathalia Wright, "Mrs. Dalloway: A Study in Composition," *College English*, V (April, 1944), 357.

circles of sound from Big Ben spread out like the beams of light. On the outer edges of these circles where the seen and the unseen, the heard and the unheard merge, light and sound survive although the human eye and ear may not record them. Mrs. Ramsay in the first section of *To the Lighthouse* is the bright beam that in the third section becomes diffused, so that Lily Briscoe effects a return of Mrs. Ramsay by capturing the unseen. At the same time the beam revolves, alternating light and dark, as the book itself alternates between light and dark— light in the first and third sections, dark in the middle section.

The return in the final section is much more than the return of the family to the island, for the actual return not only begins a new cycle but completes an old one. Mr. Ramsay, James, and Lily Briscoe return to discover a solution that Mrs. Ramsay had already discovered for herself and prophesied for them. Although the book is full of a Proustian recall of the past, there is also, as Lily Briscoe saw, "constantly a sense of repetition—of one thing falling where another had fallen" (p. 305). It is the "unseen part" of Mrs. Ramsay which returns and fills the place where once the "seen" Mrs. Ramsay had been. What makes these moments of return more Joycean than Proustian is that to the character who has the revelation comes a recognition of his role in relation to others, a sacrifice of some part of the self for the good of the whole, a sense of unity in diversity. In Proust the individual never sees himself in terms of the group. The moments of revelation of Proust's hero are of significance to him alone.

The structure of *The Waves* and *The Years* is essentially the same as that of *Mrs. Dalloway* and *To the Lighthouse*. The punctuating devices are the times of day and the years instead of the sounds of Big Ben and the beam of the lighthouse. Within these frameworks we find a constant cycle of return, and each book ends with a reunion after which the central characters, Bernard and Eleanor, have a revelation of the true nature of reality as an "eternal renewal," in Bernard's words. To Rhoda, Neville, and Bernard are given the soliloquies that conclude each section in *The Waves*, to the timid Rhoda, the delicate and lonely Neville, the interpreter, Bernard. The soliloquies of Rhoda and of Neville alternate until the conclusions of the eighth and ninth sections when Bernard speaks.

In the first section before the sun has risen, Rhoda at the end is turned and tumbled in the waves; at the end of the second section Neville, as he is about to leave the train, feels "whirled asunder" from those who have traveled with him; at the end of the third section Rhoda sees that there is "a world immune from change" but that she, "like a cork on a rough sea" (p. 107) will not be admitted to it; at the end of the fourth section Neville is seized with the horror of Percival's death; at the end of the fifth section Rhoda relinquishes herself to the flux, to trams, to omnibuses, to the waves. Then finally at the end of the sixth section Neville finds satisfaction in the fact that there is something central and permanent in a room, that is, in identity, and that although Percival has died it is possible to find another Percival, another room, if one abolishes clock time; and Rhoda, at the end of the seventh section, finds at last the door to "the world immune from change." But Bernard's discoveries in the last two sections are less personal than Neville's and Rhoda's. To Bernard on the river and on the train, one does not move in just a single direction. At the end of section eight, boys are *coming back* from a day's outing on the river, and as Bernard sleeps he clasps the *return* half of his ticket to Waterloo. Beyond Rhoda's immunity from change, which is death, is Bernard's recognition of permanence within change, of a pattern of return. And beyond Neville's sense of permanence in identity, is Bernard's sense of the unity of all being, of all those who ride against the enemy, death.

At the end of each section in *The Years*, instead of returning to a sense of flux such as that found in *The Waves* at the end of the early sections, we return to death at the end of each year. The waves bring flux, but the years bring death. 1880 ends with Mrs. Pargiter's funeral; 1891 with the leaves falling, autumn "drawing in"; 1907 with the lights going out; 1908 with Eleanor's remark of Miss Pym, "She's been dead these twenty years!" (p. 159); 1910 with the death of the King; 1911 with the blowing out of the candle; 1913 with a "He turned away" (p. 223); 1914 with "Time had ceased" (p. 278); 1917 with "cold meat"; 1918 with guns booming and sirens wailing. It is only in the final section that the cycle does not end with death but with a sense of renewal in the risen sun. The sense of return is also heightened by the use of the seasons in *The Years*, life alternating with death. Spring is followed by autumn; summer by a cruel March; spring by a searing August; January by spring; winter by summer. As Eleanor has seen, there is "a gigantic pattern."

These four novels illustrate, then, Virginia Woolf's use of a circular pattern that lies behind the circular pattern of her philosophy. The structure of the novels not discussed is also based on a sense of return as can be easily seen in *Jacob's Room, Orlando,* and *Between the Acts. Jacob's Room* ends with the clearing of the room for reoccupation; *Orlando* ends with the twelfth stroke of midnight, which for Joyce in *Finnegans Wake* was to indicate the end of one Viconian cycle and the beginning of the new; *Between the Acts* ends with "Then the curtain rose," (p. 219) rose on a new act, a new cycle of being following the cycles of the play and of the plays within the play. Erik Wiget is the only critic of Virginia Woolf to note the role of *die Wiederkehr* in her works. He sees that the reincarnation of Orlando is not in the sense of a purification but in the sense of a timeless return of cosmic energy like that proposed in the philosophy of Vico. Furthermore, Wiget points out, that this sense of return lies anchored in the events of nature which Virginia Woolf is continually using as motifs: the time of year, the trees, the fields, the animals.[49]

If it has seemed that Joyce's influence has been stressed to the exclusion of Proust's and Bergson's in this chapter, it is in an attempt to rectify the balance since most critics have discussed Proust's and Bergson's influence to the exclusion of Joyce's. It is true that Proust's revelations of the past have in them an almost mystical element in that they are not the

49. Erik Wiget, *Virginia Woolf und die Konzeption der Zeit in ihren Werken* (Zürich, 1949), pp. 68-69.

result of ordinary memory but of an instant in which our eyes become oblivious to the objects around us. In neither Joyce nor Proust are those instants transcendental in the sense that they give insight into a world of the spirit. Proust's resurrection of the past shows him that death is meaningless since the past is implicit in each moment, sealed as if in a jar and ready to be released; Virginia Woolf's instants of revelation in the later novels indicate that the individual does not die, for he is part of a larger reality, as the waves are part of the sea. In the consecration scene in the *Portrait* it is this sense of a larger reality which Stephen achieves. The individual lives by becoming aware of his role in relation to others, of unity beneath change. That people die but that their roles are permanent is the message of Miss La Trobe's pageant. Thus in return lies the synthesis of the individual with the eternal. The early novels of Virginia Woolf are more Proustian in the sense that return in these novels is more meaningful to the individual than as a universal law, but in all the novels after *Jacob's Room* the influence of Proust and Bergson and of Joyce may be perceived.

3

Almost every critic who has written of Virginia Woolf has in some way touched upon her sense of time. It will be possible then in this section to deal only with the more important contributions on the subject of time. James Hafley in his excellent book *The Glass Roof* sees a development from a Bergsonian philosophy in the earlier novels to a philosophy that emphasizes "public as well as personal values"[50] in the last two novels. David Daiches sees the relation of Virginia Woolf's work to that of Joyce, of Proust, of Bergson, but he continually stresses the fact that the matter of influences is not so important as Mrs. Woolf's developing "a view of her art which made her susceptible to that kind of influence."[51] Bernard Blackstone does not attempt to determine the kind of time Mrs. Woolf employed. Rather he emphasizes the fact that she found the conventional

50. Hafley, *The Glass Roof*, p. 164.
51. Daiches, *Virginia Woolf*, p. 155.

time sequence inadequate. Nevertheless, he writes of the "taste of eternity"[52] in her books and of their mystical affinities. Joan Bennett says that Virginia Woolf chose to elicit an order from her impressions instead of "recording impressions as they flow in upon the mind."[53] She notes that for Virginia Woolf "these islands of time in which we live [are] surrounded by the great ocean of historic and prehistoric time."[54] Mrs. Bennett also discusses the means of recapturing the past in *Mrs. Dalloway,* but she finds no system of metaphysics in the works of Virginia Woolf.

Two critics who emphasize in particular Mrs. Woolf's debt to Bergson are Floris Delattre and Ruth Gruber. Delattre writes that to the problems posed by William James and by Bergson we can relate each of Virginia Woolf's novels. Like them she refused all theories that reduced living being to abstractions; she shared their curiosity about the phenomena of the inner life, the importance they gave to intuition; she shared their interest in the multiplicity of states of consciousness, in the qualitative difference between individuals, in the universality of change and of flux, in an individual unity impenetrable by other identities.[55]

Ruth Gruber states that "the poetic concept of reality peculiar to the French philosopher [Bergson] is the kernel of her writing."[56] She believes that Bergson's definition of style, his creative *élan vital,* and his *durée* all influenced Virginia Woolf. William Troy agrees with Gruber and Delattre in finding in Virginia Woolf "the exact voice of Bergson."[57] Critics who deal in particular with the influence of Proust are Nathalia Wright, who sees the "consciousness of self" in the novels as proceeding from Proust,[58] and Erich Auerbach, who discusses

52. Bernard Blackstone, *Virginia Woolf: A Commentary* (New York, 1949), p. 47.

53. Joan Bennett, *Virginia Woolf* (New York, 1945), p. 21.

54. *Ibid.,* p. 23.

55. Delattre, "La durée bergsonienne...," p. 100.

56. Ruth Gruber, *Virginia Woolf: A Study* (Leipzig, 1935), p. 49.

57. William Troy, "Virginia Woolf: The Novel of Sensibility" in *Literary Opinion in America,* ed. M. D. Zabel (New York, 1937), p. 340.

58. Wright, "Mrs. Dalloway: A Study in Composition," *CE,* p. 353.

three new techniques that sprang from Proust—a chance occasion releasing processes of consciousness, a naturalistic rendering of these processes, and the elaboration of the contrast between interior and exterior time.[59] Winifred Holtby, however, thinks that the influence of Bergson and Proust on Mrs. Woolf was slight, for she was too good a Platonist to be classed as a Bergsonian.[60]

Most critics feel that the influence of Joyce is seen chiefly in *Mrs. Dalloway*. William York Tindall states that in *Mrs. Dalloway* Virginia Woolf follows patterns from *Ulysses;*[61] Jean-Jacques Mayoux writes that the thought of *Mrs. Dalloway* is analogous to that of *Ulysses* but that the vision is different. With Joyce all is flux; with Virginia Woolf "the soul is spatialized."[62] According to Ruth Gruber, *Mrs. Dalloway*, like *Ulysses*, revives the Aristotelian unities of time, place, and action.[63] Solomon Fishman, on the contrary, states that Joyce and Virginia Woolf differ because their values are rooted in different systems—his in a Thomistic tradition that stresses contemplation, hers in a rationalistic and humanistic tradition.[64]

Virginia Woolf's interest in "the moment" is noted by a number of critics. Isabel Gamble speaks of the moment in *Mrs. Dalloway* as "the medium for a rounded view of the entire self," important in creating "a static spatial form out of the insistent changes of time."[65] In *To the Lighthouse*, John Hawley Roberts discovers a power that "makes any given moment reflect all other moments."[66] "Her interest lay in the nature of the moment with its burden of past, present, and future, its mingling of time

59. Erich Auerbach, *Mimesis: The Representation of Reality in Western Literature*, trans. Willard R. Trask (Princeton, New Jersey, 1953), p. 538.

60. Winifred Holtby, *Virginia Woolf* (London, 1932), pp. 21-22.

61. William York Tindall, "Many-Leveled Fiction: Virginia Woolf to Ross Lockridge," *College English*, X (November, 1948), 66.

62. Jean-Jacques Mayoux, "Le roman de l'espace et du temps Virginia Woolf," *Revue Anglo-Américaine*, VII (April, 1930), 320.

63. Gruber, *Virginia Woolf*, p. 51.

64. Solomon Fishman, "Virginia Woolf of the Novel," *Sewanee Review*, LI (1943), 339.

65. Isabel Gamble, "The Secret Sharer in 'Mrs. Dalloway,'" *Accent*, XVI (Autumn, 1956), 237.

66. Roberts, "Towards Virginia Woolf," *Va. Quart. Rev.*, p. 602.

and eternity,"[67] writes William York Tindall. Peter and Margaret Havard-Williams see this moment as related to mystical experience in *The Waves* where the image of the circle predominates—Rhoda's bubbles, Louis' ring of steel, Bernard's smoke rings.[68] Another critic, James Southall Wilson, says that she has "made out of flowing time something permanent."[69] Virginia Woolf's own essay on the moment indicates its importance to her. The moment, she says, consists of visual and sense impressions. Then at the center is consciousness and self-assertion. The moment runs "like quick-silver" and yet some moments are "stabilized, stamped like a coin."[70]

Virginia Woolf's theory of time is difficult to sum up because it is composed of sometimes divergent points of view. "The more we know of people the less we can sum them up," she writes in her essay on Mrs. Thrale.[71] Aileen Pippett perhaps states the core of the matter when she says: "She has attained the kind of immortality she strove for, the seizing and sharing of the mystic moment."[72] Because of her keen awareness of the flux of life with its dangers and uncertainties, she was compelled to discover within this flux something which would prevail. This was done by means of a sense of return and by means of the arrested moment within which return was effected.

Return also was seen by Virginia Woolf as a pattern of life. Clarissa's line, "I shall come back," echoes down through all the succeeding novels. "The seim renew." There is in Virginia Woolf something of the mystic, something of the Bergsonian, something of the rationalist, something of the Platonist. "The melancholy river bears us on,"[73] she wrote in "The String Quartet," but against the flow of the river she re-creates the

67. Tindall, "Many-Leveled Fiction," *CE*, p. 66.
68. Peter and Margaret Havard-Williams, "Mystical Experience in Virginia Woolf's *The Waves*," *Essays in Criticism*, IV (January, 1954), 84.
69. J. S. Wilson, "Time and Virginia Woolf," *Virginia Quarterly Review*, XVIII (Spring, 1942), 276.
70. Virginia Woolf, *The Moment and Other Essays* (New York, 1948), p. 7.
71. *Ibid.*, p. 50.
72. Aileen Pippett, *The Moth and the Star* (Boston, 1955), p. 368.
73. Woolf, *A Haunted House*, p. 24.

past, not only the immediate past but past ages that are mean-ingful to her. Her emphasis on the moment of recall is Proust-ian; her emphasis on the unifying quality of this moment is Joycean. Her re-creation of the past is Proustian; her sense of return is Joycean. Her sense of an arrested instant is mystical; her sense of the persistence of past ages is Joycean. Her sense of flux and her sense of intuition are Bergsonian; her sense of the therapeutic value of writing down haddock and sausage is rationalistic.

In summary the essence of her belief about time, however, was that Shakespeare's sister, buried unknown by the Elephant and the Castle, "lives in you and in me, and in many other women," for "great poets do not die; they are continuing presences; they need only the opportunity to walk among us in the flesh."[74] We who read Virginia Woolf give her this opportunity.

74. Virginia Woolf, *A Room of One's Own* (New York, 1929), p. 198.

CHAPTER FOUR

ALDOUS HUXLEY:

PERENNIAL TIME

1

"In the mind, too, some coloured accident of beauty revives and makes all young again. A chance light shines and suddenly it is spring."[1]

Whereas Joyce had used *la durée* as a means of creating a sense of ubiquity in his books and whereas Virginia Woolf had from *Jacob's Room* on immersed her characters in mind time, Huxley in his novels remains aloof from the human process, creating characters who are chiefly mouthpieces for his ideas. Clock time and eternity, two abstractions on which he relies, lead him away from the flow of life into the realm of theory, so that his novels are often more truly essays to expound his ideas. "He has the power of disengaging his mind as if it were an impersonal instrument," writes Edwin Muir.[2]

Huxley's early philosophical position was close to the materialistic empiricism of his grandfather, T. H. Huxley. "I have no dislike or fear of external objects, and feel no objection to

1. Aldous Huxley, *Arabia Infelix and Other Poems* (New York, 1929), p. 7.
2. Edwin Muir, *Transition* (New York, 1926), p. 103.

immersing myself in them,"[3] he writes in *Proper Studies*. In this book he rejects an idealistic position, although he states that he is able to understand "the Platonic theory of ideas," and he also rejects the position of the philosopher like Bergson "who would chop and trim the objective world in order that it may fit the bed he had prepared for it in his mind."[4] In "Vulgarity in Literature" Huxley compares the world of the mind to a "Wombland." "Matter is incomparably subtler and more intricate than mind," he writes.[5]

Huxley's mysticism developed in spite of and because of firmly laid anti-mystical concepts. D. S. Savage's essay on Huxley shows how the earlier anti-mystical works fulfill the same function for the author's personality as the later mystical writings.[6] It is possible to show as well that his early ideas of time led to the "timeless Ground" of his later works.

Huxley early rejected the Bergsonian time scheme as an abstraction. C. E. M. Joad stresses the illogicality of accepting as Huxley did the reality of chair and table and rejecting the reality of the mental process, thought, that is equally the result of combinations of electrons.[7]

Furthermore, Huxley considered Proust decadent because he did not apply his acute analyses of personality to a moral purpose. In *Proper Studies* Huxley also deplores what he calls Proust's "discontinuity." He declares that there is a "strange moral poverty"[8] about the book and that only an invalid could afford the luxury of such a life of intermittence. In stressing this latter point in Proust's novel, Huxley shows his distrust of involuntary memory, which as Proust often indicates is the key to his work. Proust's chief significance for Huxley lay in the

3. Aldous Huxley, "Intelligence," in *Proper Studies* (New York, 1928), p. 76.

4. *Ibid.*, p. 74.

5. Aldous Huxley, *Collected Essays* (New York, 1959), p. 109.

6. D. S. Savage, "Aldous Huxley and the Dissociation of Personality," *Critiques and Essays on Modern Fiction*, ed. John W. Aldridge (New York, 1952), pp. 340-61.

7. C. E. M. Joad, "Philosophy and Aldous Huxley," *The Realist* (July 1, 1929), 99-114.

8. "Personality and the Discontinuity of the Mind," in *Proper Studies* (New York, 1928), p. 291.

more concrete realm of his magnificent psychological analyses. Often Huxley's technique imitates the Proustian technique, but imitates it in form, not in spirit.

In a very early story from *Limbo* called "Happily Ever After," a story containing an almost Jamesian touch with its American traveler in England, Guy tells Marjorie, "We've got twelve hours ... but that's only clockwork time. You can give an hour the quality of everlastingness, and spend years which are as though they had never been."[9] This remark suggests a relativistic attitude toward time, but does not reflect any particular influence.

Nevertheless, "Uncle Spencer" in Huxley's collection of short stories *Little Mexican* is strikingly Proustian in its method. Antonieke, the Belgian housekeeper, reminds the reader of Françoise in *Swann's Way*. In addition, we find the child observer, the long, involved Proustian sentence structure giving the flavor of remoteness, and opening paragraphs with general comments on memory and past time. In the same story Bergson is mentioned, not in connection with time but in connection with his *élan vital*, in a comic comparison of pigs in the Grand' Place on Saturday morning with "Bergsonian *élan vital* in a state of incessant agitation."[10] It is interesting to note that at this stage in his development, Huxley attributes to Uncle Spencer such discreditable interests as Brahmanism, Swedenborgianism, and mysticism.

The title story in the same volume, *Little Mexican*, begins also in a Proustian fashion. The sight of his moth-eaten, old green hat brings back to the narrator memories of his Italian tour in 1912. The story then proceeds with the tale of his journey and his meeting with Fabio and Fabio's despotic father. However, we find here no real connection with Proust, no acceptance of the motivating interest behind Proust's preoccupation with time.

Of the early novels *Those Barren Leaves* gives us the most pertinent material on time. Miss Thriplow as she crushes a bay

9. Aldous Huxley, *Limbo* (New York, n. d.), p. 161.
10. Aldous Huxley, *Little Mexican* (London, 1948), p. 24.

leaf between her fingertips is "suddenly back in the barber's shop at Weltringham, waiting there while her cousin Jim had his hair cut."[11] The entire scene returns for her. Mr. Chigwell, the barber, the revolving brush, the vaporizer, and then her love for Jim, who is now dead. She feels here and now the exact "delicate" passion she had felt then. The others go on talking, but Miss Thriplow is engaged in her recollection of Jim.

Huxley deals directly with the Proustian notion of time in this novel through Francis Chelifer, who considers such recollections as Miss Thriplow's dangerous. Chelifer is glad when his family home is sold, for the souls of dead events lodge themselves in objects, "a house, a flower, a landscape, in a group of trees seen from the train against the sky-line, an old snapshot, a broken pen-knife, a book, a perfume" (p. 124). One is tempted by such things to live in the past and to neglect the present, one's bodily existence. Huxley later scoffs in *Those Barren Leaves* at what he calls "the cult of the emotions" (p. 278) fostered by Bergsonism and Romain-Rollandism in the twentieth century. Actually it is easy to see that Bergson receives short shrift from Huxley: his *élan vital* compared to seething pigs in a market, his intuition accredited to dogs, (p. 253) who are good Bergsonians according to Huxley, and his theories of time satirized in the purposely satirical juxtaposition of the past, Miss Thriplow's "delicate" passion, with the present, a barber shop manned by a Mr. Chigwell.

The resolution of the matter comes in the final pages of *Those Barren Leaves* in the words of Calamy. "Human beings have selected three-dimensional space and time as their axes. Their minds, their bodies, and the earth on which they live being what they are, human beings could not have done otherwise. Space and time are necessary and inevitable ideas for us" (p. 397). So although Huxley occasionally uses the Proustian technique in this novel, he firmly rejects the motivation behind it, and the technique itself is employed with a satirical twist.

In *Point Counterpoint* one finds a good many Proustian

11. Aldous Huxley, *Those Barren Leaves* (New York, 1925), p. 55. Subsequent references to this volume appear in the text.

parallels, and sometimes they are more serious in tone than the ones in *Those Barren Leaves*. For instance, the full moon causes Elinor as she talks to her husband to change "her position in space and time" (p. 72). She is back at Gattenden in the early months of their marriage.

Usually, however, Huxley's use of involuntary memory mocks the Proustian method. Furthermore, it is used in a mechanical fashion here and there in the novel and does not by and large either expand or condense the time experience as Proust's explorations into the past do. For Walter Bidlake, the catalyst is an offensive old man,[12] in contrast to the *madeleine* or sound catalysts used by Proust. Suddenly Bidlake is nine years old, walking with his mother to visit Wethrington, the under-gardener, who is ill. He remembers the staring eyes, the clammy white skin, the skeleton hands, and the stale air of the sickroom. He longs to get into the fresh air, for Mrs. Wethrington's grief only embarrasses him.

The scene in which Spandrell, inspired by a lamp post, finds himself in the snow-covered pass where he had been as a boy is further proof of Huxley's ridicule of the Proustian method. Had it been Rampion instead of the decadent Spandrell to whom this experience occurred, one could interpret it as more significant.

However, Huxley's attitude toward Proust throughout the book is usually a caustic one. Molly d'Exergillod, a professional conversationalist who practices her repartee in bed before she gets up and who records witticisms and anecdotes in a diary, has married into a family that "has won the distinction of being mentioned in *Sodome et Gomorrhe*" (p. 85). And Mark Rampion, the positive character in *Point Counterpoint*, pronounces Proust's "horrible great book" "an endless masturbation" (p. 400).

These examples are climaxed by the description of Lucy Tantamount's laugh: her painted lips against her pale gums transport Philip Quarles without transition to the palace

12. Aldous Huxley, *Point Counterpoint* (New York, 1947), p. 13. Subsequent references to this volume appear in the text.

gardens at Jaipur where the crocodiles are fed. He sees the insides of their mouths, like "slightly glacé cream-coloured kid" (p. 293).

Aside from the fact of ridicule, these experiences do not catch the essence of the Proustian recall of the past, for they remain within the framework of clock time instead of producing a sense of the flow of mind time. Huxley removes a scene from the past and places it in the present. Because he is involved with clock time, he has no other choice.

But aside from imitation of the Proustian technique, *Point Counterpoint* shows a more general interest in the question of time. As Beatrice Gilray mends her pink silk camisole, the clock ticks, either according to Newton, the moving instant separating the past from the future, or according to Aristotle, making a little more of the possible real. And Illidge as a communist is worried by theories of Einstein and Eddington who claim "that space and time and mass themselves, the whole universe of Newton and his successors, are simply our own invention" (p. 153).

In fact, the very contrapuntal nature of the book itself reflects a theory of time. Philip Quarles's ideas on writing a novel with a "multiplicity of aspects" (p. 192) seem to the casual observer to reflect Bergson's theories. Actually they do not. Quarles recognizes that experiences or various planes of experience may be juxtaposed, one on the next, as if they had happened that way. Thus Huxley plays with time as if he were rearranging objects: first Walter Bidlake and Marjorie, then Tantamount House and Lord Edward in his laboratory, next Philip and Elinor in India. But Huxley fails to create the sense of ubiquity which pervades *Ulysses* or *Finnegans Wake* because his shuffling of scenes is external to the characters involved. Note, for example, the transitions between chapters. At the end of Chapter II in *Point Counterpoint*, we find ourselves at Lady Edward's party at Tantamount House. "Two flights up . . . ," begins Chapter 3, "Lord Edward Tantamount was busy in his laboratory." Joyce's ordering of scenes is related to the inner life of his characters rather than to their outer actions. For instance, the Nestor and Proteus episodes in *Ulysses* are ordered thus because they indicate progressive states of mind in Stephen, the search for the father developing from a seeking in the empty annals of history to a grappling with the nature of reality. Emphasis on the external world circumscribes and limits the action of the novel; with the inner world as a medium there are no boundaries of time and of space.

Philip Quarles explains his theory of multiplicity further in a later entry in the notebook. Not only should an artist see an event through the eyes of biologist, chemist, bishop, and historian, but he should be able to look through any particular object or experience, to render it diaphanous, so that in a single object one may see the entire universe. "The artistic problem is to produce diaphanousness in spots, selecting the spots so as to reveal only the most humanly significant of distant vistas behind the near familiar object" (p. 247). This idea of diaphanousness is akin to Proust's theories of past experiences hidden in an object and brought to consciousness by a sudden flash of insight as one tastes, hears, or smells the object. The obvious difference is that Huxley sees past history in any object through his intellect whereas Proust experiences the past through his senses or his intuition.

Furthermore, Quarles wishes to see the historical past in any object whereas Proust has a character experience his personal past through an object. From the smell of roast duck in an old kitchen, Quarles would glimpse spiral nebulae, Mozart's music, the stigmata of St. Francis of Assisi. Thus he steps outside of individual experience and by so doing objectifies the time values so that the character by an intellectual process is reminded of earlier events but does not relive them as Proust's character does. Quarles himself suspects that his diaphanousness could not be achieved without pedantry. Quarles's point of view is Huxley's, for neither one sees coexistence of past and present—only a transparent quality in the present that may allow certain past events to filter through.

But it is Mark Rampion (D. H. Lawrence) who pronounces the final word on the matter of time at this stage in Huxley's work. "What with their quantum theory, wave mechanics, relativity, and all the rest of it, they do really seem to have got a little way outside humanity. Well, what the devil's the good of that?" he asks Philip (p. 398). This question is a timely one for Huxley, for soon after the writing of *Point Counterpoint* he was to find the philosophy that led him far outside the bounds of humanity but that formed a kind of counterpart to his early reliance on clock time.[13]

However, it is not the novels only that tell us about time. Huxley's interest in it is further reflected in two volumes of essays, *Proper Studies* (1927) and *Do What You Will* (1929), which belong to this period. Already mentioned is the essay in *Proper Studies* in which Huxley states that Proust's work produces a sense of discontinuity. Huxley has always set himself up against the relativists, almost in fear, one senses. His sudden turning to mystical doctrine is not surprising if we realize that it in no way disturbs his basic sense of the absolute quality of reality. He simply sets up a second *modus vivendi* or *modus non vivendi* that barely touches the first. When Huxley accuses Proust of discontinuity, one is obliged to recognize that unconsciously he is accusing Proust of his own fault, for the theory of "multiplicity" in practice produces a discontinuity more striking than the breaks in continuity which Huxley sees in *Remembrance of Things Past*.

In the essay on Pascal, in *Do What You Will*, Huxley claims that "the life-worshipper lives as far as possible in the present— in present time or present eternity."[14] In this phrase, "present eternity," there is perhaps a hint of reconciliation with the adherents of mind time. Huxley mentions in the same essay his interest in J. W. Dunne's book[15] on time and the fact that the future in certain circumstances is foreseeable. For a fleeting

13. D. S. Savage in "Aldous Huxley and the Dissociation of Personality" points out that Huxley's career is shaped like an hourglass. The detachment that Huxley felt as a result of his early disillusionment toward life turns into the impersona'ity of his mysticism. Only in *Point Counterpoint*, which stands between the two bulbs of the hourglass, does he move toward "a sympathetic approach to human life" (p. 349).

14. Aldous Huxley, *Do What You Will* (London, 1949), p. 290.

15. J. W. Dunne, *An Experiment with Time* (New York, 1927).

moment he admits that time is a habit formed by our earliest ancestors and that by thinking in terms of the fourth dimension we are now breaking that habit.[16] This is a remarkable and momentary concession to the relativists against whom he persists in standing firm. "How I hate old Proust!" he exclaims in *Eyeless in Gaza*. "Really detest him."[17]

It is interesting that Bergson himself in *Creative Evolution* actually says about what Huxley has to say on the subject of discontinuity. Bergson writes: "We could not live over again a single moment, for we should have to begin by effacing the memory of all that had followed."[18] For Bergson the past *exists* in the present, is preserved in the present. Bergson's concept of time is, however, basically different from Huxley's for it involves duration, a phenomenon of the individual consciousness, and later for Bergson a phenomenon perceivable only through the individual consciousness. Huxley gave no recognition to this time of the mind. Quarles's theory of multiplicity is an intellectual abstraction imposed by the author. It retains a sense of clock time, but a clock time reinterpreted and rearranged by the ideas of a god-like manipulator. The dream or phantasy life of the characters is not a governing factor in Huxley's work.

Huxley's rejection of an inner time of the mind illustrates his need for a time medium that is reassuringly in order. His reliance on the absolute nature of time and space may have a two-fold origin. It may result both from his sense of the need for something concrete to cling to at a time when Victorian values seemed to be crumbling and paradoxically from his deeper sense that even time and space are not solid, thus his necessity for insisting that they are. Under his early rejection of those who preached a subjective time lie perhaps unconscious fears that they are right and that they may disturb his world— thus his violence in contradicting them.

16. Huxley, *Do What You Will*, p. 263.
17. Aldous Huxley, *Eyeless in Gaza* (New York, 1936), p. 6. Subsequent references to this volume appear in the text.
18. Henri Bergson, *Creative Evolution*, trans. Arthur Mitchell (New York, 1944), p. 8.

2

The change in Huxley's thinking which came after his meeting with Gerald Heard in the early 1930's is apparent in *Eyeless in Gaza* (1936), the first novel in which one sees Huxley moving away from Rampionism (D. H. Lawrence) and toward a new philosophy of asceticism and contemplation. But there are in addition numerous anti-mystical references to time in the novel. *Eyeless in Gaza* is significant in a study of time not only for its ideas but for its method. As in *Point Counterpoint*, Huxley chooses to juxtapose scenes and events occurring in separate circumstances and to diverse characters. Here, however, the discontinuity is even more marked than in the earlier novel. D. S. Savage suggests that by his method Huxley emphasizes the sense of discontinuity in the existence of Anthony Beavis.[19] And it is true that the unity that Anthony discovers in the last chapter is in sharp contrast to his sense of life as "a pack of snapshots in the hands of a lunatic" (p. 17) as he looks at some old photographs in an early scene.

"Somewhere in the mind a lunatic shuffled a pack of snapshots and dealt them out at random, shuffled once more and dealt them out in different order, again and again, indefinitely. There was no chronology" (p. 17). These words describe the time scheme behind the book. The chapters are headed by dates, and the dates are "dealt out at random" so that we move backward and forward with no regard for the conventions of time. Huxley has here pushed the method used in *Point Counterpoint* a step further, perhaps influenced by Christopher Isherwood's *The Memorial*.[20] There is no order in point of chronology. Still he does not achieve a sense of ubiquity like that in *Ulysses* chiefly because although dates are shuffled, we are still aware of chronology in the conventional sense. The mind of the reader rearranges the cards in order despite the author. Joyce opens for us a new world, a new order of time, whereas Huxley in *Eyeless in Gaza* merely plays with the hands

19. Savage, *Modern Fiction*, p. 351.
20. Jocelyn Brooke, *Aldous Huxley*, Bibliographical Series of Supplements to *British Book News* (London, 1954), p. 24.

of the clock. This is but another example of Huxley's intellectual detachment.

Furthermore, Huxley's technique of multiplicity is seen also inside the larger structure of the novel. In the funeral scene (p. 24) we find the camera shifted from face to face, from mind to mind. James Beavis trying to recall a name, Anthony sick with fright and distaste, Mary Amberly deciding not to kiss the boy, Roger Amberly observing his father-in-law: a gallery of reactions to Mrs. Beavis' funeral.

And as for Proust and Bergson, they receive no more respect in this novel than in the earlier books despite haunting Proustian parallels. In the opening pages there is a picture of Proust as "that asthmatic seeker of lost time squatting, horribly white and flabby," (p. 6) and Bergson is ridiculed as the favorite philosopher of Brian (p. 384). Huxley feels that it is a misfortune that present events sometimes invoke the past. A woman's body seemingly "uncompromisingly there" reminds Anthony of earlier occurrences. The smell of Helen's skin "at once salty and smoky" transports him "instantaneously to a great chalk-pit" (p. 16) where he had spent an hour with Brian striking flints. Later, Helen's body, brown and flat like a Gauguin, transports him to a picture gallery in Paris where Mary Amberly is showing him his first Gauguin. These scenes give us another insight into Huxley's rejection of duration, for he views the past here as full of pitfalls, reminders of guilt, Brian and Mary Amberly. In *Eyeless in Gaza* almost all the re-creations of the past are painful ones. The noise of jackdaws over the church where his mother's funeral is taking place reminds Anthony of his mother's protest when he had flung stones on a frozen pond (p. 28). The pain of the scene on the roof with Anthony reoccurs to Helen many years later in the station at Basel and causes her to wince. Huxley prefers, then, the oblivion of clock time in which the past recedes ever farther from our sense.

Although the tone of these re-creations of the past is not Proustian, the method of evoking the past is. If there seems to be an inconsistency in Huxley's using Proust's method at all, it is explained by Huxley's interest in a technique that offered new artistic possibilities, not in any basic agreement with Proustian principles. Therefore, these incidents in which the past is recalled often sound like interpolations, not integral parts of the plot. Occasionally, however, for instance in Mr. Beavis' re-creation of driving to a Christmas dance of eighty-eight with Maisie (p. 23), we find a sympathetic use of the Proustian method. Huxley's rejection of Proust cannot always be seen as final. Nevertheless, Huxley's reliance on a concept of clock time (motion in space) remained as the basis of his stylistic techniques even after his adoption of mysticism, for a sense of the "timeless Ground" is in no way applicable to the structure and methods of the novel.

The early glimmerings of Huxley's mysticism are exemplified by Anthony Beavis. "God is not limited by time. For One is not absent from anything, and yet is separated from all things" (p. 99). This contemplation of unity and diversity which begins for Anthony at the dinner party given by Gerry Watchett receives adult confirmation in the person of the Scotchman, James Miller. By allying himself with Miller, Anthony fulfills the destiny that Brian's death has laid at his feet. In Miller's philosophy Anthony discovers the unity of all life. The last chapter in *Eyeless in Gaza* is a forerunner of what is to come in *The Perennial Philosophy*. Miller is, one sees, Gerald Heard with his pacifist activities and philosophy of unity in diversity. Anthony achieves release with his liberation from the consciousness of being separate, and he departs for his meeting in the last chapter with a serene sense of well being. Time here is the timeless present, and yet it in no way disturbs the Huxleyian conception of the reality of clock time, the absolute nature of which is indissoluble but which may be ignored through a contemplation of the 'timeless present.' We find ourselves with Huxley in a new world, but one that in no sense refutes the old one.

As a transitional book, then, *Eyeless in Gaza* stands between the two distinct phases in Huxley's life, looking backward to the earlier anti-Proustian time theories and forward to the mystical timelessness of Mr. Propter and Sebastian Barnack. In *After*

Many a Summer Dies the Swan Mr. Propter claims that even history is evil, albeit evil at a distance. According to Huxley we may live on the animal level or on the spiritual level, but try to mix the two, and we have the evil of human time.[21] Past and present are only ersatz for the experience of eternity and reaching eternity is worth the difficulty it involves. All good is primarily outside time, and by forgetting our egos we are finally able to achieve some of our potentialities in eternity. The human organism functions according to its own laws and achieves what limited good it is capable of. One must note here that Propter does not refute Rampion; he merely changes the emphasis. The end for Rampion was the good that the organism could achieve per se. Now Propter, while admitting that some good may be achieved by the organism in time, declares that there is another higher good, one of which Rampion was not aware. Although Spandrell in the last pages of *Point Counterpoint* seemed to be moving toward Propter's position, Rampion was not moved even by Spandrell's dramatic declamations. Now with the backing of the Sankara, Meister Ekhart, John of the Cross, and others, Spandrell becomes the respected Mr. Propter (Prompter, Prop, and Proper are all suggested by the sound of the name) and later the wise Bruno.

In *Time Must Have a Stop,* through Bruno and Sebastian Huxley fully expresses his mystical concepts. The influence of Proust has about disappeared, for Uncle Eustace reading Proust manages only ten pages at a time and often less. However, Huxley's mysticism has given him kindlier feelings toward the relativists. Although Eustace cannot imagine his mother-in-law changing her "conduct to fit the principles of relativity,"[22] still Huxley states that the Einsteinian revolution has changed the whole course of scientific thinking, "brought back idealism, integrated mind into the fabric of nature, put an end forever to the Victorian's nightmare universe of infinitesimal billiard balls" (p. 87). Furthermore, Eustace is interested in Professor

21. Aldous Huxley, *After Many a Summer Dies the Swan* (New York, 1939), p. 117.
22. Aldous Huxley, *Time Must Have a Stop* (New York, 1944), p. 86. Subsequent references to this volume appear in the text.

Whitehead's theory of location: there is "no such thing as Simple Location, only location within a field" (p. 89). For instance, Sebastian noticing a beetle crawling across the left knee of a statue wonders what the beetle would say it was doing.

But Huxley chooses the path of Plotinus, Eckhart, and Boehme instead of trying to apply theories of relativity to his writing or to accept them as part of reality. He prefers his double world. From now on his readers receive disquisitions on the "divine Ground," the "all embracing field." In keeping with his pattern of detachment, he never really integrates his concepts of timelessness with his writing. Compare Huxley's treatment of mysticism in *Time Must Have a Stop* with Virginia Woolf's use of the "moment of vision" in her books and the point is clear. Huxley's double vision of life is emphasized by the observation of Jocelyn Brooke that the more Huxley progresses toward non-attachment, the more he becomes interested in the unpleasant aspects of the human body.[23]

Eustace when he dies loses all sense of time; past, present, and future hold no meaning for him. He sees Jim Poulshot die in a war that has not yet occurred. He has achieved the second world of timelessness, timeless good, and until Madame Weyl, the medium, contacts him, he is bathed in an "incoherent succession" (p. 261). The relativists consider that time is the result of our own perceptions, but they do not invent a second world of timelessness, leaving that step to the mystics and considering such a state of simultaneity as a part of life, not a state separated from bodily existence.

Eustace's trips back and forth from the spirit world to the material world illustrate for Huxley the difference between time and timelessness. An uncomfortable wrench heralds his return to the spirit world where he feels "the chaos and delerium of unfettered mind" as against succession and matter. In the flux of images two things stand out for Eustace—one, the "tender ubiquity of light" and, two, the knowledge that flesh and blood stand ready to foster him (p. 264).

23. Brooke, *Aldous Huxley,* p. 24.

But it is the final passage from Sebastian's notebook which clarifies Huxley's stand on time. Here Sebastian takes as his point of departure Hotspur's speech from *Henry IV*, Part 1, from which the title *Time Must Have a Stop*, is, of course, derived.

> But thought's the slave of life, and life time's fool,
> And time, that takes survey of all the world,
> Must have a stop.[24]

We learn that there are three steps in existence, the eternity of the animal world, the "human world of memory and anticipation," and "the world of spiritual eternity" (p. 282). This life of the spirit is the complete mortification of memory, a life led entirely in the present. It is a life out of time. Furthermore, in such a state one finds no separateness, only identity with the infinite.

Our actions, therefore, while we exist in time should be directed toward achieving what lies beyond time, achieving this identity with the infinite presence, the unitive knowledge that is the purpose of human life.

It is interesting to compare these ideas with the proclamation of Rampion, "Well, what the devil's the good of that?" when he suggests that the relativists are getting outside of life. Now Huxley feels that we must get outside of life, that Bergson, Adler, Freud, the pragmatists, the behaviorists make thought the slave of life, that they may be right as far as they go, but that they don't go far enough. For Hotspur's speech concludes that time must have a stop, and, says Huxley, time *does* have a stop. Only by recognizing the fact of eternity can we keep thought from becoming a slave to life. "The divine Ground is a timeless reality. Seek it first and all the rest . . . will be added" (p. 298).

What stands out in observing the philosophies behind Huxley's writing are the striking dualisms. He argues for the reality of time and space and at the same time employs a Proustian recall of the past which rests on the idea that mind time is

24. Act V, Scene 4, lines 81-83.

real, clock time an abstraction. His preoccupation with the scatalogical aspects of life rivals that of Swift; at the same time he preaches mysticism. His interest in problems of world population and food supply comes at a time when he is writing on non-attachment. He explores the possibilities of the chemical sources of visions through mescaline while ascribing to a religious position which holds that visions are God given.

In Huxley's later books the dualism between flesh and the spirit is used to indicate both that life is an inferior copy of eternity and that transcendence on this earth is a poor substitute for grace. Thus *Ape and Essence* (1948) begins on the day of Gandhi's assassination as well as with Bob Briggs, who is "all the Romantic Poets rolled into one."[25] Like Swift, Huxley attempts to shock his readers into accepting his remedy; the vulgarity of the "ape" is outlined in the minutest detail in order that "the eternal essence" may appear by contrast more desirable. Mysticism is more attractive to the man who sees the physical world as repulsive, and Huxley is telling us in *Ape and Essence* that attention to the material world will lead to destruction and to a new civilization even more crass than our present one. Tallis' path of non-attachment is the alternative, although this path is barely evident in the story. Huxley understands that within life there are means of self-transcendence, but that these are inferior to an adoption of non-attachment. In the epilogue to *The Devils of Loudun* Huxley has discussed "some of the more common Grace-substitutes."[26]

It is Helen and Katy who form the contrapuntal action of *The Genius and the Goddess,* much as the dead Tallis and Dr. Poole had presumably interacted in *Ape and Essence.* Helen has taught Rivers that memory is a dangerous drug and that the immediate experience is God. "If you want to live at every moment as it presents itself, you've got to die to every other moment."[27] Katy represents animal grace; her being is dependent on and renewed by animal contact. Helen, on the other

25. Aldous Huxley, *Ape and Essence* (New York, 1948), p. 1.
26. Aldous Huxley, *The Devils of Loudun* (New York, 1952), p. 313.
27. Aldous Huxley, *The Genius and the Goddess* (London, 1955), p. 9.

hand, is able to make the synthesis between the spiritual and the animal to achieve what Huxley calls "human grace."

Ideally we should be able to accept the spiritual, the human, and the animal. Helen's position in this last novel seems to resolve the dichotomy between the human and the non-human which persisted in the novels through the writing of *Ape and Essence*. The picture of animal grace in Katy is entirely sympathetic; only at the end when her broken body lies on the road is the reader graphically aware that there is for Huxley a further stage, the grace achieved by Helen who lives on in Rivers, whereas Henry Maartens cannot recover Katy because Katy minus body is nothing. Huxley succeeds in this last novel in finding a middle road between spirit and flesh through Helen, but there is some doubt that he is really able to demonstrate Helen's way since Helen is dead when the novel opens, and it is Katy who dominates its pages. Both Tallis and Helen haunt their respective books but indicate at the same time the difficulties of writing about non-attachment. Short of the séance, which Huxley had used almost with tongue in cheek in *Time Must Have a Stop*, one is forced if one is to illustrate non-attachment to rely on an absent character, bound to be unconvincing. Since Helen, however, before her death presumably achieved "human grace," her actual appearance in the novel would have been meaningful in illustrating Huxley's point about transcendence. Nevertheless, in the characterizations of Helen and of Katy, Huxley in this novel is notably less pessimistic about the possibility of some positive achievement in the development of human life.

Huxley himself makes a distinction between what he calls "eternity philosophers" and "time philosophers,"[28] the latter often obsessed with the past. While as a young writer Huxley rejected Bergson's and Proust's time theories as decadent and unrelated to the realities of time as we act by it, he later came in *The Perennial Philosophy* to reject the importance of clock time except as a step that would lead to the reality of the timeless spirit. In each case D. S. Savage's sense of dissociation is

28. Aldous Huxley, *The Perennial Philosophy* (New York, 1945), p. 193.

clear: the dualism between the ideal and the actual in the earlier period and, with the possible exception of *The Genius and the Goddess,* between the human and non-human in the later period. The only difference lies in his present point of view as a "positive accentuation of futility"[29] and his early point of view as a negative "accentuation of futility." In both periods Huxley refuses to make external reality the slave of the inner world and in this lies the thread of continuity to be found in considering his theories of time. Time and eternity for Huxley are absolute, despite our perception of them or reaction to them. One cause for Huxley's point of view toward reality is to be found in his own definition of his position as "moderately extraverted." Therefore, he seeks an order in time outside of himself. Joyce finds in Vico, T. S. Eliot in neo-Thomism what Huxley finds in Eastern mysticism, the submergence of the individual in the universal, of the particular in the general, but because of the extreme detachment of the mystical position Huxley is forced to write "about" it rather than to make it an integral part of his novels.

29. Savage, *Modern Fiction,* p. 361.

PART III

GERMANY

INTRODUCTION

The working out of the time problem in the German writing to be discussed here may be seen to have produced different results from the working out of the Bergsonian thesis in French, English, and American writing. Although Bergson eventually saw duration as the essence of life itself, those influenced by him have interpreted *la durée* chiefly in terms of the individual consciousness. The influence of German philosophers like Hegel has been, on the contrary, to cause writers to stress Being more than individual being. The fact that both groups of writers had equal access to Freud's work shows even more clearly the importance of the two philosophical backgrounds.

In literature Bergson's influence is often seen through Proust, who has been considered, if erroneously, an interpreter of the Bergsonian rationale. It is partly because of Proust's emphasis on the *moi* that Bergson's *durée* in English and American literature is often synonymous with the process of the individual consciousness. On the other hand, the pervasive influence of the Hegelian identification of abstract truth with reality, despite modern existentialist influence, has had in the German culture a strong hold causing even the literary proponents of existentialism to deal often with *man* instead of with *men*. The blending of the abstract and the concrete, of the essential and the material, which has characterized the German *Weltanschauung,* persisted in spite of existential thinking.

In contrast to the works of Joyce and Virginia Woolf stand the works of Kafka where identification of subject and object is approached in an entirely different way. Kafka objectifies inner reality without sacrificing any of its inward nature. Therefore, instead of finding ourselves observing the workings of the mind of Molly Bloom from the outside, as if the author, like a surgeon, had shown us a cross-section of the human brain, we discover in Kafka's work that we are plunged into this inner world by virtue of the fact that the author treats it as others treat the outer world—as reality per se. Through the objectification of the inner world, Kafka avoids the *as if,* for the dream, the phantasy, the world of the spirit *exist* for him. The stream-of-consciousness technique, on the other hand, implies another level of reality, particularly when it is coupled, as it is in most of the works where it appears, with sections dealing with the outer world. Thus in *The Waves,* for instance, we find the introductory portions describing the time of day alternating with the *monologue intérieur* of the characters. In fact, at the very core of the technique of Joyce and Virginia Woolf lies the interaction of the external world with the inner world, of the clock with *la durée.* It is through this interaction that the truth of the inner world is perceived, whereas the time of the clock is seen by comparison as a mechanical abstraction.

In the works of Kafka, there is no such interaction: Joseph K. actually is executed in *The Trial;* K. actually is a land surveyor in *The Castle,* a land surveyor who never surveys land. With Kafka the extraordinary does not appear as extraordinary. So convincing is Kafka's witnessing of the inner world that the reader himself eventually becomes convinced that for Gregor Samsa to become a beetle is perfectly natural. The closest approach to this technique in the English literature discussed is the objectifying of Bloom's fantasies in the Circe episode or of Virginia Woolf's own fantasies in *Orlando.* In the stream-of-consciousness method, however, the extraordinary is seen as fantasy or dream. Even in the Circe episode the fantasy is pretty clearly fantasy.

Mann in his work is less inward in his treatment of time than Kafka. In *The Magic Mountain,* for instance, there is some comparison of the inner time of Hans Castorp and of mechanical time, yet this comparison is usually treated by means of exposition rather than through a technique worked out in the book. Like Huxley's characters Mann's often expound ideas. There is one long passage of *monologue intérieur* in *The Magic Mountain* when Hans Castorp is lost in the storm, but on the basis of this passage one cannot call Mann a Bergsonian. Nor can one feel that the inner approach to reality like that in "The Wardrobe" is more than an anomaly for Mann. Instead of putting individual experience before essence, Mann often makes us feel that essence precedes individual experience, as in the conversations of Naphta and Settembrini.

But Kafka is not free of abstractions either. Whereas Joyce sees with Bergson that reality consists of the rich and varied flow of consciousness of man, Kafka deals with the dream as an abstraction. *The Trial* and *The Castle* are the dreams of K., told by Kafka not from the dreamer's point of view but from that of Kafka, who is awake and observing the dream. For this reason Kafka is able to impose some order on what tends to become disordered flux in *Finnegans Wake.* The essence of Kafka's method is not to state to the reader that it is a dream he relates; in this way he is able to present the dream as if it were actually happening.

The stream-of-consciousness technique, therefore, shows us inside the mind of a character in a different way from Kafka's. The terms *past* and *present* are retained by Joyce and Woolf, even though past and present are coexistent. Duration is life itself ever plunging into the future. What was real for Kafka was not the mental process but the image produced by the mental process. This image stood beyond change and was subject to no past, present, or future. Thus he invests the images produced by K.'s mind with an objective being of their own, like Platonic essences. The emphasis in *Finnegans Wake* is not on the objectification of the dream but on the dream as a subjective expression of the dreamer. The emphasis in Kafka's work is on the dream as an objectified representation of the dream of all mankind. In *Finnegans Wake* although the dream may represent the dreams of all mankind, it is the dreamer himself who may *be* all mankind. It is this sense of being which the use of Bergson's *durée* produces, freeing the author from intellectual abstractions and essences beyond the flow of life. On the other hand Kafka's method is often more effective than Joyce's in producing a sense of identification with the main character for the simple reason that as a more abstract figure than HCE, K. embraces more variations than even Joyce could invent about his hero, for duration is life, not an eternal essence, and as such is limited by its finite character.

Another approach to time is *die ewige Wiederkehr*, Nietzsche's famous concept, which has found many adherents in contemporary literature. Other circular concepts, like Vico's, have also been of great importance. These represent another means of counteracting the flow of the river of time. In fact, reality seen in the form of a circle presents even more security against flux than Bergson's assurance that the past is never lost, for it promises a reincarnation that may offer redemption. In Bergson's definition of reality, on the other hand, the future is unpredictable. Eternal recurrence is, like *la durée*, a principle or pattern inherent in life itself. Sometimes, as with Vico, it is imposed on life from outside by a Creator; sometimes, as in Nietzsche, no outside influence is predicated.

For Thomas Mann the concept of circular reality brought no escape from time but rather as for Joyce a discovery of eternity in time. Mann was strongly influenced by Nietzsche and by his concept of eternal recurrence. But Mann reverses the process that Joyce followed. Whereas Joyce takes figures from the contemporary scene and invests them with mythical significance, Mann in the *Joseph* books takes figures from the remote and legendary past and invests them with universal significance. Even the characters in *Dr. Faustus,* although contemporaries, have an archaic quality. Furthermore, in seeking a symbol of recurrent reality Joyce chooses an ordinary figure from everyday life whereas Mann chooses the extraordinary figure, the artist or the hero. The influence of Nietzsche encouraged Mann to see life in terms of this hero whereas the influence of Vico while stressing the heroic and the divine also stressed the human.

Mann, however, when not concerned with working out the theme of circular reality in terms of myth often chooses the ordinary figure, like Thomas Buddenbrook, for his protagonist; for the ordinary interested Mann no less than the extraordinary, and his own background led him to see life in terms of the conflict between these two elements in society. It is no accident, however, that he does not invest his "ordinary" heroes with mythical status, or that his mythical heroes are not ordinary men. The very nature of the myth prevents the hero from being ordinary—one of the attractions of the myth for Mann. Joyce defined the terms *ordinary* and *extraordinary* in a different way. Whereas for Mann the term *extraordinary* referred often to social status or to outward achievements as well as to inner victories, for Joyce in *Ulysses* Bloom is heroic simply because of his overcoming of self. On the other hand, HCE in the heroic age does overcome the Duke of Wellington, but this sort of accomplishment is symbolic and by itself does not receive the central emphasis in *Finnegans Wake.* Mann's emphasis is, of course, also on inner accomplishment, but he approaches his figures from the outside, not from the inside.

Closely connected with eternal recurrence is the use of the myth and the archetypal figure. They give one a sense, as T. S. Eliot has pointed out, that all of literature has a simultaneous existence. Joyce chooses mythical archetypes from world literature. Mann's mythical figures come from the Old Testament, from Germanic legend, from early Christian history. Kafka provides an interesting comparison here, for he sometimes invents a legendary background as in "The Great Wall of

China" or in "An Old Manuscript." He suggests thus a sense of
the spirit of the past without a sense of its pastness. He achieves
the same archaic quality of experience that Mann achieves
even though he is not writing about the past as Mann is, but
about an eternal present of the inner world of man. Thus
we sense as we read "An Old Manuscript" that "nomads from
the north" threaten us each morning as we prepare for the day.
Kafka appeals to atavistic fears, the fear of the animal as light
approaches bringing with it dangers, removing the protective
dark and the possibility of concealment. These atavistic fears
and urges to which Kafka appeals have been largely ignored by
critics, but they lie at the basis of the powerful impact of his
stories. Kafka goes behind and beyond the myth and the
legend, which are safe areas compared with fears of the day,
fears of the night, of the burrow, of violence, of metamorphosis
which lie suppressed but ready to break out in man. The veneer
of civilization, trials and castles, barely covers our primitive
fears of the knife twisted in the breast or of our pursuit of the
unknown which stalks us in turn, silent and waiting like the
officials in *The Castle.*

The myth, the archetypal figure, as they appear in Thomas
Mann's work pertain much less to the subconscious than Kafka's
figures. Often in Mann's stories subject and object are united,
but in other parts the reader is conscious of Mann as the
manipulator, his observations remaining separate from those
of the characters and the characters remaining separate from
the world that surrounds them. In the treatment of Tonio
Kröger, Gustav Aschenbach, and Hans Castorp, the inner and
outer worlds often merge, but in the treatment of Joseph,
Adrian Leverkühn, and Grigorss the inner and outer worlds
more often remain separate. This separation is emphasized
sharply by the narrator device in *Dr. Faustus.*

The fact that the myth was employed by Mann in a long
narrative about the time that the myth of Nordic supremacy
was being exploited politically in Germany is perhaps no
accident. A sense of mythical counterparts, of the continuation
of the heroic past in the present, of the mystery of remote times

was abroad. Mann's use of the biblical myth for a constructive purpose acted as a small antidote to the poison created by the Nordic myth. But Mann personally found in the Joseph myth a screen between inner and outer reality—as if outer reality had become so fearsome that the inner man no longer could see himself in terms of it.

Mann's sense of myth enables him to put the emphasis on his characters in conflict with forces outside of them. Even the devil is objectified in *Dr. Faustus* whereas in "Death in Venice" evil within Aschenbach is synonymous with the foul contagion that infects Venice and in "Tonio Kröger" the alienation of the central figure is synonymous with the loneliness of the girl he sees without partners. As long as evil remained for Mann the perversion of the Aschenbachs and the alienation of the Tonio Krögers, he was able to meet it on its own terms, but in the face of mass racial slaughter, a merging of outer reality with the inner man was no longer possible. In the *Joseph* books Mann felt that the human being and the contagion that threatened to infect him were separate phenomena. From this he drew hope for the future. Abstract values like social justice in the *Joseph* books, the power of evil in *Dr. Faustus,* penitence in *The Holy Sinner* often dominate his work. The remoteness of the mythical figure encouraged the split between subject and object in Mann's novels. Mann's use of the myth is, then, partly the result of social forces by which he was surrounded. Kafka's world of fantasy had revealed some years before the rise of National Socialism that the beast lurks in the jungle. And the atavism that made Mann turn toward abstractions had been fully exposed by Kafka, who in a strange way predicts the Germany of the 1930's.

Turning back now to Aldous Huxley, the subject of the preceding chapter, we can note that like the later Mann, although for different reasons, Huxley in his approach to reality keeps subject and object distinct from one another. Furthermore, both Huxley and Mann often see their novels as vehicles for the expounding of abstract ideas. Both authors, Mann to a lesser extent, evidence an interest in mysticism and occultism.

But Mann in all three of these positions is less extreme than Huxley. Mann takes no sharp position against the flow of mind time; with Mann the outer world is often only the reflection of the inner one, and Mann approaches occultism with extreme caution proposing nowhere in his works a "divine ground" of the spirit. Dr. Krokowski's séance is, in fact, one of the finest pieces of mockery in *The Magic Mountain*. It is essentially because of this better synthesis of the inner and outer realities that Mann achieves a larger view of life than Huxley despite Huxley's brilliant insights into segments of his material.

CHAPTER FIVE

THOMAS MANN:

THE CIRCLE OF TIME

1

Thomas Mann saw reality both in terms of will and of idea, of the concrete and of the abstract, of the individual and of the universal. Mann's ability to merge these two areas is an ability that is inherent in the German temperament. It is significant to note that Mann was early attracted to both Schopenhauer and Nietzsche. Wagner and later Freud and Goethe were also especially influential in forming Mann's *Weltanschauung*. In *A Sketch of My Life* Mann states that he came to Nietzsche before Schopenhauer and that whereas Nietzsche's influence was intellectual and artistic, Schopenhauer's was chiefly spiritual.[1] Nietzsche's influence was a profound one for Mann for the better part of three decades. Nietzsche's hostility to mind, to intellect, to aesthetic escape had on Mann a "deepening, strengthening, formative" effect.[2] Nietzsche stressed that life was in danger of being overwhelmed by spirit although Mann was later to say he "will not agree that there

1. Thomas Mann, *A Sketch of My Life*, trans. H. T. Lowe-Porter (Paris, 1930), p. 24.
2. Thomas Mann, "Freud and the Future," in *Essays of Three Decades*, trans. H. T. Lowe-Porter (New York, 1947), p. 413.

is any real world at all."[3] Nietzsche defined time by his doctrine of the *ewige Wiederkehr,* a conception that was to be "the great test." "Who can bear the thought?" he asked.

It was Nietzsche's attitude toward intellect which led Mann to Schopenhauer and to his doctrine of Will. Here Mann discovered the possibility of aesthetic escape from Will, which interested him chiefly during the period when he was concluding *Buddenbrooks.* Although the world is the product of Will, it is also the product of idea, the process of the individual mind, and idea can, according to Schopenhauer, occasionally wrench itself free from Will to achieve the aesthetic state. Mann states that he was not so much concerned with the doctrine of the conversion of the Will as with "the element of eroticism and mystic unity"[4] in Schopenhauer, but it is the interplay of these two conceptions, Will and Idea, which is the basis of Mann's early work. And throughout all his writing, the Schopenhauerian "idea of species" is counteracted in Mann by a sense of individual destiny. Mann speaks of "the profound, even shattering impression" made on him by the philosophy of Schopenhauer.[5]

A third influence on Mann's sense of time was that of Wagner. In Wagner Mann found what he felt to be the essence of Schopenhauer's philosophy, the erotic "focus of the will" accompanied by psychological and mythical music. "It is the language," says Mann, "of 'once upon a time' in the double sense of 'as it always was' and 'as it always shall be.' "[6] Wagner, like Nietzsche opposed to the artificial, uses myth in a purgative sense, as an antidote to the complexity of culture; for him it represents the simple, the purely human.

Schopenhauer and Wagner stand behind the mystic and aesthetic attitudes toward time found in many of Mann's early heroes. Opposed to these attitudes stands Nietzsche's defense

3. Thomas Mann, "Schopenhauer," in *Essays of Three Decades,* trans. H. T. Lowe-Porter (New York, 1947), p. 403.

4. Mann, *A Sketch of My Life,* p. 24.

5. Thomas Mann, "Freud and the Future," in *Essays of Three Decades,* trans. H. T. Lowe-Porter (New York, 1947), p. 415.

6. Thomas Mann, "Sufferings and Greatness of Richard Wagner," in *Essays of Three Decades,* trans. H. T. Lowe-Porter (New York, 1947), p. 313.

of life, of time itself, which nevertheless ran in circles of eternal recurrence. Freud and Goethe, to be discussed later, appear as influences in Mann's thinking after the writing of *The Magic Mountain* and modify the essentially pessimistic contours of the early works.

The early influences on Mann are evident in the treatment of time in the short stories preceding *Buddenbrooks*. The detachment of Little Herr Friedemann is a detachment that is repeated in various forms in the other early stories. The stranger in "Disillusionment" confesses that he has no sense of actuality, that he wants the infinite from life, and the hero of "The Wardrobe" has lost track of time and space. Like Nietzsche, Mann sees this extreme detachment as evil, as leading to destruction and decay. It is a detachment that he often connects with the artist as in "The Dilettante." Gerhard Jacob suggests that Mann was influenced in his criticism of the artist by Nietzsche's second or third period when Nietzsche saw the artist as the epitome of decadence.[7]

The earliest example of Mann's later extensive use of myth and legend may be seen in "Tobias Mindernickel." The dog, Esau, sells his birthright of freedom for food, like all dogs, and like his biblical prototype. As a result he falls into the clutches of Tobias or the biblical Tobiah, who appears in the books of *Nehemiah* and of *Tobit* as an authoritarian leader. Tobias wields the power of life and death over Esau alone; at one point he compares himself to Napoleon. The dictatorship of Tobias, however, is pictured with typical Mannian irony since Tobias' kingdom consists of a single room and a dog.

A more mystical use of myth is evident in van der Qualen's experience in "The Wardrobe." Arriving in a nameless city, the hero passes by an old gate and crosses a river, the Styx. Below the bridge a man, Charon, sculls an ancient boat. "Here is *the* river," thinks van der Qualen to himself. A later use of this same imagery is found in *Death in Venice* in the passage of Aschenbach to the Lido. Having crossed the river, van der Qualen has

7. Gerhard Jacob, *Thomas Mann und Nietzsche, Zum Problem der Decadence* (Inaugural Dissertation, University of Leipzig, 1926), p. 55.

entered Hades with all its torments, which his name implies that he will undergo. His detachment as well as that of Tobias leads to disaster.

In *Buddenbrooks*, however, Mann's attitudes toward aesthetic detachment and the life principle are reversed, to some extent. It is here that the mystic unity Mann found in Schopenhauer achieves a positive status. But the role of the artist is still suspect for Mann. The musical Gerda and her son Hanno, rapt in a Wagnerian nirvana or in contemplation of the sea, Christian with his interest in the theater, are seen as spiritual weaklings contributing to the collapse of the Buddenbrooks. It is rather to Thomas, who has suppressed his love for literature in the interests of the "firm," to whom Mann gives the Schopenhauerian vision of eternity as a preparation for his death.

The Buddenbrooks' attitude toward time changes throughout the generations, and this attitude may be seen to relate to the worldly achievements of each generation. The old man, Johann, had been "jovial, simple, sturdy, humorous."[8] His son, the Consul, deplores that his father has so little taste for old family records. Old Johann's time is held within him; it is an instinctive knowledge of the past and of his position in time which does not depend on family Bibles and genealogies. His instrument is the flute, even his musical taste is simple and instinctive, the flute deriving from the pipes, suggesting perhaps the pipes of Pan in this instance. Under old Johann the firm flourishes.

But his son, the Consul, is more self-conscious about time: for him the relation of the past to the present becomes an outward preoccupation, a fanatical conning of old records, not an inner knowledge. As a result his hold on the present becomes less certain, his decisions about the firm and the fate of his family less adroit. His knowledge about Herr Grünlich is entirely of an outer nature; never does he consider the man's inner qualifications, and it is fitting retribution that he should be duped by him.

8. Thomas Mann, *Buddenbrooks*, trans. H. T. Lowe-Porter (New York, 1935), II, 129.

Of the Consul's children, saturated in family history, Thomas and Tony are the ones to carry on their father's devotion to the images of the past. Tony, the innocent victim of her father's blindness to inner values, is herself equally blind. True, she is aware from the beginning of Herr Grünlich's evil character, but this is simply because she is involved personally. Had she been in her father's position, she would have acted exactly as he acted. Even as a child she walks about the town "like a little queen," and when her marriage to Herr Permaneder fails, she admits to her brother that it was not her husband who was to blame so much as the fact that in Munich there was no status attached to the name of Buddenbrook. At last Thomas understands what has happened and presses her no longer to return to her husband. At the basis of Tony's failure in life is the fact that she sees the past as if it were a badge to be worn on one's sleeve. Neither Tony nor Thomas has absorbed the spirit of old Johann although of the two Tony, because she is not "consumed by the inexpressible," comes closer to her grandfather. It is this attitude toward life, the emphasis on artificiality rather than on instinct, which Mann learned from Nietzsche to deplore.

According to Nietzsche, Thomas Buddenbrook would have earned no solution to his problems. It is, therefore, surprising to find Schopenhauer's doctrine of aesthetic escape, a doctrine that Nietzsche denied, introduced near the end of *Buddenbrooks*. Until this point the philosophical assumption behind the book has been that life, instinctive life, is thwarted by the Buddenbrooks who are chiefly concerned with the artificial processes of living: genealogies, the social ladder, the burgher hierarchy. Now near the end, mind takes over and elevates Thomas Buddenbrook beyond life, to "float free in a spaceless, timeless night."[9] Life, the life of the body, is seen as a prison from which death liberates one so that one becomes united with all those who have ever said "I."

It has been Thomas' wish that Hanno might develop the qualities of old Johann, his simplicity and his sturdiness, but

9. *Ibid.*, p. 259.

now he realizes that all children are part of him and he part of them, that somewhere a child is growing up, strong, and well-grown, and that in this child his own Will will be merged. The understanding of time in the book changes then from an understanding that time in itself is important, the present everything, as it was to old Johann, to an understanding that time in itself is nothing, an illusion created by the limitations of the individual personality. It was a spiritual escape from life which Mann was never again to see as a satisfactory solution. Nietzsche's influence was the stronger. Thomas' conversion to Schopenhauer is of course only temporary, for he is soon won back to the burgher life of forms. The decline of the burgher class is piped in on the notes of the simple flute, gathers force in the adherence of that class to forms behind which the untended forces of life grow rank and decay into physical weaknesses, artistic withdrawal, empty religious poses, and moral corruption. The impossibility of the resurrection of old Johann in the flesh leads to Thomas' mystic doctrine of the eternity of the Will. *Buddenbrooks* suffers under the divisive influences of will and of idea, two attitudes toward time, two attitudes toward life inconsistent with each other, yet each proposed by Mann at different points in the book as ideal. In terms of Mann's work as a whole the temporary "conversion" of Thomas Buddenbrook seems like an anomaly; in terms of *Buddenbrooks* it is scarcely a convincing interpolation.

In *Reflections of a Non-Political Man,* Mann states that in *Buddenbrooks* only the Schopenhauer-Wagner influence was present, whereas Nietzsche comes to the forefront in "Tonio Kröger."[10] The ethical, the pessimistic, the epic, and the musical of Schopenhauer and of Wagner Mann sees as the basis of *Buddenbrooks* and of what he regards as his failure to make real characters of the Buddenbrooks. He feels that the grasp of life itself eludes him here. But Erich Heller has expressed the weakness of *Buddenbrooks* in another way: "At one moment Schopenhauer is accepted: the world is Will and the spirit is

10. Thomas Mann, *Betrachtung eines unpolitischen* (Frankfurt am Main, 1956), p. 83.

its enemy. At the next moment Schopenhauer is ousted by Nietzsche: the Will is good, and the enmity to it is wicked."[11] Herein lies the basic contradiction in *Buddenbrooks*. Even in Thomas' revelation, there is Nietzsche's influence, for if the Will is evil as Schopenhauer saw it to be there is no reason for the peace that Thomas gains from his insight. Neither the fascination of the world of the spirit which Mann was to see and reject in *The Magic Mountain* nor the "Lebensbegriff" of Nietzsche is fully enunciated in *Buddenbrooks*. Not until *The Magic Mountain,* in which these influences had been fully absorbed by Mann, is the real drama of the opposition of spirit and life, eternity and time finally played out. A sense of the past which Mann was to integrate creatively with the present in the *Joseph* books appears by comparison artificial in *Buddenbrooks,* like the machinery of a Wagnerian opera.

It was in "Tonio Kröger" that Nietzsche's influence was to come fully to bear and to create the artistic and philosophical unity that *Buddenbrooks* lacked. Around "Tonio Kröger" are grouped three short stories: "Tristan," "The Hungry," and "The Infant Prodigy," all of which mirror attitudes found in the longer work. In "Tristan" we find in addition a parody of the Wagnerian Tristan. The rejection of life and of time in the sanatorium, the withdrawal from life of Herr Spinell, and his seduction of Herr Klöterjahn's wife into his nirvana are evil influences seen in perspective against the affirmation of life found in the mythical Tristram. Tristram, by implication, mediates between the burgher qualities of Herr Klöterjahn and the decadent qualities of Herr Spinell. Wagner's Tristan music had been criticized by Nietzsche as emphasizing spirit at the expense of life. Thus, under Nietzsche's influence, it is the burgher screams of joy of the youthful Klöterjahn which put Herr Spinell to rout. These joyful screams have in them more of the inner affirmation of a real Tristram than do the melancholy perceptions of the would-be lover, Spinell, whose name contains connotations of spiders and of madness.

The withdrawal of Detlef in "The Hungry," his longing for

11. Erich Heller, *The Ironic German* (Boston, 1958), p. 62.

life, the simple, the instinctive, the dumb life from which he is shut out, connects him with the red-bearded, hollow-cheeked beggar who like him is excluded, but in a different way. Like Tonio Kröger he yearns for a "little friendly, devoted, familiar human happiness."[12] And in "The Infant Prodigy" the artist is seen as a worthless charlatan. These stories lead up to "Tonio Kröger," in which Mann explores the relationship between life and art more extensively, concluding with Nietzsche that cultivation of the intellect leads to insoluble problems for the artist.

What does Mann mean in terms of time when he speaks in *A Sketch of My Life* of the linguistic leitmotiv in "Tonio Kröger" having been transferred to the realm of idea and emotions?[13] Instead of stressing external history, he has turned in "Tonio Kröger" to the internal history of his hero.[14] Tonio's adventures are basically those of the inner man, and the chronological and external narrative of *Buddenbrooks* has been abandoned. Divided between the two extremes that his name implies (note that Lisabeta always addresses him by both names), Tonio Kröger represents both artist and bourgeois. But Nietzsche's influence, as Mann acknowledges, is the paramount one in the story. Surrendering to the power of the intellect leads Tonio as it had Nietzsche to torment and then to solitude. Literature is not a calling but a curse, he tells Lisabeta, for one must die to life to become a creater. He speaks of being "sick of knowledge" in the same way that Nietzsche expresses hostility to mind.

Nietzsche's *ewige Wiederkehr* with its accompanying despair is Tonio Kröger's experience too. Events in Tonio's life keep repeating themselves. For instance, he returns to his parents' house in his native town, but he finds it transformed into a Public Library, a projection into reality of the public library that has for a long time been within Tonio himself. In

12. Thomas Mann, *Stories of Three Decades*, trans. H. T. Lowe-Porter (New York, 1941), p. 169.

13. Mann, *A Sketch of My Life*, p. 31.

14. For a discussion of the leitmotiv in "Tonio Kröger," see Hans Eichner, *Thomas Mann* (München, 1953), pp. 27-28.

each room a poor creature sits writing behind a counter. The condition of the house and of the grounds mirrors Tonio's own inner experience, too. The breakfast room, the bedroom, the garden where life had been lived have become desolate, and the walnut tree groans and creaks in the wind. The tempest that takes place during the passage to Copenhagen is a repetition of the tempest that Tonio has provoked within his own depths by devoting himself to the intellect. The wind keeps him from conversing with the stranger who addresses him.

The chief scene of repetition occurs on a day that Mann introduces by a favorite word, *festal,* a word that later for Mann is to describe the essence of recurrence, the feast celebrating the essential unity in all experience. At the seaside resort where Tonio hovers "disembodied above space and time," all at once it came to pass: Hans Hansen and Ingeborg Holm enter the room, not in reality the same Hans Hansen and Ingeborg Holm but figures who represent them, represent most poignantly for Tonio Kröger the other world, the world of the living, which he yearns for. Behind the glass door he stands observing the dance of life which goes on without him as it always has, the glass separating him from life as the glass in Goethe's tale in *Lotte in Weimar* separates the real from the appearance of reality in the picture. Near him a girl who has not danced implores him with "black swimming eyes," but he ignores her. The dancers gaze at Tonio Kröger as he gazes at them, each in turn the observer and the thing observed. Because he is separated from their gaiety, his only participation can be in helping up those who like him have fallen, for he lifts up the fallen dancer and receives her thanks. But in his heart he feels icy desolation and longs for "the blond and the blue-eyed, the fair and the living."[15] Time has swung about in its full circle, bringing once more his sense of isolation from the Hanses and Ingeborgs. With Nietzsche Mann is also saying that participation in time is real, that the *ewige Wiederkehr* brings for the artist the almost unbearable repetition of experience because of his necessary withdrawal from time. Tonio Kröger's

15. Mann, *Stories of Three Decades*, p. 132.

withdrawal is not, however, into the mystic realm of Hans Castorp. What Mann is pointing out here is the extraordinary anguish of the artist caught between life and art. As Tonio Kröger himself says: "I stand between two worlds."

Although Mann wrote that the distinction between *Geist* and art is much clearer in *Fiorenza* than in "Tonio Kröger,"[16] nothing that Mann has written is more difficult to interpret than his play. The glass that in "Tonio Kröger" separated life and art has been removed in *Fiorenza*, and Mann attempts to integrate life and art and to oppose to them, *Geist*, that term that for the German means more than just spirit. *Geist* indicates the ability to distinguish no longer between personal and supra-personal problems, the ability to feel a personal responsibility for the condition of the world, the ability to reduce the distance between oneself and the masses by forming a bridge between theory and reality.[17] This ideal man of *Geist* is, presumably, the Prior, whereas Lorenzo represents the man of art, although this distinction is not clearly maintained.

Despite Mann's intention to create a hero of Savonarola, he is an unsympathetic character as well as an ambiguous one. In fact, Nietzsche's influence itself was always somewhat ambiguous for Mann. Therefore, in Savonarola there appear Nietzschean characteristics, some of which Mann accepted, others of which he inwardly rejected. The morality of the ascetic, under which the Prior labors, was uncongenial both to Nietzsche and to Mann. But both the Prior and Lorenzo suffer from an illness that like Nietzsche they strive to overcome. Mann has said that above all else in Nietzsche he saw the overcoming of self.[18] Lorenzo through art attempts to compensate for a crippled body; Savonarola through religion attempts to compensate for a wounded ego. Each fails in his own way to possess Fiorenza, Savonarola because of his "morality" and Lorenzo because of his devotion to art for art's sake. As Lorenzo sees, the Prior is the wooer of death, of nirvana, of eternity, and as the Prior

16. Mann, *Betrachtung eines unpolitischen*, p. 84.
17. Erich Kahler, "The Responsibility of Spirit," in *The Stature of Thomas Mann*, ed. Charles Neider (New York, 1947), p. 443.
18. Mann, *A Sketch of My Life*, p. 21.

sees, Lorenzo's worship of beauty is a worship of decay. Both are ill; both seek power. And yet the Prior lives whereas Lorenzo dies. He rejects Fiore's suggestion that he should renounce life and live as a monk, he loves the fire, he expresses contempt for the masses, and he desires power. He is ambiguous because as well as a man of *Geist* we see in him the contours of the Nietzschean superman with his secret will to power. Because of the ambiguity of the central figure, *Fiorenza* suggests no solutions to the problem of the opposition of *Geist* and of art; what it does, however, is to present some of the tensions that exist in this opposition.

One of these tensions is that between time and eternity which underlies the debate between Lorenzo and the Prior. To Lorenzo beauty is dependent on time; to beauty, the Prior opposes spirit that exists in eternity. Lorenzo's art is dependent on the eyes whereas the Prior's art is holy and without dimension. The Prior asks for eternal peace, but Lorenzo sees that this is to be won at the expense of the wings of life. And yet as a man of *Geist* the Prior cannot renounce life but must form the bridge between theory and reality by sacrifice of himself. Thus time is important to him as well as eternity, but his time is not external to himself as is Lorenzo's but rather internal, the internal fire that will destroy him and purify in so doing. The indecision that Mann exhibited in *Buddenbrooks* between time and eternity is in *Fiorenza* to some extent resolved in the figure of Savonarola in the sense that through his inner recognition of his role in relation to humanity he serves both time and eternity. In *Buddenbrooks* time and eternity had been two separate areas. Nevertheless, the reader can not help but sense that Mann feels with Lorenzo that there is that in Savonarola which is evil. Because of his lust for power he does not succeed as a man of *Geist,* and in his lust for power lies his failure to integrate the personal and the supra-personal, time and eternity. The Prior is ambiguous because he would withdraw from time and simultaneously he would embrace time, and this is essentially the ambiguity which underlies much of what Mann has written.

Art and *Geist* were divisive influences that Mann felt instinctively in the Germany of the early twentieth century, and as a play *Fiorenza* dramatizes these influences. The fact that Mann himself calls the hero of "Gladius Dei" "grotesque"[19] may be a key to his feelings about Savonarola. On the other hand, Herr Blüthenzweig is no less unattractive. "At the Prophet's" provides another satirical treatment of a Savonarola as well as of the artist, the novelist, who hungers for Maria Josepha's hand as a wolf does for his supper.

Between spirit and life, time and eternity, Mann finds serious oppositions that he fails to reconcile until he integrates the early influences of Nietzsche, Schopenhauer, and Wagner. Mann finds difficulty in harmonizing Nietzsche's *Lebensbegriff* with Schopenhauer's eternity and Wagner's nirvana. In *Royal Highness*, Klaus Heinrich attempts to reconcile "the claims of society and the solitary,"[20] form and life, in his marriage to Imma Spoelmann. He succeeds in his attempt, in achieving a sense of the *Lebensbegriff*. But according to another definition of time in the book, time is illusion and "truly viewed, all happenings stationary in eternity,"[21] a Schopenhauerian eternity in which the Will may float. It is not clear then which view of time Mann himself advocates, particularly since the characters in *Royal Highness* appear as mere shadow figures. "How to equip the typical with individuality, how to win freedom from that which is fated ... this was the persistent problem of Thomas Mann," writes Erich Heller.[22] Mann is more aware of the roles of his characters in *Royal Highness* than he is of them as individuals. Thus he creates a double vision, for the individual and the symbolic fail to merge unless each is given sufficient force.

With *Royal Highness* Mann groups "The Blood of the Walsungs" and "Felix Krull," which have in common the isolation-motif. In "The Blood of the Walsungs" figures from the more

19. Mann, *Stories of Three Decades*, p. vii.
20. Mann, *A Sketch of My Life*, p. 34.
21. Thomas Mann, *Royal Highness*, trans. A. Cecil Curtis (New York, 1916), p. 342.
22. Heller, *The Ironic German*, p. 193.

virile past, the original Siegmund and Sieglinde, by implication underscore the decadence and withdrawal from life of their prototypes in the nineteenth century. The past is used here as it had been in "Tristan," and both stories reveal the degeneration that results from devotion to art for art's sake. This view of time which indicates a Schopenhauerian pessimism toward the development of Will is the exact opposite of the view of time Mann was to come to in the *Joseph* books in which past and present are creatively integrated so that they interact rather than act in opposition to one another. The sympathy and detachment[23] that Mann felt simultaneously toward tradition also enabled him to produce "Felix Krull," in which the venerated tradition of *Dichtung und Wahrheit* is linked with the autobiography of a criminal. The oppositions in Mann's early work spring essentially from the basic oppositions inherent in his background: the artist versus the burgher, the black-eyed versus the blue-eyed, the mystic versus the humanist. Toward time too, as has been shown, Mann's attitudes were ambivalent: time was both everything and nothing, the past was both revered and viewed with detachment as a means of irony.

But in *Death in Venice* as in "Tonio Kröger" Mann's attitude toward time is more consistent, for here Nietzsche's rationale predominates again. The immeasurable space, the sense of eternity, provided by the sea, which causes Gustav Aschenbach's time sense to falter, are seen distinctly as leading to the disintegration of Aschenbach. In *Buddenbrooks* the role of the sea had been an ambiguous one: for Tony it had been the setting for the one vital experience of her life whereas for Hanno it had contributed to his withdrawal from life. One bit of irony lies in the fact that Tony, who says she understands Hanno's devotion to the sea, cannot have the slightest inkling of its meaning for Hanno: for her it represents life, for him it represents death—each it is true an escape from the meaningless existence of the Buddenbrooks, one escape effected, the other not. The sea in "Tonio Kröger," which enabled him to enjoy

23. Mann, *Stories of Three Decades*, p. vii.

"profound forgetfulness," is one of the influences that intensifies his conflict as an artist. In "A Man and His Dog" the hero becomes "lost to time" by the sea. Later in *The Magic Mountain* Mann is to equate "the abiding present" with the effect of the sea.

It is toward this eternity of the sea that Gustav Aschenbach, whose surname indicates the elements of life and of death equally balanced within him, is gradually beckoned. His trip to Venice is the classical trip to the underworld. The gondolier who takes him to the Lido is Charon. It is by the ocean that he first meets Tadzio, who appears to Aschenbach like a young god from a primeval legend. The seduction effected by the sea loosens Aschenbach's rigid hold upon the present, upon reality, a hold that was so rigid as to have become meaningless like that of the Buddenbrooks. Eternity is seen here as the enemy of life and not as an escape from life as it appears temporarily to Thomas Buddenbrook.

The sea has a rotten swamp scent and fever-bearing winds, foul-smelling lagoons represent the death that the sea is to bring to Venice and to Aschenbach. In Aschenbach's attempt to escape death he is defeated by himself. From a life that had been too rigidly disciplined Aschenbach turns to the other extreme, abandonment of discipline. It is on a beach, which looks autumnal, on which stands an empty apparatus, an abandoned camera, for Aschenbach has abandoned the apparatus of his artistic career, that the Summoner from the sea smiles and beckons to Aschenbach. Schopenhauerian eternity leads to disintegration as does Aschenbach's earlier devotion to intellect. Mann would feel that both influences are in opposition to Nietzsche's concept of life.

As in "Tonio Kröger" what happens to Aschenbach is an externalization of what is happening to him inwardly.[24] At the moment when he stands before the mortuary chapel waiting for the tram that will return him to the safekeeping of Munich, there appears in the door of the chapel a man with the air of a pilgrim. At this moment there crystallizes in Aschenbach that

24. R. Hinton Thomas, *Thomas Mann* (Oxford, 1956), p. 76.

part of him which is the pilgrim, which seeks new worlds. His thoughts almost at once turn to tropical vegetation that is to be the background for his dream later when he has gone far on the road to disintegration. What he needs, he thinks, is a break, but the break he takes is a break first from outward normalcy and then from life.

For some time Aschenbach's style has been too "fixed and exemplary, conservative, formal, even formulated."[25] This is an important clue to his decline, for his over-rigidity opens the door to his corruption, to Venice. His ticket to Venice is issued by a man who reminds Aschenbach of a circus director; in a larger sense this man directs the eternal circular motion of life, for the whole story is one of going and of return, of travel, and of travel to the grave, which is both going and return. The dandy on the ship is in essence what Aschenbach himself is becoming inwardly and what later he is to become outwardly after he visits the hotel barber. All his experiences are ones that represent his own inward disintegration, and all experience is circular. The man who appears with the band of singers at the hotel is like the two earlier figures, the man before the mortuary chapel and the dandy on the boat to Venice. Like them this singer has a skinny neck, reddish eyebrows, and a snub nose. The contortions, the hilarity, the suppressed giggling of the repulsive singer act as a kind of mockery of the relation between Tadzio and Aschenbach. In his actions they could, if they would, see their own attitudes, but both remain grave.

Nevertheless, the morass into which Aschenbach sinks is not without a beauty of its own, the beauty of the luxurious foliage of the jungle. And before his death he does produce one short piece of perfect prose now that he is freed from an over-formulated style, a page and a half of perfect prose for which the price has been high. Essentially Aschenbach's seduction by death is possible because of the forces that have led him to abandon life entirely in his devotion to form. But neither the time of the clock nor the timelessness of the sea is seen by Mann as a fruitful influence upon the artist. Some compromises

25. Mann, *Stories of Three Decades*, p. 387.

must be found between life and art, spirit and life, time and eternity, but *Death in Venice* does not tell us how these compromises are to be effected—rather it describes the results when they are not effected. The fate of the artist is viewed with more pessimism here than even in "Tonio Kröger." Those who reject life, Mann sees with Nietzsche, experience the horrors of the damned.

Mann is consistent in *Death in Venice* in advocating participation in life for the artist; Schopenhauerian eternity stands in this story for death and for disintegration. Aschenbach, caught between the clock and the sea, both agencies outside himself, could have been saved had he understood what Mann understands in his treatment of the story, that real time is based on one's inner perceptions of it. In other words, Aschenbach allows himself to be controlled by forces outside himself instead of realizing that effective control lies within him, in the synthesis of passion and of reason. Follow reason exclusively and one makes a god in the image of oneself as Aschenbach had in his early years; follow passion exclusively and one makes a god of something in the physical world outside oneself, like Tadzio, subject to decay and rotting and disease that lead to disease in oneself. Aschenbach, unable to make the synthesis between beauty and truth, becomes a victim of his art. There is in every artist something of Gustav Aschenbach, and the core of the creative problem is exemplified by his experiences.

In *The Magic Mountain* Mann succeeds in reconciling some of the oppositions he had found in Nietzsche, Schopenhauer, and Wagner through Hans Castorp, who avoids the extremes of Settembrini and of Naphta. *The Magic Mountain* aims "to *be* that of which it speaks."[26] Thus it depicts the timeless enchantment of Hans Castorp and at the same time seeks to abrogate time in the novel by means of the leitmotiv, "the magic formula that . . . links the past with the future, the future with the past."[27] Mann has called this novel a time-romance for

26. Thomas Mann, "The Making of *The Magic Mountain*," in *The Magic Mountain*, trans. H. T. Lowe-Porter (New York, 1953), p. 725.
27. *Ibid.*, p. 720.

two reasons: first, because it attempts to present the inner significance of an epoch, and, second, because time is one of its themes, both the time of Hans Castorp and the time of the book itself.[28]

Hans Castorp's time adventure starts with the disquieting feeling that the silver dish his grandfather shows him evokes for him. Like the family records in *Buddenbrooks,* this dish suggests both change and stability, but its meaning is not perceived by Hans's grandfather, who wears black in a kind of worship of the past for its own sake. Later in a conversation with Naphta, Castorp remembers the air-tight food jars in his grandfather's home. These jars, hermetically sealed, contain eternity. The silver dish and the jars symbolize the two time experiences that Hans Castorp is to undergo at Haus Berghof and that are to determine the direction of his life: eternity and a creative acceptance of the past. A third time is that of Joachim, Hans's cousin, whose time is that of the flatlands, clock time.

Hans's illness causes him to be sealed hermetically in a kind of jar. When Castorp knows he is ill, time takes on for him a continuity, "a continuous present, an identity, and everlastingness." Its units disappear, and it is marked only by "a dimensionless present in which they eternally bring you the broth."[29] A period of illness at the sanatarium is only the same day repeating itself. It is in a Schopenhauerian eternity or a Wagnerian nirvana that Hans loses himself.

As rationalist and humanist Settembrini sees this loss of identity as dangerous and unwholesome. The silver dish had been disquieting for Hans Castorp, disquieting because it had marked out for him his role in time in relation to the past and to the future. It is easier to preserve oneself hermetically in the rarified atmosphere of Haus Berghof. Nevertheless, it is this second sense of time, an inward reckoning of time, which at the end of the book replaces the dimensionless present of the sanatarium. A beginning of Hans's education in time comes

28. *Ibid.,* p. 725.
29. Mann, *The Magic Mountain,* pp. 183-84.

early in the book when he realizes that "time *isn't* 'actual.' When it seems long to you, then it *is* long."[30] Time itself has no divisions; it is we who demarcate it. In the vacuum of Haus Berghof, the only time of any significance is the seven minutes when one holds the thermometer between one's lips. Hans is even able to live again in his own past, for Mme Chaucat's eyes remind him of those of Pribislav Hippe, a school friend, and he is rapt back into the past so strongly that it is as if his body were dead as it lies on the bench.[31]

But it is not this inner knowledge of time which predominates at this point in Castorp's experiences. He must descend into the pit in order to be reborn. His illness intensifies his sense of detachment. Since we measure time by means of a circular motion, this motion might as well be described as rest. Each day is the same day in the rhythmic monotony of time's flow. On June 21 we are told by Mann that our ancestors celebrated the longest day of the year in sheer despair, "an act of homage to the madness of the circle."[32] Nietzsche's *ewige Wiederkehr* is Castorp's experience. Lost in the snow, which replaces the sea for Mann in this novel, Hans moves round and round in bewildering circuits. At Haus Berghof, to counteract the timeless atmosphere, Hans would sometimes sit with his watch before him, but it had no feeling for time limits. It never paused. Naphta, like Schopenhauer, states that it is impossible to have knowledge of time.

Near the end of the book when Hans's watch is broken, he does not have it fixed on the same grounds he had had when he had given up using the calendar, the grounds of his freedom from time. It is through sickness, however, that Castorp overcomes his attraction for nirvana and "arrives at an understanding of humanity that does not . . . scorn the dark, mysterious side of life, but takes account of it without letting it get control over his mind."[33] Mann sees the enchantment of the mountain as "a state of sin," both dangerous and tempting at the same time. Hans is received back into the world "sternly, solemnly,

30. *Ibid.*, p. 66.   31. *Ibid.*, p. 120.   32. *Ibid.*, p. 371.
33. Mann, "The Making of *The Magic Mountain*," p. 726.

penitentially" as a sinner.[34] The war is a dark penance that he must undertake in order that he may return to life and be reoriented in a time that is inwardly meaningful to him. Hans Wolff points out that the outbreak of the war comes almost as a release. "The release motif connects the end of the novel with the beginning. He who loses his life will again be given life, not in order to live but in order to die."[35]

As well as Hans's time, there is the time of the book itself, which as Mann has said runs parallel to the time of the hero. At one point in *The Magic Mountain* Mann draws a line between the plastic arts and music and poetry, showing that whereas the plastic arts exist in the shortest instant of the present, music and poetry need duration in which to exist. He goes on to say that with music the time element is single, whereas in literature there is the time of the piece itself and the time of the content. Time can become both the subject and the medium of the narrative.[36]

Time is seen as the medium of the narrative in *The Magic Mountain* through the use of the leitmotiv by Mann to preserve the "inward unity and abiding presentness of the whole."[37] The magical *nunc stans* in which Hans finds himself is established by means of this technical device. As Erich Heller points out the leitmotiv is for Mann a "literary symptom of a metaphysical belief towards which he inclined."[38] The use of the leitmotiv also creates a sense of the circular in time which was Hans's experience as well. The pencil that Hans gives to Clavdia Chaucat and that recalls the pencil he had once borrowed from Pribislav Hippe is one frequently cited example of Mann's use of the leitmotiv. The pencil not only unites past and present but indicates the circular nature of reality, for Hans's love for Pribislav had been as unyielding of results as his love for Clavdia is likely to be. Both represent regressive forces in society. Hermann Weigand lists other examples of the leitmotiv

34. Mann, *The Magic Mountain*, p. 711.
35. Hans M. Wolff, *Thomas Mann* (Bern, 1957), p. 74.
36. Mann, *The Magic Mountain*, pp. 541-42.
37. Mann, "The Making of *The Magic Mountain*," p. 720.
38. Heller, *The Ironic German*, p. 194.

such as Settembrini's checked trousers, Frau Stöhr s rabbit's teeth, and Hofrat Behrens' blue cheeks and bloodshot eyes.[39]

The word *hermetic* is a central leitmotiv in the book: it contains associations with the classical god of magic, Hermes Trismegistus; it serves to remind us of the enchantment of the mountain; it is used in connection with the séance at which Joachim is to be resurrected; and it describes the glass jars of sealed food. The use of the leitmotiv leads according to Hans Mayer to even more than a sense of timelessness. The characters in *The Magic Mountain* are "a company of enchanted peaks characterizing a lapse of time without events, history, goal, or change. They do not age since they experience nothing. . . . The process of physical aging is connected with spiritual growth. And that is possible only in relation to concrete reality."[40] Hans Castorp alone returns to life because he experiences both concrete reality and the striving for spiritual growth. The leitmotiv, however, freezes the other characters.

On a third level *The Magic Mountain* abrogates time in that it presents "the inner significance of an epoch, the pre-war period of European history."[41] It is a symbolic novel in that each of the characters represents something beyond himself. Settembrini is the exponent of the West, "of the bourgeois-capitalist world," Mme Chaucat represents the East as against the West, Naphta represents medieval mysticism and nihilism. Peeperkorn[42] stands for Christianity combined with the life of the body.[43] Castorp himself may be seen as Germany subjected to these influences, both political and philosophical. Early in the novel as he had talked to Settembrini, Castorp had remembered a scene from his own past. He saw himself rowing across a lake. In the east the landscape was moonlit; in the west

39. Hermann Weigand, *Thomas Mann's Novel "Der Zauberberg"* (New York, 1933), p. 90. For further discussion of the leitmotiv in Mann's work, see R. Peacock, *Das Leitmotiv bei Thomas Mann* (Bern, 1934).

40. Hans Mayer, *Thomas Mann* (Berlin, 1950), p. 115.

41. Mann, "The Making of *The Magic Mountain*," p. 725.

42. Hans Wolff sees Peeperkorn as a caricature of Nietzsche's "dionysischen Menschen." "Unterordnung des Geistes unter das Gefühl ist Nihilismus par excellence" (*Thomas Mann*, p. 73).

43. Hermann Weigand, "The Magic Mountain," in *The Stature of Thomas Mann*, pp. 162-63.

it was still broad daylight. Castorp looked from one scene to
the other. In a sense, this is his position throughout most of
the novel—a position between the magic of the rising mists of
the East and the fixed and glassy daylight of the West as it was
Germany's position. These symbolical significances are what
Mann means when he speaks of *Steigerung* in the novel. At the
end, Hans is released into life in the same way that Mann feels
Germany was forced out of the metaphysical and individual
stage into the social through World War I. As a penance war
comes and imposes discipline. Germany is received back into
life as a sinner.

On a more universal scale, Hans Castorp is the *Bildungsreisender,* the young man who, through his experiences, is
educated or transformed in some way. Howard Nemerov even
sees in Hans the prototype of the quester hero and thus links
the story with the myth of the search for the Grail.[44] Castorp
gains insight from the various influences to which he is subjected and becomes through them a kind of genius in living.
Interpreted in this way the novel indicates that the time of
Hans Castorp is abrogated by the more universal time of all
young men who strive for goals.

In *The Magic Mountain* Mann has been able to reconcile
the contradictions he felt in the philosophies of Nietzsche and
of Schopenhauer, for here he has succeeded in some measure
in reconciling the typical and the individual, time and eternity.
Royal Highness had lacked *Steigerung* because the characters
were to begin with merely shadow figures and as such were
able to carry little intellectual or ideal significance. We are told
that *Royal Highness* is the allegory of the artist, that it is even
more, a myth, but it is difficult to accept this dual level when
the reality on which the symbolic level is based is flimsy. The
power of Kafka's stories, for instance, rests on the fact that the
everyday level is so everyday.

In *The Magic Mountain* Mann comes to terms with Nietzsche, who believed that life, time itself, was the supreme
experience, even though it might lead to a discouraging round

44. Mann, "The Making of *The Magic Mountain,*" pp. 727-29.

of repetition; and he rejects Schopenhauer, who saw in the merging of the individual Will in the collective Will, an existence in eternity. This eternity, which Settembrini decries, is according to Mann an experience that is destructive and unwholesome. It is to be distinguished from the growing time sense that Castorp achieves in the midst of nirvana and despite it. It is not this isolation from life which Mann hopes to achieve despite what he has to say about creating a magical *nunc stans*. It is true that the occult, the magical have always held a fascination for Mann, but it has been a fascination that he has seen again and again as evil, an evil culminating in the figure of Cipolla in "Mario and the Magician." To participate in life, to create life in his novel, time and not eternity must be emphasized. Past, present, and future are not abrogated by the use of the leitmotiv but they are integrated. It is an integrated attitude toward time, one that sees that time is what the individual makes it that Mann achieves in *The Magic Mountain*.

Thus Hans at the end although he has abandoned his watch has done so because in spite of the enchantment of the everlasting soup he has learned that the only thing that is meaningful is his inner sense of time. He has freed himself from the clock time of the flatlands without succumbing to the rarefied atmosphere of death. And Mann has freed himself from the chronological order of *Buddenbrooks* without like Gustav Aschenbach succumbing to the power of the ocean. The time of the individual is significant, but a sense of eternity may be achieved through seeing this individual, if he is real enough, as a symbol. Castorp and Mann both understand that a sense of one's role may be learned only by participation in, not withdrawal from life. Thus Castorp returns to the flatlands to participate in the war. Mann in *The Magic Mountain* succeeds in creating more than just shadow figures; he creates real people who may serve as prototypes. Mann's difficulty in *Fiorenza*, for instance, had been that he tried to create prototypes before he created individuals. Eternity sought for itself leads to death, but seen in relation to time it may become meaningful.

It is for this reason that it is possible to see some similarity between Mann's and Bergson's concepts of time. Mann has said in a letter to Richard Thieberger: "Ich habe nie etwas von Bergson gelesen und Proust erst lange nach Beendigung des Zbg. kennengelernt."[45] Nevertheless, the letter expresses interest in Thieberger's work on the relation between Bergson and Mann and states that he often wonders how much connection exists between contemporaries without there being any direct influence or contact.

To equate Nietzsche's *Lebensphilosophie* with Bergson's vitalism is accurate only in that both saw the intellect as a force that "distorts the living flow of reality."[46] However, for Nietzsche everything was appearance, even the so-called "reality" that was distorted by intellect. Mann was to see this later when he said in his essay on Schopenhauer that Nietzsche would not admit that there was any real world at all. For Mann there was in addition the spiritual force of Schopenhauer, who proposed an eternity for the collective Will. This doctrine with its Platonic overtones is in direct opposition to what Bergson taught. Although some of Hans Castorp's experiences with time are Bergsonian in character, particularly the experiences in which a scene from his personal past recurs, and his recognition that real time is inner time is Bergsonian, the essence of Castorp's and Mann's experience with time in the book is that individual duration is meaningless unless the individual is aware of his role. Hans's personal past, the scene with Pribislav Hippe, is chiefly significant as a leitmotiv, even though it is recalled by Hans in the same way that the past was recalled by Proust's hero. Mann's idea of time differs essentially from Bergson's in that the sense of individual duration which Bergson saw as reality is merged by Mann with the symbolic. Thus after combating the infinity represented by the snow in the chapter "Snow," Hans recognizes the claims of life, not only the "temps homogène" but a sense of his role, his role as *Bildungsreisender*. This is clear when Hans understands that

45. Richard Thieberger, *Der Begriff der Zeit bei Thomas Mann* (Baden-Baden, 1952). Letter printed at front of book, no page number.
46. Thomas, *Thomas Mann*, p. 75.

"in the center is the position of the *Homo Dei,* between reck-lessness and reason, as his state is between mystic community and windy individualism."[47] One critic has stated that Mann's time sense differs from Proust's in that Proust encourages "introspection and brooding over things gone" whereas Mann encourages a sense of reality that is meaningful not only for the individual but for the society of which he is a part.[48] The Platonic background of Mann's heritage caused him to see that man is important as well as individual men. Mann achieved in *The Magic Mountain* the merging of the individual and the typical, of the particular and the general, of time and eternity by seeing his characters as something more than themselves.

2

It is in *The Magic Mountain,* then, that Mann breaks with some aspects of Schopenhauer and Wagner; with Schopenhauer's pessimism, his doctrine of the individual's return into the collective Will; with Wagner's sense of decay, his emphasis on the dark, and his sympathy with death. These influences Hans Castorp forsakes for participation in life, which Nietzsche advocated, but which was integrated by Mann with a Platonic sense of universals. But Mann raises himself above Nietzsche's nihilism at the same time that he denies Schopenhauer's pessimism. Hans Wolff suggests that he does this by means of irony—as his last works from the *Joseph* books on show. In one respect he is in these works nearer to Schopenhauer than to Nietzsche since Mann shared with Schopenhauer the belief that there is a solution to suffering and that art plays a leading role in this solution.[49]

Gradually after World War I, Goethe and later Freud gain importance for Mann. The fact that Goethe was fundamentally friendly to life and that he saw that "In the end, the only way to move is forward"[50] counteracted the earlier influences on

47. Mann, *The Magic Mountain,* p. 496.
48. Harry Slochower, *Three Ways of Modern Man* (New York, 1937), p. 91.
49. Wolff, *Thomas Mann,* pp. 142-43.
50. Thomas Mann, *Last Essays,* trans. Richard and Clara Winston, Tania and James Stern (New York, 1959), p. 140.

Mann. Goethe's interest in primal types also influenced Mann, but Mann writes that Goethe "does not celebrate the myth, he jests with it, treats it with affectionate, teasing familiarity."[51] Mann's own approach to the myth, an approach that he has called both sympathetic and detached, is often like Goethe's.

Friedrich Sell has pointed out that Freud showed Mann the solution to Naphta's irrationalism. Progress can be made by increasing consciousness, by investigating the relation between instinct and reason.[52] Another critic, Henry Hatfield, puts it that Mann saw Freud as the great explorer, investigating the subconscious for the sake of the conscious.[53] In one of his own essays on Freud, "Freud and the Future," Mann has indicated that his interest in "the primitive foundations of the human soul" springs from Freud. For the myth is the foundation of life; it is the "formula into which life flows when it reproduces its traits out of the unconscious."[54] It is this life of myth which Mann sees in terms of the festival, a word that becomes a leitmotiv in the Joseph books.

The influences of Goethe and of Freud led Mann to a creative use of the past through myth. In "Disorder and Early Sorrow," coming before *Joseph*, Mann had seen that a worship of the past for its own sake was a worship of death and contained in it a hostility to the present.[55] This attitude had been maintained by Mann from *Buddenbrooks* through *The Magic Mountain*. Now in *Joseph* Mann adopts a new attitude toward the past. In his preface to the *Joseph* novels Mann states that in these books he treats "the birth of the ego from the mythical collective."[56] Myth, he says, is nothing but the integration of the present with the past, in short, tradition. In the return of the

51. Mann, "Sufferings and Greatness of Richard Wagner," *Essays of Three Decades*, trans. H. T. Lowe-Porter (New York, 1947), p. 357.
52. Friedrich Carl Sell, "The Problem of Anti-Intellectualism," in *The Stature of Thomas Mann*, ed. Charles Neider (New York, 1947), p. 492.
53. Henry Hatfield, *Thomas Mann* (Norfolk, Connecticut, 1951), p. 161.
54. Mann, *Essays of Three Decades*, p. 422.
55. Mann, *Stories of Three Decades*, p. 506.
56. Thomas Mann, "The Joseph Novels" in *The Stature of Thomas Mann*, ed. Neider, p. 226.

ego to the collective, Mann neutralizes the difference between
isolation and community. It is a continuation and deepening
of the process he had begun in *The Magic Mountain* of invest-
ing his characters with symbolic significances, of *Steigerung*, as
he calls it. It is a mixture of psychology and myth which in
"Sufferings and Greatness of Richard Wagner"[57] (1933) Mann
saw in both Wagner and Nietzsche, who he writes anticipated
Freud. "I thought it might be amusing to attempt by means of
a mythical psychology, a psychology of myth," writes Mann in
A Sketch of My Life.[58] Sometimes overlooked among the influences on Mann's interest in myth is Lessing, of whom Mann
wrote that he was the first founder of a mythical type.[59] Also to
be considered is the fact that Mann had read Jung and that
Hegel's synthesis and antithesis were of interest to him. Mann's
interest in the ideal may spring partly from Hegel, to whom he
attributed in "An Experience in the Occult" the idea that "spirit
is the ultimate source of all phenomena."[60] The eternity of
Schopenhauer and the eternal recurrence of Nietzsche modified
by later influences no longer result in despair for Mann.

Another influence that Mann has acknowledged in the preface to the *Joseph* books is Sterne's *Tristram Shandy*, but as
Jonas Lesser has pointed out, it is difficult to see any relation
between *Joseph* and Sterne. Lesser suggests, however, that
Mann could have observed how Sterne abandons the old novel
form and fashions something new from the novel. Mann could
have asked, "Shall we then write new books always in the same
way like the apothecary who puts together prescriptions?"[61] It
is even more likely that Sterne's sense of time interested Mann.
Sterne defends his breach of the unity of time, as Mann often
does, by reminding the reader that "the idea of duration, and of
its simple modes, is got merely from the train and succession
of our ideas."[62]

57. Mann, *Essays of Three Decades,* p. 311.
58. Mann, *A Sketch of My Life,* p. 60.
59. Mann, "Lessing," in *Essays of Three Decades,* p. 191.
60. Thomas Mann, *Three Essays,* trans. H. T. Lowe-Porter (London, 1932),
p. 258.
61. Jonas Lesser, *Thomas Mann in der Epoche seiner Vollendung*
(München, 1952), p. 323.
62. Laurence Sterne, *Tristram Shandy* (New York, 1950), p. 105.

In the *Joseph* books each character has his own time sense. The time sense of Joseph and of Jacob is a leisurely one like that of the novelist. For Jacob seven years do not seem long because of his intuition of his one-hundred-and-six years of life. For Rachel, with only forty-one years, the period is longer. Furthermore, each character is aware of his role in time, and of the fact, as Joseph tells Benjamin, that the feast is "not *again*. ... It is always the one and the only time." Jacob confuses himself with Abraham, the Cain-Abel situation recurs, the Set-Osiris story. Even old Eliezer confuses himself with Abraham's servant, also called Eliezer, and tells the boy Joseph tales of his wooing Rebecca for Isaac. Geneviève Bianquis considers that this confusion of identity rests on the difference between civilized and primitive time.[63] Between Jacob and Abraham there were twenty generations, but primitive time is more uniform than ours and events tend to repeat themselves in the same way. The man who recognized in his own life an event that he knew had occurred in the history of his family felt reassured. With Freud, Mann had said, "Jedes wirkliche Leben ist eine gelebte Vita." In the recognition of his role, man finds a kind of defense against the disasters of life, for seen as collective experience they are divested of some of their terror. Thus Joseph is able to go twice into the pit and still preserve his sense of destiny, for he is aware of the story of Adon and Ashtaroth. Thus Jacob at Shechem is Abraham "come from the east, buying from Ephron the ploughed land and the field of the double cave."[64] In Esau, Jacob recognizes Edom, the Red; Set, the brother of Osiris; and Cain, the murderer of Abel. Joseph in Egypt comes once more to serve Laban, who "in his present form bore an Egyptian name and a high-flown title."[65] The death of the steward Montkaw is less bitter for Joseph because he can believe that no event is lost: "*Forever* you will

63. Geneviève Bianquis, "Le temps dans l'oeuvre de Thomas Mann," *Journal de psychologie normale et pathologique*, XLIV (January-June, 1951), 364.

64. Thomas Mann, *Joseph and His Brothers*, trans. H. T. Lowe-Porter (New York, 1938), p. 174.

65. Thomas Mann, *Joseph in Egypt*, trans. H. T. Lowe-Porter (New York, 1938), p. 178.

come across the court with your little wedge-shaped beard, your ear-rings, and the tear-sacs."[66]

This sense of the revolving sphere is what Erich Heller has called "the tectonic principle of *Joseph and His Brothers*— together with ideas of incarnation and metempsychosis."[67] For it is not only the past but the future as well which Mann enables the reader to see in each event. Mut-em-enet is Cleopatra; Joseph is Christ; Joseph's three years on Potiphar's island are like Christ's three days in the tomb. The Egyptians believed in the revolving sphere, and even the Jews accepted the belief in part. Alfred Jeremias' *Handbuch der Alt-Orientalischen Geisteskultur*,[68] one of Mann's sources for the *Joseph* books, mentions the revolving sphere in Sumerian-Babylonian mythology.[69] For Mann this sphere is different from the *ewige Wiederkehr* that had dominated his earlier work. Like Nietzsche he had found the *ewige Wiederkehr* a pessimistic concept. But under the influence of "the revolving sphere" events in Mann's works are often modified for the better. Thus although Cain killed Abel, Esau does not kill his brother; Joseph's brothers do not kill him, but only tear his coat to pieces. And although Adonis is slain in the pit, Joseph in the pit dies only to his earlier life.

This more optimistic attitude toward repetition comes also partly from Goethe's attitude toward progress and partly from Freud, who enabled Mann to attain "a smiling knowledge of the eternal,"[70] since he had shown him that some balance could be struck between the ego and the id and that the human will alters its purpose through experience, moving toward increasing socialization.[71]

This attitude toward repetition enabled Mann to achieve in the *Joseph* books a better balance between the individual

66. Mann, *Joseph in Egypt*, p. 368.
67. Heller, p. 241.
66. Mann, *Joseph in Egypt*, p. 368
67. Heller, p. 241.
69. Heller, *The Ironic German*, p. 241.
70. Mann, "Freud and the Future," in *Essays of Three Decades*, p. 422.
71. Frederick J. Hoffman, *Freudianism and the Literary Mind* (Baton Rouge, Louisiana, 1957), p. 225.

and the typical than he had been able to achieve heretofore. It is the individual who effects the change in each revolution of the sphere. It is he who reinterprets eternity. It is for this reason that Mann speaks of psychology and myth as becoming united in the *Joseph* books. As well as a reply to Wagnerian nirvana, Mann's myth is, as Harry Slochower points out, a reply "to the vogue of 'Things Past.' "[72] Mann had once quoted Goethe, who had observed that "there is nothing past that one should yearn to have restored, there is only something eternally new formed out of the expanded elements of the past."[73] "Mann's Platonic universals are invaded by an Aristotelian dynamics that prevents his universe from being 'shut.' "[74] Hans Castorp had had to taste "the everlasting soup" to become aware of his role; Joseph begins at the point that Hans has achieved at the end of *The Magic Mountain*. Instead of war and death, it is death and rebirth that Joseph experiences so that he may in the end become Joseph the provider.

The leitmotiv is again used as the chief technical means of creating the sense of repetition in the books. In *Joseph*, the leitmotiv applies in its broadest sense, not only to words but to situations and events. The resurrection motiv is the central one in the novel. In addition there is the enmity between brothers, relationships between father and son, the favorite son, and the son as rival. The festival, the pit, the womb, the moon, the well, the grave are all important leitmotivs.[75]

Through modifying his sense of time so that it now includes a sense not only of the symbolic but of the mythical, Mann at once broadens and humanizes the scope of his work. Hans Castorp, even in his quester role, is more restricted in scope than Joseph, who is compared with and who is aware of many prototypes. Furthermore, by placing his hero halfway between the dark past and the present, Mann is able to imply prototypes

72. Harry Slochower, "Thomas Mann and Universal Culture," *Southern Review*, IV (April, 1939), 743.

73. Thomas, *Thomas Mann*, p. 116.

74. Harry Slochower, *Thomas Mann's Joseph Story* (New York, 1938), p. 13.

75. Hatfield, *Thomas Mann*, p. 101.

that would be in the future for Joseph but in the past for us, his readers. Thus he achieves almost a sense of prophecy, so that the reader sees that not only do we re-enact roles, but that these roles will be re-enacted again in the future. Prophecy, like a sense of repetition, provides a feeling of security for the primitive mind in that the unknown is believed to be known.

Between *Joseph in Egypt* and *Joseph the Provider* came *Lotte in Weimar* in which Mann, abandoning myth for the time being, subjects the matter of return, of recurrence to a close analysis. Mann is interested in this book in examining the individual's attitude toward time and its effect on his actions. Even the subject of the revolving sphere is not spared Mann's irony, for *Lotte in Weimar* is both a tragic and a comic, both a tender and an ironic commentary on repetition, on recurrence. The tension of the book rests on two different interpretations of time, that held by Goethe and that held by Lotte, if Lotte's may indeed be called a conscious interpretation. In Mann's eyes her tragedy is that she is unable to see herself in terms of her role, an inability that gives rise to comic overtones as well. The role is as important as time and space for Mann, as the individual, and the individual is important chiefly in terms of his roles. It is a kind of ironic judgment on this theory of time that Lotte in the novel is on the whole a more appealing and human figure than Goethe, who is thoroughly aware of his role. Yet Goethe's existence is justified by his work, and Lotte does not see that the sacrifice of her individuality is justified by her having been immortalized by Goethe. For her this is not enough. And she returns, as Goethe says, to be kissed.

Goethe is as well aware of the revolving sphere as he is of the principle of forms. Before Lotte appears in Weimar, he knows that she will appear—in fact he has been rereading *Werther.* Thus when August brings him the news, he is not in the least surprised and begins a discourse on the hyaline quartz he has just received which is highly pertinent to the situation although August, who is unperceptive enough to order the raspberry dessert, perceives nothing. Lotte is like the hyaline quartz; in her present form she is a dead being for Goethe. To kiss her now would be like stressing the importance of the glass in front of a beautiful picture, as he tells her symbolically at the dinner. Return must be understood in the book in a double sense. Lotte returns to a man whom she thought she knew and whom she is disquieted to find she no longer does. To her, return, which was to be a "coming home," becomes a bitter disappointment. For forty-four years, she tells Riemer, the situation has retained for her its "full freshness and immediacy." Her mistake is to return literally and in the flesh.

Interpreted in a different way, for Goethe return is symbolic of the unity in change. Metamorphosis, the containing of youth in age and of age in youth, is an underlying principle of life. Taken symbolically, then, Lotte's return is good although Lotte, who cannot understand it on this level, is insulted by Goethe's mention of the trembling of her head and by his refusal to use the *thou*. The essence of Lotte's sacrifice is that she has in one sense remained throughout her married life the young girl in the pink bows; she has been frozen by Goethe's genius. Throughout her life she has seen herself always as this girl simultaneously as she became wife and mother. To live with this double personality has caused her the pain that makes her seek out the "might have been" in an attempt to live out an experience that never had been lived. Her conflict arises because she is unable to recognize the passage of time whereas all of her dreams have been connected with an experience that occurred within time. Thus time is for her both nothing and everything. She lacks, perhaps excusably, Goethe's ability to transform the experience, to realize that both the experience in itself and time in itself are nothing. Real triumph over time consists in time's being inside one, not outside, in an inner sense of recurrence. Even death is for Goethe but transformation, and he tells Lotte that they will "awake together." But even then Lotte's response is uncomprehending as she whispers, "Peace to your old age!" It is Mager, not Goethe, who can offer her solace as he runs up to help "Werther's Lotte out of Goethe's carriage," thus reinforcing the confusion in her mind between form and matter.

Goethe's coldness and aloofness is not, however, justified entirely by his greatness or by his meaningful sense of time. It is typical of Mann's irony that he is able to apply it to subjects with whom he at the same time feels community. This same coldness is one of the causes of Adrian Leverkühn's pact with the daemonic and of Gustav Aschenbach's downfall. Mann's attitude toward the artist was always ambivalent; only with Joseph, who was an artist in living rather than in the fine arts, does he feel complete sympathy. Joseph the provider is a commentary on Goethe.

Mann returned to myth in *The Transposed Heads* and in *The Tables of the Law* before he started on *Dr. Faustus. The Transposed Heads,* based on a Hindu legend, reaches even further into the well of time than the *Joseph* books had. It is pre-history searching into the very depths of unconscious racial knowledge and indicating through its story what man has always known instinctively, that spirit and mind govern matter. The characters here can look to no antecedents; their significance lies in their future that is our past.

In *The Tables of the Law* Mann jests with the biblical myth of Moses. The faithful servant women find in the revolving sphere a means of interpreting the Princess' indiscretion in having borne Moses at all. Rather than the discovery of a foundling, they see in the incident a re-enaction of the old fairy tale of Akki, the water-bearer, finding Sargon in the reeds. At the same time, Mann is stressing here what he had stressed in the *Joseph* books—the willingness of primitive man to see himself and others in terms of roles. The birth of myth lay in this very capacity of primitive man, and Thomas Mann feels for the process both veneration and a sophisticated amusement that the abrogation of time, the great truth that it is an inner sense of time which is meaningful, should have its origins in rationalizations of human follies and fears. Like Adrian Leverkühn, Mann finds it difficult to keep from laughing at that which is most serious. This ironic attitude toward myth stands out even more clearly in *The Tables of the Law* than in *Joseph.*

In *Dr. Faustus* there is also a sometimes ironic rendering

of myth. Of all Mann's books this one is the most complex in its interweaving of time levels. Serenus Zeitblom (the serene blossom of time) is frequently at pains to inform his readers of these various levels and to apologize for skipping backwards and forwards in time. By using the narrator in *Dr. Faustus,* Mann says that he acquired the possibility of letting the story play on two levels of time, of interweaving the experiences, which shock the narrator as he writes, polyphonically with those that he is describing so that the trembling of his hands may have both a double and a single significance.[76] Zeitblom points out that there is the time of the book and the time of the narrator as well as the time of the reader. There is the time of Adrian from 1885 through 1941, the time of medieval Germany, re-created through the atmosphere of Kaiseraschern and of Halle, and the time when Zeitblom writes the account, that of the fall of the Third Reich. According to Erich Kahler "What happens to Adrian comprises not only the fate of modern art and the intellectual; it comprises also the tragedy of Germany, it comprises the general crisis of our world."[77]

The word *osmosis,* which Mann uses as one of the leitmotivs in the book, describes what happens to the various levels of time. They merge and blend and are absorbed in one another. One critic has called it an Eleatic universe that Mann creates in *Dr. Faustus.*[78] The doddering absent-mindedness of Zeitblom serves to dissolve the time barriers even further, for he often forgets just where he is in the narrative and skips ahead to hint of the future of a character whom he has not yet introduced. "While aesthetic philosophy may assert that music and literature in contrast to the plastic arts depend on time and succession," says Mann in his diary, "music and literature always strive to be present in their entirety at every moment. In their beginning exists their middle and their end, the past invades

76. Thomas Mann, *Die Entstehung des Doktor Faustus* (Amsterdam, 1949), pp. 32-33.
77. Erich Kahler, "Thomas Mann's 'Doctor Faustus,'" *Commentary,* VII (April, 1949), 354.
78. Philip Blair Rice, "The Merging Parallels: Mann's 'Dr. Faustus,'" *Kenyon Review,* XI (Spring, 1949), 204.

the present, and even the most extreme attention to the present is invaded by concern for the future."[79]

In addition to a complex treatment of time levels, the means by which these time levels are integrated, the use of leitmotiv, is a complicated one in *Dr. Faustus*. Both events and words are repeated in the weaving of the themes of the book. The farm at Pfeiffering resembles Buchel; there is the dog, Suso become Kaschperl, the tree, linden become elm. The pond, the mother, the maid reappear. Adrian's experience with the pimp is repeated in his later experiences with the devil. There is the theme of polyphony, first the polyphony of the songs the children sing with Hanne, the stable girl, and later the polyphony of Adrian's compositions. The central leitmotiv is perhaps the repetition of experiences with the daemonic, emphasized through the frequent use of the words *daemonic, witchcraft, deities of the depths, the tempter, poison, hermetic,* and such.

The chapter describing Jonathan Leverkühn's experiments is a fertile source of the leitmotiv. *Hetaera esmeralda*, introduced here, becomes a compelling image throughout the book. She loves the dusk of heavy foliage, and for Adrian she becomes a seductress. The osmotic growths are later compared by the devil to the music that Adrian will produce under evil power. The devouring drop becomes the drop in the bucket, the diving bell in which Adrian embarks in his fantasies. By means of the leitmotiv, Mann often connects two times: thus, for instance, Europe beleaguered by invasion forces is compared to a madhouse bringing to mind the madhouse that Adrian is to enter, Adrian who is also beleaguered by hostile forces. Adrian's headache occurs often on festal occasions. "Root treatment," "the lusts of hell," "turn out," and many more expressions are used by Mann to make of *Dr. Faustus* a time mosaic.

The scholastic *nunc stans* of Kaiseraschern and the timelessness of figures like Adrian or Nepomuk, who is compared by Zeitblom to Christ on earth, contrast in *Dr. Faustus* with the truth recognized by the devil that it is not time, but "the

79. Mann, *Die Entstehung*, pp. 192-93.

manner of time" that matters.[80] This sense of qualitative time is like the time sense that Hans Castorp had achieved on his magic mountain after he has renounced nirvana, but whereas Hans combines his inner sense of qualitative time with a sense of his role, the devil's point of view indicates that an inner sense of time by itself may lead to chaos. Adrian is unable to combine an inner recognition of time with a sense of role. Like Goethe in *Lotte in Weimar* he is detached from time; he is cold and aloof. His failure to recognize that it is the manner of time which matters is the cause of his pact with the devil as it had been the cause of Gustav Aschenbach's decline. Instead of rank vegetation, it is osmotic growths that accompany the ruin of Adrian. There is something uncanny about Adrian's art as there is about osmotic growths. Hans Castorp and Joseph, who are not concerned with art in the narrow sense, work through the conflicts between isolation and community, spirit and life, time and eternity to achieve balance.

With Goethe in *Lotte in Weimar,* however, we see Mann turning again to the theme of the artist in isolation which had been for him always a source of conflict and which he now in *Dr. Faustus* sees not only in relation to his own problems but as a source of the tragedy of Germany. Osmotic growths are now more appropriate symbols than rank vegetation, for Adrian does not degenerate but despite his isolation he produces works of genius. The reason for this is that at the same time Mann deplores the necessary isolation of the artist, he feels that it is justified in terms of the greatness of the art produced. To come down from the mountain would be for Goethe or for Adrian death to their art, as it was for Gustav Aschenbach's. Goethe and Adrian do not long for the blond and the blue-eyed as Tonio Kröger had. This tension has for them been resolved. But the price that Adrian must pay as an artist is a terrible one, like the price those about Goethe are forced to pay. For this reason Mann has seen Leverkühn as an ideal figure, a hero of our time because he bears the sorrows of the age by himself,

80. Thomas Mann, *Doctor Faustus,* trans. H. T. Lowe-Porter (New York, 1948), p. 230.

and he accepts his crucifixion.[81] Unlike Goethe he does not sacrifice others to his genius. Goethe himself in *Lotte in Weimar* is seemingly untouched by suffering, but in *Dr. Faustus* Mann has seen that the artist too must bear the responsibility of his art.

That the music that Adrian produces is great, even though osmotic in origin, is proof of the "daemonic" theory expressed in a discussion early in the book that good and evil are inter-dependent. Mann is saying that for the artist reconciliation between art and life may be achieved only at the expense of art, that isolation is necessary for the artist, and that if great artistic heights are to be reached, great depths must be plumbed. Hans Castorp's sacrifice is petty in terms of the eternal damnation incurred by Adrian Leverkühn. Through a pact with evil, great art may be produced as a long chain of Adrians from Beethoven to Schönberg to Mahler to Nietzsche to Kierkegaard to Baude-laire to Rimbaud to Rilke have proven.

Mann turns from dealing with genius in the fine arts to dealing again with the genius in living in his next book, *The Holy Sinner*, in which in terms of another legend the question of penance is explored. Whereas the central character in *Dr. Faustus* had been contemporary and the legend of Faust implied, the process is again reversed in *The Holy Sinner*, so that, as in the *Joseph* books, we are now dealing directly with ancient figures who may have counterparts in the modern world. Grigorss, like Joseph, caught in the revolving sphere, goes down into the pit to be reborn, first when he is placed by Sieur Eisengrein in the plump little cask, "a new mother-womb," and pushed out to sea and much later when he returns again to the sea, to the womb, to exile on the islet. Grigorss experiences a sense of timelessness on the islet as Hans Castorp had experienced it on his magic mountain. Without events, time becomes meaningless, and shrunken to the size of a hedge-hog, a foetus, he knows time no more. Out of this withdrawal comes redemption for Grigorss as new mental resolution had come for Hans Castorp from his withdrawal on the mountain.

81. Mann, *Die Entstehung*, p. 81.

But it is the attitude toward withdrawal which matters. Whereas Hans's withdrawal is undertaken at first with no very serious motivation and only gradually becomes an education, Grigorss from the first knows the purpose of his seclusion. It is this motif of burial, of rebirth, and of salvation, which is central to Christianity, which enables Grigorss to become like Joseph, Grigorss the provider. Mann's hopes for Germany's future alternate with his fears for it as one can see in *Dr. Faustus*. Mann seems to say in his later works that if Germany is to achieve salvation, it must be through the socialization won by Joseph and by Grigorss rather than by the dangerous path of the artist followed by Adrian Leverkühn.

The incest theme and the Oedipus theme in *The Holy Sinner* go even further than the legend of Grigorss to relate this book to the primitive foundations of the human soul. These primeval patterns lie hidden in all men, and Mann has treated or implied both themes in other works. There is direct treatment of incest in "The Blood of the Walsungs." In the isolation that Mann has seen from the beginning as sinful, the embrace of the sister is more natural than that of an outsider. In the ingrown Buddenbrook family, Thomas and Tony cling together in a way that neither achieves with a mate. Tonio Kröger makes a confidante of Lisabeta because like him she is in the family of artists. On the day of his sister's wedding Adrian Leverkühn develops one of his headaches. The Oedipus theme, though never treated by Mann so outspokenly as in *The Holy Sinner,* lies behind all the homosexual episodes in Mann's work: the attachment of Tonio Kröger to Hans Hansen; of Hans Castorp to Privislav Hippe; of the magician to Mario; of Tadzio to Gustav Aschenbach. Another basic theme in many of Mann's books is that of the return to the womb—seen in the withdrawal of his characters from life. It is perhaps no chance that these themes are explicit in a novel about salvation, for Freud had seen that health could be achieved by bringing hidden guilt to light. *The Holy Sinner* may act as a kind of catalyst which caused Mann to turn from Adrian Leverkühn to a character like

Felix Krull, who confesses all. *The Holy Sinner* may be seen as the timeless myth of rebirth and of salvation on many levels.

"To continue with *Felix Krull* after thirty-two years," says Mann in his diary, "everything I did between might be seen as an interpolation, claiming a whole lifetime." That he went on with the story at all was the result of his attraction to the idea of the unity of all existence.[82] Mann has returned in his last work to a theme of which he had said earlier that it expressed both a sympathetic and detached attitude toward tradition in that it burlesqued and at the same time honored the literature of confession. Even Mann's ideas of time and of space are burlesqued in that they are put into the mouth of Kuckuck.[83] Reality is seen again in this book as circular in that people and events recur in different guises, and time is once more abrogated by the timeless figure of the main character. The artist is again Mann's subject, the artist whom Adrian Leverkühn had compared to the charlatan. Adrian Leverkühn's "charlatanism" is in a sense repeated in the figure of Felix Krull, for the imposter is now the humorous imposter. Mann in his diary realized the inner relation of Felix Krull to the Faust material— the theme of isolation in Faust was related to a tragic mysticism, he says; in Krull to a humorous criminality.[84]

Rather than achieving the social orientation of Joseph and of Grigorss, Krull is a complete success in a kind of social disorientation. That the resolution of the conflicts of the artist may be found in a blatant mockery of society is perhaps the supreme irony of Mann's many ironies. It is the same solution that Henry James had found for Morris Gedge in "The Birthplace." That it happens to be the last word that Mann spoke on the problems of the artist does not mean that it was meant to be Mann's final word, but at least it is a means of throwing light on the contradiction inherent in *Dr. Faustus*. If good springs from evil, then the artist may as well cultivate evil, for it is likely that it is society, not the artist, which errs, that the

82. *Ibid.*, p. 84.
83. Thomas Mann, *Confessions of Felix Krull*, trans. Denver Lindley (New York, 1955), pp. 272 ff.
84. Mann, *Die Entstehung*, p. 26.

art that the charlatan produces is better than society deserves. Perhaps Felix Krull has found the happiest way of resolving these tensions, for society is none the worse from his activities and the artist achieves detachment through his irony and thus has no need of literal isolation.

Humor, Mann had said, quoting Kierkegaard, is the attitude of mind that can not help thinking of God always in juxtaposition to something else, something opposite to the idea of God.[85] Mann is saying in *Felix Krull* that the tragedy and the comedy of the world lies in its divisions, its divisions between good and evil, between life and art, between time and eternity.

From little Herr Friedemann to Felix Krull, Mann's central theme, the relation of the artist to society, has persisted, although it has been treated in many guises. It is remarkable, says Frau von Tümmler to her daughter, how the crocus resembles the autumn colchicum.[86] *(The Black Swan)* But whereas the hunchback, Herr Friedemann, falls to the ground rejected by Frau von Rinnlingen, Felix Krull, the imposter, is at the end borne to ecstasy in the embrace of Dona Maria Pia. In the revolving sphere through which Mann abrogates time, he sees the principle of progression. Although there can be no spring without death to precede it, each resurrection produces new combinations, new solutions in the weeding out of the spiritual weakling.

In conclusion, it may be said that for Thomas Mann as for Nietzsche, time is circular. Mann sees further that we constantly return to earlier points of existence because the Adon feast happens in essence only once. Time itself merges for Mann with the eternal at the point where the individual "defies the 'always' and breaks the never-ending round."[87] It is this sense of progress in time, which Mann had from Freud and from Goethe, which causes his Platonic universals to be "invaded by Aristotelian dynamics."[88] Time is circular then only

85. *Ibid.,* p. 78.
86. Thomas Mann, *The Black Swan,* trans. Willard R. Trask (New York, 1954), p. 109.
87. Heller, *The Ironic German,* p. 242.
88. Slochower, *Thomas Mann's Joseph Story,* p. 13.

in so far as it is literally repetitive. The chosen ones, the elect, have the power to influence the course of eternal recurrence in an upward direction. Arthur Eloesser has seen Thomas Mann as primarily a moralist rather than a philosopher or a historian.[89] Mann's concept of time cannot in fact be separated from his concern with good and evil because his first interest has always been life itself.

89. Arthur Eloesser, *Thomas Mann sein Leben und sein Werk* (Berlin, 1925), p. 81.

CHAPTER SIX

TIME AND REALITY

IN THE WORK

OF FRANZ KAFKA

1

Although Max Brod notes a relation between Kafka's work and Plato's doctrine of ideas, Kafka's primary interest was not, apparently, in developing a particular system of metaphysics. Unlike Thomas Mann, whose early writing Kafka admired, Kafka was not interested in introducing the dialectics of philosophy into his novels. Philosophical precedents are implicit, not explicit, in Kafka's fiction.

Kafka's diaries and letters indicate that he read a number of philosophers, especially Kierkegaard, but his remarks about them show little interest in their concepts of time. At Frau Bertha Fanta's Kafka took part in study and discussion of Fichte, Kant, Hegel among other philosophers.[1] Once in his letters Kafka quotes Schopenhauer to the effect that there is nothing more beautiful than suffering.[2] Critics have counted

1. Wilhelm Emrich, *Franz Kafka* (Bonn, 1958), pp. 413, 421.
2. Franz Kafka, *Briefe, 1902-1924* (New York, Schocken Books, 1959), p. 310.

Nietzsche among his spiritual forebears, but Kafka never expounded the influence, although a childhood friend, Frau Selma Robitschek, describes how Kafka and she often sat under an oak while he read Nietzsche to her.[3] That Kafka read widely in Kierkegaard is clear in the diaries as well as in the letters. He compares him to a star over an inaccessible region, and complains that he does not really understand Kierkegaard although in March, 1918, Kierkegaard is so much with him that he has not read any other books for a long time.[4] Kierkegaard's philosophy shows that life may be examined either forwards or backwards or in both directions at once, he writes.[5] Bergson is not mentioned in the diaries or letters, nor had Kafka ever heard of Proust.[6] And yet the revolt against Hegelian intellectualism, led by Schopenhauer and Nietzsche, nurtured by Kierkegaard, by William James in America, and by Bergson in France, is a tradition of which Kafka was at least partially aware. His awareness of it in his fiction is, however, implicit rather than explicit. Nor do his characters engage in discussions of metaphysics on a purely intellectual level like the ones between Settembrini and Naphta in *The Magic Mountain.*

Nevertheless, because for Kafka time and space as they appear were not necessarily real, he employed a technique to interpret the reality behind the illusions by which we are surrounded. A great deal has been written about this technique. Erich Kahler in 1953 argued that Kafka's works are neither symbolic nor allegorical because by the symbol thought is directed from the concrete to the abstract and by allegory thought is directed from the abstract to the concrete. Kafka's work is rather like a daydream in which subject and object are one. Kafka's K. lives for Kahler in a dreamlike day of human existence. Kahler preferred, therefore, the term *parable* as a description of the technique, for with the parable there is "a time-spanning simultaneity."[7] In 1958 Wilhelm Emrich re-

3. *Ibid.,* p. 495.　　　　　　　4. *Ibid.,* pp. 190, 234, 237.
5. *Ibid.,* p. 235.
6. Max Brod, *Franz Kafka, eine Biographie* (Berlin, 1954), p. 42.
7. Erich Kahler, "Untergang und Übergang der epischen Kunstform," *Neue Rundschau,* LXIV (1953), 38.

examined the question of method in Kafka and concluded that none of the terms *allegory, symbol,* or *parable* were exact in describing Kafka's technique. Kafka's works are not parables, says Emrich, because they have no metaphysical background in religion or philosophy. There is, in fact, says Emrich, no name for Kafka's technique; it introduces a new epoch in writing. Kafka depicts the totality of all life and thought, but he has to use everyday speech, images, and ideas to represent this.[8]

Emrich's clarification of Kafka's method is valuable. However, the totality of all life and thought is seen in Kafka through his investigation of the inner world of mankind. Kafka tells the history of this inner world using the language of the outer world. Kafka does indeed introduce a new epoch in literature, and one reason for this is that he introduces a new means of dealing with the unconscious, a method differing from the "monologue intérieur." Since Kafka was dealing with man's unconscious rather than with *a* man's unconscious, the "monologue intérieur," which employs the language of the inner world of an individual, did not suffice. One should note in this connection that critics have not yet decided who is speaking in Joyce's *Finnegans Wake*. Kafka avoided this dilemma by stationing his conscious self within the dream and recording his surroundings literally. In this way he achieved an objectivity impossible with the stream of consciousness method. He becomes thus a kind of reporter at large in the dream world. It is interesting to note that Kafka early became acquainted with the concept of the unconscious in the work of Freud.[9] Max Brod in pointing out the relation between Kafka and Kleist indicates the essence of Kafka's effect when he writes that with both writers the most insoluble, most secret, and darkest areas are treated with the greatest possible clarity, simplicity, and sharpness.[10]

An important source of Kafka's approach to reality may be found in some of the authors in the German-Austrian-French

8. Emrich, *Franz Kafka*, p. 78.
9. *Ibid.*, p. 421.
10. Brod, *Franz Kafka*, p. 50.

literary background of Kafka. In 1922, speaking of one of Stifter's stories, "Zwei Schwestern," Kafka wrote in a letter that it appeared to be a dream that many had dreamed.[11] This is a significant statement, for Kafka's own stories are dreams that many have dreamed. His indebtedness to Stifter is clear. In Stifter's *Der Nachsommer,* which Kafka read and admired,[12] one finds the characters subordinate to the ideal of unity which Stifter sets up. Stifter wrote of *Der Nachsommer* in a letter to Heckenast (February 29, 1856): "The entire situation and the characters shall, according to my intention, represent something higher than themselves." One critic points out that in *Der Nachsommer* there is hardly any difference between the speech of the characters, as if souls were communing, not living humans. Because Stifter is dealing with ideas and not with material shaped by time and space, it is as if he were creating time and space. Stifter's characters lack "Körperlichkeit" because he is striving after a greater truth as Kafka later did. "He presents the permanent content of experience made transient in our lives by the incidentals of time and space."[13] Walther Rehm sees *Der Nachsommer* as a book beyond time, a book that gives the impression of being the painting of a dream. The landscape in the book is, according to Rehm, a spiritual landscape.[14] And Emil Staiger states that what Stifter writes lacks reality. "It is an ideal world which never was and never will be."[15] *Der Nachsommer* should be classed, he says, with *Wilhelm Meister's Wanderjahre* and Plato's *Republic.*

The theme of transcendent truth is also found in some of the works of Grillparzer to whom reality was not restricted to mere material facts. The higher reality that the poetic genius and the artist seek is to be found as the subject of the plays *Sappho* and *Medea.* Kafka's experimentation with dream and the dream within the dream has definite connections with Grillparzer's

11. Kafka, *Briefe,* p. 420.
12. Brod, *Franz Kafka,* p. 63.
13. Eric Blackall, *Adalbert Stifter* (Cambridge, 1948), p. 328.
14. Walther Rehm, *Nachsommer zur Deutung von Stifters Dichtung* (Bern, 1951), pp. 35, 101.
15. Emil Staiger, *Adalbert Stifter als Dichter der Ehrfurcht* (Ostern, 1943), p. 32.

Der Traum, ein Leben. But particularly influential for Kafka was Grillparzer's "Der arme Spielmann" which Kafka mentions as significant for him in *Letters to Milena.*[16] Although Kafka admits that the story has "ridiculous and dilettantish features," he states that "there is no more beautiful fate for a story than for it to disappear, and in this way."[17] Jacob, the musician in the story, finds that reality is not that which his father, who is a statesman, his successful brothers, or even his beloved Barbara consider it. He discovers that he perfers to play his violin in the streets rather than in the halls and houses because in the crowds he finds kinship with perhaps a few. People play Mozart and Bach, he complains, "aber den lieben Gott spielt keiner." Barbara, who has earlier enjoined Jacob to leave music and concentrate on "important" things, at the end of the story refuses a high price for the old man's violin while the tears stream down her face. In a diary entry in 1847 Grillparzer wrote: "The artist must also have the gift of forgetting, if necessary, his formal education,"[18] a remark that represents Grillparzer's attitude toward the artist and the sort of attitude by which Kafka was undoubtedly influenced. According to Max Brod, Kafka preferred Grillparzer's diaries to his other works, and it was no wonder, comments Gerhart Baumann, for Grillparzer's diaries are like the background of a long journey. In them one sees that the writer is continually forced to make new justifications and new examinations of his position; his trial never comes to an end.[19]

Grillparzer's characters, says Baumann, have that free movement of soul life, which under changing circumstances continually surprises us with its new facets.[20] They live to give themselves up entirely to the dream world in order to defeat reality. One frees oneself from that which is transient only if

16. Franz Kafka, *Letters to Milena,* ed. Willy Haas, trans. Tania and James Stern (London, 1953), p. 79.

17. *Ibid.,* p. 97.

18. Franz Grillparzer, *Tagebücher und literarische Skizzenhefte* (Wien, 1924), V, 177.

19. Gerhart Baumann, *Franz Grillparzer* (Wien, 1954), p. 152.

20. *Ibid.,* p. 206.

one goes through the continually open door where time and space are only empty names, says Grillparzer.[21] For Grillparzer "life acquires the character of a dream and the dream maintains an uncanny reality."[22] Grillparzer sought, says Ernst Alker, to describe the the interior of the personality behind the façades. Although he writes of the phantasy world, he pays strict attention to form. "Der arme Spielmann" can be considered as "ancestor of the modern novel, stressing psychological relationships more than events."[23]

The theme of the artist in exile stressed by Grillparzer may be seen as well in Goethe, Kleist, and Hölderlin—all of whom Kafka read. Brod takes particular notice of the relation between Kleist and Kafka, stating that their talent for realistic detail is counterbalanced by their tendency to create a dream atmosphere.[24] In a letter, Kafka compares visiting an art gallery to a visit to Weimar and speaks of the difficulty of grasping the creator himself rather than the physical details that surrounded him.[25] Brod writes that Kafka's love for Goethe's work never changed,[26] and in the diaries Kafka's strong interest in Goethe is evident. Both Kafka and Goethe rendered individual experience in general form.

Brod and Kafka read together *The Temptation of St. Anthony* and *A Sentimental Education*. Brod feels that Flaubert sacrificed everything to his idol, literature. In fact, his devotion to idea was so strong that Frédéric Moreau in *A Sentimental Education* lives, according to Lionel Trilling, in a kind of "ideological zoo."[27] At the end of the novel when Madame Arnoux comes back to Frédéric with the purpose of giving herself to him, he decides against taking her in order not to degrade his ideal. In *Bouvard and Pécuchet*, the books, not the people, constitute reality for the heroes. And in *The Tempta-*

21. *Ibid.*, p. 87.   22. *Ibid.*, p. 85.
23. Ernst Alker, *Franz Grillparzer, Ein Kampf um Leben und Kunst* (Marburg, 1930), p. 197.
24. Brod, *Franz Kafka*, p. 50.   25. Kafka, *Briefe*, p. 403.
26. Brod, *Franz Kafka*, p. 67.
27. Lionel Trilling, "Introduction," in Gustave Flaubert, *Bouvard and Pécuchet*, trans. T. W. Earp and G. W. Stonier (Norfolk, Connecticut, 1954), p. ix.

tion of St. Anthony all the movement is in the realm of the spirit; Anthony remains stationary in time and place.

By the time of Kafka's death in 1924 the only works of Thomas Mann in print were those preceding *The Magic Mountain*. Nevertheless, Kafka wrote to Brod in 1917 that Mann belonged among those after whose work he hungered.[28] Brod assures us that Kafka "loved Thomas Mann's *Tonio Kröger* and reverently searched out every line of this author's in *Neue Rundschau*."[29] Kafka speaks of "re-reading" "Tonio Kröger" as early as 1904.[30] "Tonio Kröger" like "Der arme Spielmann" stresses the alienation of the artist. What Kafka found in "Tonio Kröger" that interested him was probably the close identification of subject and object, so that Tonio in a sense becomes the objects or people that he views, the house turned into a library, the ship tossed by the storm, or the girl who stumbles on the dance floor. Although Mann often abrogates time in quite a different way from Kafka (in *Buddenbrooks* through Schopenhauer or in "The Blood of the Walsungs" through legend), a story like "The Wardrobe," which Kafka could have read, describes a man similar to K., a man absolved from time in a hypothetical city, in a phantasy world. At the sea resort in Denmark, Tonio Kröger, like the hero of "The Wardrobe," "enjoyed profound forgetfulness, hovering disembodied above space and time."[31] The way in which Kafka's idea of reality parallels and extends that set up by these earlier writers will be examined in what follows.[32] Kafka's relationship to these

28. Kafka, *Briefe*, p. 182.
29. Brod, *Franz Kafka*, p. 58.
30. Kafka, *Briefe*, p. 31.
31. Thomas Mann, *Stories of Three Decades*, trans. H. T. Lowe-Porter (New York, 1938), pp. 123-24.
32. A great deal has been written by critics on the subject of time and reality of Kafka, and a brief review of some of the foremost contributions is essential in an examination of this subject, one of the most controversial subjects on the contemporary literary scene.

There are those who explain how Kafka's abrogation of time values takes place. Willy Haas, for example, claims that the real hero of *The Trial* is *das Vergessen* ("Meine Meinung," *Literarische Welt*, II [June 4, 1926], 1-2). Peter Reichmann says that in Kafka through the atmosphere of dreams the conventions of time are overcome ("Franz Kafka and New Trends in Europe," *Canadian Bookman*, XXI [June-July, 1939], 17-19). Ezequiel Martínez Estrada explains that Kafka's world is one of hollows, not of objects and beings; in such a world intuition is the only instrument of understanding ("Intuition," in *The Kafka Problem*, ed. Angel Flores [New York, 1946], pp. 348-53). And Austin Warren calls Barnabas' appearances and disappearances "sheer magic" ("Kosmos Kafka," *Southern Review*, VII [Autumn, 1941], 357).

Then there are explanations of the quality of the time experience in Kafka. Erich Heller writes that "Kafka's novels take place in infinity. Yet their atmosphere is as oppressive as that of those unaired rooms in which so many of their scenes are enacted. For infinity is incompletely defined as the ideal point where two parallels meet" (*The Disinherited Mind* [Cambridge, 1952], p. 158). Heinz Politzer shows that in Kafka "der Charakter des Überwirklichen besteht in seiner Undeutbarkeit und die Aufgabe des Kafkaschen Realismus in seiner Symbollosigkeit" ("Problematik und Probleme der Kafka-Forschung," *Monatschefte*, XLII [October, 1950], 276). Eugen Gürster comments that "die tiefe Unwirklichkeit der Welt vor dem Geist ist gerade Kafkas zentrales Erlebnis" ("Das Weltbild Franz Kafkas," *Hochland*, XLIV [April, 1952], 337). Philip Rahv understands Kafka's time values as "an example of neurotic regression" ("The Death of Ivan Ilyich and Joseph K.," *Southern Review*, V [Summer, 1939], 181). In them he sees the conception of Moira, an impersonal fate, dominating life without regard for law, justice, or rights. Thus the struggle lies between real historical forces, the civilized mind, and the primordial forces of destiny. In a later article Rahv explains that Kafka's works are speculations, not so much findings about reality as methods of exploring it. Thus history is abolished, there is only one time, the present, and his characters move "within the dimension of personality" ("Franz Kafka: The Hero as Lonely Man," *Kenyon Review*, I [Winter, 1939], 71).

William Phillips, expressing this idea in different terms, speaks of Kafka's rendering of "total experience" at all times. Instead of moments when the hero relives his entire life or chronological recounting of instants, Kafka maintains "a kind of permanent crisis, which loads each particular experience with the sum of all experience" ("The Great Wall of Criticism," *Commentary*, III [June, 1947], 595). This idea of crisis is interpreted in theological terms by John Kelly, who sees in Kafka the concept developed by Kierkegaard and Barth of the revelation of God as the turning point in man's life. One cannot, therefore, seek God by falling back on the past, but one's true self is found in the present moment, in the crisis of revelation ("Franz Kafka's 'Trial' and the Theology of Crisis," *Southern Review*, V [Spring, 1940], 748-66).

Other writers note the unreality of Kafka's world. Edwin Muir observes that Kafka's values continually shift between the metaphysical and the actual ("A Note on Franz Kafka," *Bookman*, LXII [November, 1930], 235-41), and James Burnham notes that Kafka dissolves all connective tissue between dream and waking, reality and illusion ("Observations on Kafka," *Partisan Review*, LIV [March-April, 1947], 186-95). H. S. Reiss speaks of Kafka's awareness of relative values and changing conceptions of reality ("Franz Kafka's Conception of Humour," *Modern Language Review*, XLIV [October, 1949], 534-42). In his book he refers to Kafka's world as "ein geistiges Niemandsland," a superstructure over the everyday world. The juxtaposition of the real and the unreal is the essence of Kafka's work. "Kafkas Kunst ist Spiegel und Abglanz seines gequälten Geistes" (*Franz Kafka Eine Betrachtung seines Werkes* [Heidelberg, 1952], p. 167). Felix Weltsch in his analysis of Kafka's humor compares reality in Kafka to "Metageometrie." As "Metageometrie" stands to Euclid's geometry, so Kafka's world is to our daily world. "Diese eigenartige Irrealität führt zu einer tiefern Auffassung der Realität." The unreal courts, defendants, and arrests make one conscious that the real theme is the guilt hidden behind appearances (*Religiöser Humor bei Franz Kafka* [Winterthur, 1948], p. 113).

Significant French criticism on this subject is that of Albert Camus and of Robert Rochefort, the German edition of whose book contains an important preface by Romano Guardini. Camus says that Kafka's significance lies in the perpetual balance of the natural and the extraordinary, of the individual and the universal, of the tragic and the everyday, of the absurd and the logical. In Kafka's work the spirit projects into the concrete its spiritual tragedy and in doing so illustrates Nietzsche's words, "The great problems are in the street" (*Le Myth de Sisyphe* [Paris, 1942], p. 174).

Guardini in his introduction to Rochefort's book points out that Kafka belongs to a tradition, springing from the work of Feuerbach, Comte, Marx, and Nietzsche, which secularizes that which is spiritual while retaining an atmosphere of the divine. Hölderlin and Rilke, like Kafka, belong to this tradition. With Kafka the personality of God dissolves, becomes anonymous, but at the same time there is still a divinity (*Kafka oder die unzerstörbare Hoffnung* [Wien, 1955], p. 20). Through a detailed discussion of the works, Rochefort develops this theme. Rochefort writes: "Kafka erstrebt den mystischen Zustand, das Leben über dem Leben: das Gewissen treibt ihn und die Unruhe um das 'höhere Ich,' die er lange Zeit für die Ursache seines Niedergangs halt" (p. 81).

On memory, the tool of time, a valuable comment is that of William Hubben, who notes the curious lack of memory in the Kafka novel and relates this to the Freudian theory of guilt caused by the lost content of events ("Kafka's Apocalyptic Message," *Christian Century*, LXIV [October 1, 1947], 1172). Kafka, unlike Proust, makes no attempt to recall these events, and thus Kafka's characters submit to no punishment and admit failure. In his book Hubben relates this absence of memory to Kierkegaard's statement that "he who lives ethically has memory of his life, whereas he who lives aesthetically has not" (*Four Prophets of Our Destiny* [New York, 1952], p. 135).

Another important treatment of Kafka's attitude toward reality is the discussion of Wilhelm Emrich. Although for Kafka there is no transcendent God, writes Emrich, there is in man something immortal, the "being" of man, his consciousness, feeling, and desires. Man is both human and divine and he must keep these two spheres sharply differentiated, but at the same time bring both into harmony (p. 58). Emrich shows how Kafka's belief in the immortal residing in the being of man does not enable him to be identified with Heidegger. Kafka could not share Heidegger's reflections on the relation between nothing and being. Paradoxically, "Für Kafka aber ist das Sein das alles Nichtende" (p. 61).

Max Bense, however, sees Kafka's position as existential and contrasts it with Pascal's classical position on time illustrated by Proust's work. Bense sees that Kafka's writing "als Phänomene inneren Zeitbewusstseins im 'epischen Bewusstsein' verständlich werde, demonstrieren sie die eigentliche ontische Zeit als fundamentalontologisch deutbare Zeit der bewussten Existenz selbst, als 'Zeitlichkeit des In-der-Welt-seins,' wie der Terminus Heideggers lautet, als Zeit der Möglichkeiten, nicht der Realität" (*Die Theorie Kafkas* [Berlin, 1952], p. 63). One may agree with Emrich that Kafka was not existential in terms of Heidegger's philosophy, but in a more general sense, in his identification of subject and object, there can be no question of his relation to a larger existentialism.

Another critic, Clemens Heselhaus, sees Kafka's short stories as "Anti-

authors has only been sketched here. His affiliation with German and Austrian as well as with Russian literature has yet to be explored satisfactorily.

2

In investigating the question of time and reality in Kafka's work, one finds many valuable insights in the letters and diaries. That Kafka is aware of the relativity of time is apparent in the letters to Milena in which he speaks of his life lasting one night,[33] of a "year-letter, an eternity letter" (p. 152), or of the lengthened journey of his life because he is a Jew (p. 47). (Kafka's Jewish heritage, like Joyce's Irish-Catholic heritage, resulted in two attitudes toward time—his inward sense of myth was often transformed into outer rebellion against tradition, and his feeling as a Jew was that "everything has to be earned, not only the present and the future, but the past too") (p. 219). In the diaries there are many entries on the relativity of time and space. Emrich says that in the home of Frau Bertha Fanta, Kafka had heard Einstein's theory of relativity, Max Planck's quantum theory, and Cantor's theory of transfinite numbers discussed.[34] In one diary entry Kafka notes that after twenty years a person becomes small under the trees that have been grow-

---

märchen" and points out in detail how Kafka blends and opposes reality and unreality in the two stories "A Country Doctor" and "The Metamorphosis." The novels Heselhaus describes as "Antiromane" in which many of the same patterns apply as do in the "Antimärchen." He concludes that "Auf der Grenzscheide von Realität und Irrealität müssen wir überhaupt das eigentliche Zentrum von Kafkas dichterischer Welt suchen" ("Kafkas Erzählformen," *Deutsche Vierteljahrsschrift für Literaturwissenschaft und Geistesgeschichte*, XXVI [1952], 353-76). Friedrich Beissner, on the other hand, sees Kafka as chiefly a "realistic" writer who only occasionally hints at the transformation of reality. His talent is in representing his dreamlike inner life. Kafka succeeds in metamorphosing an inner reality into a completely structured work of art in everyday language, writes Beissner (*Der Erzähler Franz Kafka, ein Vortrag* [Stuttgart, 1952], p. 42).

A review of this criticism gives some indication of the immense impact and significance of Kafka's writing. That interpretations differ so widely is owing to the universality of Kafka's appeal. Kafka holds up a mirror to mankind, and readers find in his work what they want to find, the image of themselves.

33. Kafka, *Letters to Milena*, p. 38. Subsequent references to this volume appear in the text.

34. Emrich, *Franz Kafka*, pp. 413, 421.

ing.[35] Or if you change the position of your bed in relation to the window, "the window keeps moving around you" (1910-1913, p. 27). Kafka mentions Zeno's notion of the flying arrow which rests if observed in one of a series of positions (1910-1913, p. 34). Relative to the size of a nation are the advantages literature confers. In a small nation the influence of dead writers becomes so great that it can take the place of contemporary writing (1910-1913, p. 193). In a letter to Brod, Kafka is impressed by Kassner's point that an attempt to examine the physical world around us is doomed to failure, for objects seize us before we have reached them, and we fall into them as into a hole which was only a shadow on the path.[36]

In the diaries the theme of dread of future events dominates much of the writing. One discovers here incessant worries about even the distant future—fear that he will unfold future sufferings so far in front of him that his "eye must pass beyond them and never again return" (1910-1913, p. 162).

Kafka's whole attitude toward time is, of course, deeply colored by his personal problems of adjustment to life. His fear of the future reflects his pessimism toward the possibility of a solution to the painful relationships with his father, his mother, Milena, or the women to whom he was engaged. As a Jew his relationship to the community was also an involved one. These unsolved relationships led to conflicts between the inner and the outer man, so that he eventually took cover in his writing in the dream world as a refuge from the impingements of the world of action and event. Transcendence of time is for Kafka a successful defense, for clock time leads irrevocably to the dreaded future and is the medium of the community wherein his problems lie. "The clocks are not in unison," Kafka writes.[37] His inner being runs on ahead of the outer one. He foresees that the two worlds will split apart (death) or clash (insanity). The

35. *The Diaries of Franz Kafka, 1910-1913*, ed. Max Brod, trans. Joseph Kresh (New York, 1948), p. 27. Subsequent references to this volume appear in the text.
36. Kafka, *Briefe*, p. 61.
37. *The Diaries of Franz Kafka, 1914-1923*, ed. Max Brod, trans. Martin Greenberg and Hannah Arendt (New York, 1949), p. 202.

dreams and actual narratives related in the diaries are scarcely differentiated (1910-1913, p. 312) as if in his writing he could staple together the two halves of his life in an attempt to postpone his inevitable fate. And yet he writes to Brod in March, 1918, that struggling man must set himself against himself in order to save what is godlike in him.[38]

Kafka is aware of his talent for portraying his "dream-like inner life" (1914-1923, p. 77). This inner world penetrates the pages of the diaries not only in the relating of specific dreams but in the atmosphere that surrounds everyday incidents such as a walk with Weltsch (1910-1913, p. 189) which despite wind and rain passes as quickly as if they had ridden or watching a young man on a trolley, a young man who because of his inner excitement has no real relation to the trolley (1910-1913, p. 254). "All is imaginary," Kafka writes, "family, office, friends, the street . . . ; the truth that lies closest, however, is only this, that you are beating your head against the wall of a window-less and doorless cell" (1914-1923, p. 197)—a remark that could be regarded as a statement of theme of his two main novels. As Kafka's illness grows, one notes in the later pages of the diaries the connection of fear and the inner world; he is forced to place ordinary life against "the terror that would seem to be more real" (1914-1923, p. 225).

Any interest in the past and its connection with the present is practically lacking in Kafka. "What is there," he asks, "to tie me to a past or a future? The present is a phantom state for me" (1914-1923, p. 126). One sees in Kafka a deep fear of remembering, which accounts in part for his blindness on the subject of recovering the past. "I am afraid," he says, "of the almost physical strain of the effort to remember, afraid of the pain . . . " (1910-1913, p. 303). When his memory does come alive, he suffers from insomnia (1914-1923, p. 193). Once he remarks that past and future are barely distinguishable, for "the end of the future is really already experienced in all our sighs, and thus becomes past" (1910-1913, p. 27). However, in general Kafka's anxiety about past and future lead him to see

38. Kafka, *Briefe,* p. 239.

the present moment as a transcendent instant in the existence of the human race.

These themes in his diaries and letters indicate some of the personal reasons that led him to feel that time and space are illusory. "The watch is subject to time," (1910-1913, p. 292) he writes. It is from such attitudes—his interest in relativity, his fear of the future and of the past, his stress on the inner life—that his fictional method develops.

Although Gustav Janouch was not an Eckermann, there are recorded in the conversations several themes of importance to this study. In the conversations one again sees that Kafka's idea of reality is an inner one. "Nothing can be so deceiving as a photograph," he says. "Truth, after all, is an affair of the heart. One can get at it only through art."[39]

In the conversations Kafka also mentions his reliance on tradition and myth. He is interested in the abiding significance of the Moses story and in the Abraham myth used by Kierkegaard. "Moses is still a reality," he says to Janouch. As Abiram and Dathan opposed Moses, so the world still opposes him with anti-semitism (p. 66). In a diary entry the theme of the Moses story is related to the universal fate of man. Moses' dying vision of Canaan is symbolic of man's destiny. "Moses fails to enter Canaan not because his life is too short, but because it is a human life" (1914-1923, p. 195). As Goronwy Rees says in the preface to the conversations, "Kafka found a myth so closely related to universal reality that through it he was able to express . . . his entire response to the human situation" (p. vii). In Kafka's interpretation of Moses, one may see perhaps Nietzsche's *ewige Wiederkehr*. In the diaries Kafka often speaks of life as a circle (1910-1913, p. 200). Although Max Brod in *Franz Kafkas Glauben und Lehre* writes that in the history of

39. Gustav Janouch, *Conversations with Kafka*, trans. Goronwy Rees (New York, 1953), p. ix. Subsequent references to this volume appear in the text.

Other remarks in the conversations which show that truth for Kafka is an inner affair are: (1) his insistence that despite the disappearance of the old Jewish quarter in Prague, "the unhealthy old Jewish town within us is far more real than the new hygienic town" and (2) his claim that in "The Metamorphosis" "the dream reveals the reality, which the conception lags behind" (p. 35).

the last hundred years Nietzsche is almost the exact mathemat-
ical opposite of Kafka,[40] it is possible to see in their approach to
reality—even though the results of the approach are different—a
common bond. Günther Anders sees that Nietzsche's *ewige*
Wiederkehr had become, if not an effective model, at least a
philosophical precedent.[41] What Kafka shares with Nietzsche,
according to Anders, is the *doubt* that all problems may be
answered by a nihilistic approach to life.[42] Furthermore, Erich
Heller sees Nietzsche as "in many respects a legitimate spiritual
ancestor of Kafka." Kafka's despair, says Heller, springs from
the same motivations as Nietzsche's *ewige Wiederkehr*,
"existence, as it is without meaning or goal, but inescapably
recurrent."[43] Nietzsche's superman is strong enough to with-
stand this cursed existence, but Kafka's heroes are engulfed
by it.

A third theme brought out in the conversations is that of
change. As a Jew, Kafka says that he cannot depict things
statically. "We see them always in transition, in movement, as
change" (p. 86). Again he complains that "one never knows the
living. The present is change and transformation" (p. 51). As
well as its relation to his Jewish background, Kafka's interest in
change may well be, like Thomas Wolfe's, a fascinated preoccupation with the forces that are spinning one's death. All
that matters, says Kafka, is hope, prospects, yet sorrow has no
prospects so in sorrow "only the moment counts" (p. 57). It was
probably because of his fear of change that Kafka developed a
static form for his art rather than employing a stream-of-consciousness technique. However, the conversations cannot be
approached with the same sense of trust as the diaries and
letters.

What the diaries and letters (and conversations) show us is
that for Kafka time itself was a threat. Even the remote past,
that of Moses and Abraham, was perhaps too close for comfort,
for Kafka did not choose as Mann did to tell his stories in terms

40. Max Brod, *Franz Kafkas Glauben und Lehre* (Winterthur, 1948), p. 56.
41. Günther Anders, *Kafka Pro und Contra* (München, 1951), p. 75.
42. *Ibid.*, p. 48.
43. Heller, *The Disinherited Mind*, p. 163.

of biblical legend. Furthermore, that which Kafka observed in the world around him did not exist in its own right, but chiefly in terms of the viewer. Plato's doctrine of ideas appealed to Kafka as we know from Brod and from the diaries, although Kafka would not have ascribed completely to Plato's eternal essences since his view of reality was essentially subjective. On the other hand, the technique employed in his stories and novels is an attempt to erect an objective framework for the recounting of deep, subjective experience. Furthermore, Kafka's interest in universals owes a good deal to Platonic thinking.

3

In *The Great Wall of China* and *The Penal Colony,* the nature of Kafka's time is seen. The first volume contains "Investigations of a Dog" and "The Burrow," stories in which the emphasis is not on external events that are infrequent, but on the processes of the mind. However, Kafka is not here recording the processes of a single mind but the processes of the mind of man. Kafka generalizes about human experience, and the specific event is not important for him. The singing dogs or the burrow are not real creations from a living past. Rather their purpose is to focus the attention of the reader on certain inner states common to mankind.

In these stories there are two passages directly related to the time problem—the passage describing the burden of racial history discovered in "Investigations of a Dog" in which a generation fails as a partial result of earlier actions of other generations[44] and the description of the discovery in "The Burrow" that up under the moss where the animal can keep in touch with both inner and outer worlds, he feels at peace, "uplifted above time" (p. 143). The first theme underlines Kafka's ambiguous attitude toward his Jewish heritage, his innate sense of its importance and his rebellion against it as he rebelled against meaningless ritual that his father wished him

44. Franz Kafka, *The Great Wall of China: Stories and Reflections,* trans. Willa and Edwin Muir (New York, 1946), pp. 45-48. Subsequent references to this volume appear in the text.

to adopt. One's distance from God, Kafka felt, is imposed by time and the accumulation of empty symbols. In Kafka we frequently find the simultaneous existence of opposites, so that as he condemns past generations, he at the same time may stand in awed respect before them. Heinz Politzer has noted that "from whatever standpoint one approaches Kafka's work, one always meets a paradox."[45] The second story emphasizes the fear of time and change which Kafka exhibits, change which time brings and which may be abolished by stationing oneself apart from the anxieties of the burrow and the dangers of life—a position where as in death or unconsciousness one may escape.

In the story "The Great Wall of China," although the distance between the villagers and the emperor is chiefly emphasized as a spatial one, there is also a suggestion of temporal removal. Long dead emperors are set on the throne and proclamations of mythical emperors read. The more distant in time, the more glaring their deeds. The living present is ignored and ancient history replaces it. This seems to be a reversal of Kafka's usual practice of ignoring the past.[46] However, the past in this story is not real for Kafka in any sense. It is a hypothetical past, the kind of past with which Kafka could feel at peace, a past even further removed than Moses and Abraham. Time in its conventional sense becomes distorted for the villagers, forced by their position to view reality through a mist of distance. They fear and distrust the present. Kafka concludes that a life thus conceived is "free and unconstrained" (p. 171) and yet moral. The story illustrates yet another method of escaping both from the burrow and from life, for the present is abrogated and the remote past that replaces it is a sphere beyond the inner, guilt-ridden conscience of man. The villager, viewing himself as if he were a stranger, is governed by laws that relate not to his situation but to one that is now

45. Politzer, "Problematik und Probleme der Kafka-Forschung," *Monatschefte*, p. 273. See p. 176, above.

46. In one of the aphorisms in the same volume, Kafka notes, nevertheless, that forgetting the past gives rise to melancholy, unrest, uncertainty, and "longing for vanished ages." But he feels that this longing is essential because it is human effort itself (p. 269).

a myth. In terms of the inner man, the story is one about walls, walls that shut in and shut out communication. "The high command has existed from all eternity, and the decision to build the wall likewise," Kafka writes (p. 162).

In another story, "A Common Confusion," Kafka emphasizes the reality of inner time. A.'s first trip to the city takes ten minutes, the second trip ten hours, and the trip back one second. Although all accessory circumstances are the same, the time values actually shift for A.—there is no *as if* used here.

On the subject of time in "Reflections on Sin, Pain, Hope, and the True Way," Kafka makes several comments. Since the moment of human development is continuous, writes Kafka, revolutionaries are right to discount the past, for nothing has yet happened (p. 274). The last judgment is a kind of summary jurisdiction; only our false concept of time allows us to speak of it as "last" (p. 287). And the expulsion from the Garden of Eden is an eternal event; thus it is possible that we live continuously in Paradise (p. 293). This sense of "eternal recurrence" which abrogates time forms one basis of Kafka's method.

The volume *The Penal Colony* contains further indications of Kafka's ideas on the reality of time. One notices in Kafka's later writing that the emphasis is more and more on an inner dreamlike state and less on the external event as reality. In other words, the architecture shows less as his style develops. Thus even if one were not sure of dates, one would probably place "Investigations of a Dog" later than "A Country Doctor" and "A Country Doctor" later than *America*.[47] The particular quality of "A Country Doctor" is a result of Kafka's idea of reality. Thus the entire story is dictated by the inner state of the protagonist. The horses in the pigsty, the powerful groom, or the wound in the side of the patient give the cumulative effect of making the story itself a correlative of the doctor's emotions of frustration, fear, insecurity, and despair. What happens to the doctor is not so much an outer as an inner

47. For the chronology of Kafka's stories, see Emrich, p. 415. Also see Meno Spann, "Die Beiden Zettel Kafkas," *Monatschefte,* LXVII (November, 1955), 321-28.

experience, not of an individual but of man. The story centers around the theme of the alienation and frustration of man in seeking a goal, in this story of those isolated (country) few who seek to help others. The theme points up the false pride of these self-appointed helpers. The doctor's horse is dead; a blizzard rages. The only person who stands by him is his servant girl, Rose. Fate conjures up in answer to the doctor's need a daemonic pair of horses and a daemonic groom. He must sacrifice his one friend, Rose, to the groom if he is to reach his patient. Those who would do good must often, ironically enough, utilize evil in order to accomplish their ends.

Further frustration comes at the home of the patient when the boy begs that he may be left to die. Those whom we want to help do not even wish it. After the doctor discovers on second examination a large wound in the boy's side and knows that he is past helping, the boy, of course, begs to be saved. At the doctor's realization of his inability to cure him, the villagers punish the doctor by stripping him of his clothes and laying him beside the boy. Now he is able to tell the boy that wounds are only a matter of perspective. Returning home on the slowly moving horses, he feels that he has been betrayed, but as in Kafka's novels, the efforts of the hero avail nothing for fate is indifferent. Through this story Kafka reveals many of the hidden threats to man in reaching a desired end. He is threatened by even those who are faithful to him, for if he must protect even Rose he is not a free agent. The greatest threat comes, however, from man's own wounds that like the boy he cherishes and at the same time wishes to be rid of.

Clemens Heselhaus, approaching the story from a different angle, points out the peculiar relation of reality and unreality in this story. With the ringing of the night bell, he says, the extraordinary world steps into the ordinary. In this extraordinary dream world the reader senses a higher truth, but the doctor does not recognize this. Since, however, it is impossible to bring into agreement the extraordinary and the customary, the doctor is placed in an absurd position and the story takes on a didactic purpose. Heselhaus calls the story an "Antimärchen," that is "it is only apparently realistic, while its hero remains a man subject to human failings and miscarriages of justice." The "Antimärchen" reveals the world, not as it really is, but "as it might not be." Thus the wound of the boy is really there for the reader, but at the same time it is "unearthly."[48]

"The Metamorphosis" is, of course, another example of Kafka's strong attachment to the inner world. This is a tale of guilt, of fear, and of masochism in which the reader sees subject and object coincide in the beetle. Gregor *is* the beetle because he thinks he is, just as Anna Livia *is* the river. However, with Joyce we view from the outside the minds of his characters. With Kafka we *are* inside the mind of Gregor and are forced to accept this world of Gregor and to recognize it as our own. Kafka exposes us to our own suppressed selves and this is one reason that critics have found his stories "extraordinary."

Other examples of emphasis on inner reality may be seen in this volume in "Conversation with the Supplicant" in which because the author thinks of the supplicant as always in motion, he seems continually to be "slithering past"[49] or in which the supplicant by making people stare tries vainly to prove that he is actually alive and not "fleeting away" (p. 14). In "Children on a Country Road" (which with its detailed recounting of memories and emotions of childhood reminds one of the early Hofmannsthal) the author feels that as the birds soar they are not rising but he is falling (p. 21). And the hero in "The Tradesman" exists not in the monotonous routine of his daily work but in his mind world.

Time values are dependent upon our idea of them rather than upon the clock. The doctor in "A Country Doctor" arrives at the home of his patient in a few seconds (pointing to his desire to arrive and the force of public opinion), but the trip home (when he is naked and exposed) is long and slow. In "Up in the Gallery" Kafka shows that our appreciation of an event depends on its time. If an exquisite equestrienne were to

48. Heselhaus, "Kafkas Erzählformen," *Deutsche Vierteljahrsschrift*, p. 358.
49. Franz Kafka, *The Penal Colony: Stories and Short Pieces*, trans. Willa and Edwin Muir (New York, 1948), p. 10. Subsequent references to this volume appear in the text.

continue her act for months on end, the observer would be forced to shout, "Stop!" (p. 144). In "The Next Village" life is so short that even a normal span may not give one time to ride over to the next village (p. 158), and the ape in "A Report to an Academy" feels that the five years since he became human have been infinite (p. 173).

Kafka's stories do not contain elements of unreality, for they describe the world of the dream where the terms *reality* and *unreality* have no meaning. The form he chooses enables Kafka to present the dream world with a literalness that is the essence of the humor in Kafka, a dream presented as if it had occurred in the world of touch, sound, and sight. The method of Joyce's *Finnegans Wake*, for instance, does not provide us with this contrast; the unconscious is described by Joyce in terms of the unconscious.

4

In turning to the novel *America*, one observes how Kafka first used in a long piece of fiction some of the techniques springing from his concept of time and reality. One can see in *America* shadows of Kafka's treatment of reality in the two other novels. The long, empty corridors in the mansion in which Karl becomes lost or the sudden and unexpected appearance of Mack in the next room bring to mind the corridors of the law courts and the inns and the uncanny appearances of Barnabas. Wilhelm Emrich's piece on Kafka in *Deutsche Literatur im zwanzigsten Jahrhundert*[50] was first to shake the traditional concept of "growth" in Kafka, as established by Brod and other early interpreters. Emrich saw the basic ideas and the fundamental style of Kafka already developed in the diaries in 1911. Nevertheless, the fact remains that in *America* there is little emphasis on the baffling and the irrational. The inner world and the outer world coincide to a greater degree in this novel than in his other pieces. The source of this change in technique, a change that makes *America* more akin to conventional fiction,

50. *Deutsche Literatur in zwanzigsten Jahrhundert*, Hermann Friedmann and Otto Mann, eds. (Heidelberg, 1954), pp. 230 ff.

is probably to be found in Kafka's own admission that in this novel he was influenced by Dickens. Edgar Johnson in his biography of Dickens has pointed out that "Dickens—as always when he is most deeply moved and most profound—is speaking in terms of unavowed allegory." "But," says Johnson, "the allegory of Dickens is in one way subtler than the allegory of writers like Kafka and Melville. . . . Dickens . . . leaves the surface action so entirely clear and the behavior of his characters so plain that they do not puzzle us into groping for gnomic meanings."[51] If it is true that Kafka is following Dickens in *America*, then this novel is an anomaly, for it is thus an allegory with a second level of meaning. However, there are breakthroughs into the realm of the unconscious in the passages already mentioned and especially in the last chapter where the angels on the platform welcome Karl, and he is taken through a long series of offices until in a room for intermediate European pupils, he recognizes an attendant who closely resembles an old schoolteacher.

The more conventional story in *America* gives Kafka freedom to deal with the past, for in order to re-create the past it is necessary to have a present in which the re-creation takes place. The technique describing an inner world employed elsewhere by Kafka eliminates distinctions between past, present, and future. As Karl hears his uncle tell the group on the ship about the affair with the maid, Johanna Brummer, involuntarily he re-creates her. "Hemmed in by a vanishing past, she sat in her kitchen beside the kitchen dresser."[52] Then for a moment Karl sees and feels all the details of the affair as he had experienced them. Later as he plays a song of his native country on his piano, there is re-created through the music a scene from Karl's earlier life when he had heard soldiers in the barracks singing to each other from window to window (p. 43). Superimposed on the great, bustling, New York street over which he has no outward control is this simple scene from his homeland en-

51. Edgar Johnson, *Charles Dickens: His Tragedy and Triumph* (New York, 1952), I, 489.

52. Franz Kafka, *America*, trans. Edwin and Willa Muir (London, 1938), p. 27. Subsequent references to this volume appear in the text.

abling him to erase the present. And finally there is the passage in which Therese telling the story of her mother's death to Karl realizes that "the most trifling circumstance of that morning was still stamped exactly on her memory after more than ten years" (p. 157). Passages like these make it seem impossible that Kafka had never heard of Proust and are, as Brod says, "what cause the ordered mind of the investigator to revert to the dark of universal world disorder."[53]

America must be seen then both in terms of time and of the timeless inner world. Because of his emphasis on "surface action," an emphasis that was natively alien to him, *America* is perhaps the least successful of Kafka's longer works. He is more at home with the phantasy life of his inner world. Kafka's abandoning of the Dickens experiment in the other two novels is the result of his innate preference for the conception of time as illusory.

Kafka once wrote in an aphorism that one of his most important wishes was "to attain a view of life in which life, while still retaining its natural full-bodied rise and fall, would simultaneously be recognized no less clearly as a nothing, a dream, a dim hovering."[54] This remark describes with some accuracy the style and mood of his two central works *The Trial* and *The Castle*, for in these works life *is* a dream.

The dreamlike quality of time values and the assumption of an interior time recognized alone by the officials and K. appear throughout *The Trial*. In a passage deleted from the first chapter, Kafka had written that the riskiest moment of the day is the moment when one awakes. "It requires great presence of mind to find everything in the room in exactly the same place that one left it the evening before."[55] Because K. this morning has found his world different from the way it was the evening before, we understand that part of the dream world has intruded into his everyday world. The opening of "The

53. Brod, *Franz Kafka*, p. 43.
54. Kafka, *The Great Wall of China*, p. 267.
55. Franz Kafka, *The Trial*, trans. Willa and Edwin Muir (New York, 1957), p. 319. Subsequent references to this volume appear in the text.

Metamorphosis" may be compared with this passage in *The Trial*.

On his first Sunday in court, K. hurries to arrive at nine o'clock "although he had not even been required to appear at any specified time" (p. 43). Despite the fact that he is late he walks more slowly as he approaches the house of the examiners, as if he now had abundant time. Kafka is, of course, more adept at creating the dream than the "full-bodied rise and fall" of life. When K. leaves the examining room, the magistrate mysteriously gets to the door before him as in a dream people appear at the beck and call of our fears and wishes.

In the unfinished chapter "The House," we find the curious juxtaposition of dream upon dream. As K. lies down on the couch in his office, his thoughts hover between dream and reality, only here reality is that of K.'s waking life, which is like a dream to the reader. Thus Kafka makes us aware of various levels of reality—the dream within the dream. Of this technique Kafka had probably found examples in the Spanish-Austrian theater. Grillparzer's *Der Traum, ein Leben* may also have been influential here. K.'s first dream represents his alienated situation as he views Frau Grubach's boarders, many unknown to him, for he had for some time not bothered himself about concerns of the house. Then as he turns from the group and hurries into the law court, corridors and rooms become familiar "as if he had always lived there" (p. 307). As K. becomes more deeply implicated in the court, the details of living lose for him their significance, the dream becomes more like the inner dream.

In connection with the dream it should be noted that K. is often "in the dark." Heavy curtains hang over the windows in the advocate's bedroom; in the cathedral K. by mistake extinguishes his lamp, and "He stood still. It was quite dark and he had no idea which part of the church he was in" (p. 324). In this dream world one loses one's bearings; and since K. is lost inwardly, his physical relation to objects and places is an uncertain one, too.

When the student enters the examining room where K. stands alone with the woman who occupies the apartment outside, K. experiences his first meeting with a representative of the official group on human terms as a rival (p. 69). This meeting implies the recognition that the trial is on a different level from "the full-bodied rise and fall." Nevertheless, it is interesting to note that the meeting takes place in the same examining room where K. had had his first hearing. Kafka thus creates a link between the two worlds (inner and outer), a link which gives artistic unity to the passage.

A scene in the lumber room in the bank leads to further insights into the time experiences in *The Trial*. When K. returns to the lumber room on the second evening in Chapter 5, he finds everything exactly as he had left it the night before. The whipper is still standing in the same position in front of the warders. As K. opens the door, the warders at once cry out, "Sir!" Time has not moved on this level of experience although K. has lived through a whole day of clock time. K. deals with this situation in the realm of action by asking the clerks to clear out the lumber room the next day although unconsciously he recognizes that his experience is an inner one, for he would not ask them to do this if he thought that the whipper and the warders were there for the clerks to see. It is K.'s fault that the warders are being whipped; thus the scene represents hidden guilt. He asks the clerks to clear it out knowing that he cannot remove the imprint of the scene from his mind other than by the destruction of its outward symbols. Time has stood still in this back room of K.'s consciousness. It is not the past superimposed on the present, but rather a trick that Kafka's concept of the idea of time as illusory makes possible. The scene does not "recur"; it persists.

The appearance of K.'s uncle and the mention of his daughter, Erna, are among the few insights we have into K.'s past. K.'s uncle understands, without being told, the facts of K.'s case. K. is aware that he has known all along that his uncle would turn up, for the uncle, like the rest of the characters in the book, has reality only in relation to K.'s inner life. As a molder of K.'s past, the uncle, too, like the family of Amalia in *The Castle*, is implicated. The uncle is part of the everlasting present of K.'s mind time, neither past nor present having reality except as they are viewed by K. The character of Kafka's idea of time is clear when we observe that K. is everyman, not an individual, so we are dealing here not with a specific relationship of past and present but with a general one.

In the uncompleted chapter "Journey to his Mother," we find the same general relation between past and present. K.'s mother is almost blind, so unlike the uncle, she is ignorant of K.'s plight. Her refusal to be implicated in K.'s problem is further shown by her present indifference to K.'s visit, for earlier she had been anxious to see him. The mother, like the uncle, is part of K.'s mind, but the blind part, that which is suppressed: "she believed him to be the Bank Manager and had done so for years" (p. 294). In another unfinished chapter, "Prosecuting Counsel," K. attributes to the early death of his father and the mistaken tenderness of his mother a childish quality he possesses (p. 303). Thus despite her 'blindness' the mother is implicated in K.'s fate. But the conscious recognition of his mother remains in the background; for several years he had intended to visit her, but he had never done so, and the fragment ends before the visit is made.

That the characters are projections of K.'s mind appears again in his interview with the advocate who at once knows all about K.'s case although, as K. reflects, this advocate is attached to the court at the Palace of Justice, not to the one with skylight. As he ponders this incongruity the Chief Clerk of the Court (the one with the skylight) appears in a corner of the room where K. had not noticed him. The link between the two courts is thus inwardly established for K. The interview progresses and the advocate asks K. no questions; he either talks of his own affairs or strokes his beard. K. is, Kafka shows, his own advocate and as such the facts are known to him. K. learns that since the proceedings are not public, legal records are inaccessible to the accused and to his counsel—records of earlier acts that in life are often inaccessible because pressed into the unconscious. That this unconscious level is unreasonable and primitive is seen in Huld's remark that the officials are children (p. 152). The court and its officials exist in every life, in every time and place. And K. comments that "so many people seem to be connected with the court" (p. 169). *The Trial* represents man's self-trial to determine his success or failure in the pursuit of an inner ideal.

To claim, as critics have, that Kafka's books represent a specific theology, psychology, or philosophy misses the point of Kafka's writing, which was to embrace all quests without pointing to any one as *the way*. The search for and following of an inner ideal is an old theme in literature put into words by innumerable writers, but Kafka's distinction seems to lie not in his theme but in his all but indefinable technique that depends to a large extent on his abrogation of the time values of the outer world so that his odyssey is described in terms of the inner world where in the final analysis all our odysseys take place. "You see, everything belongs to the Court," (p. 188) the painter tells K.—even the girls on the stairs outside the painter's room. When Titorelli opens the door behind his bed, K. recognizes the same Law-Court offices even though the painter lives in a different part of the city. "There are Law-Court offices in almost every attic," Titorelli explains. "Why should this be an exception?" (P. 205.) And when Huld reflects that "after a certain stage in one's practice nothing new ever happens" (p. 233), he is expressing in different terms the universal nature of the human quest.

The scene in the cathedral should, therefore, not be interpreted to mean that the end of the quest is to be found in orthodoxy of any kind. Rather the cathedral symbolizes an inner spiritual goal that has no relation for Kafka to the cathedral as such.

As K. nears the end of his quest in the cathedral square, he is startled by the recollection that even when he was a child the curtains in this square had been pulled down (p. 255). Inside the cathedral he watches the verger, whose limp reminds him of his childhood imitation of a man riding horseback (p. 259). These two simple memories serve, not to re-create the past as in Proust, but as touchstones of the world of objects

and of the "full-bodied rise and fall" of life. As links their existence in the passage is important, for through them Kafka
reminds us that his purpose is to mirror life, but a life disguised
so that it is in the semblance of all lives.

Clemens Heselhaus sums up the question of reality in *The
Trial* by pointing out that the court itself is not real; only the
reactions of K. to the court are real. One cannot say that the
court means this or that. One can only say that the physical
realization of the court is made concrete in the physical reactions and deeds that destroy a life.[56]

Kafka's extraordinary use of phantasy and dream reaches its
culmination in *The Castle*. Günther Anders writes that the
strange element in K.'s experiences is not that so much strange
happens, but that nothing that happens, even the self-evident,
is self-evident. There is no distinction between the ordinary and
the extraordinary.[57] The reader fills in the emotional content,
the philosophical content, directed by such things as the beards
of the assistants or the soft luxuriousness of the sleigh cushions.
Normal space and time values are abrogated so that reality
is that which exists within the mind, not independent of it.

When K. returns to the inn early in Chapter 2 of *The Castle*,
he is surprised to see that darkness has set in. "Had he been
gone for such a long time? Surely not for more than an hour or
two, by his reckoning. And it had been morning when he left."[58]
As in Kafka's short story "A Common Confusion," the length
of the trip does not determine the time it takes. Kafka does not
write: K.'s trip seemed to take a whole day. Rather despite all
of K.'s outward reckonings, the inner time of the subconscious
mind prevails, and it is *actually* dark when K. reaches the inn.
The Castle is related in terms of the primitive, unreasoned
drives and evaluations of our unconscious lives which for Kafka
are more real than what appears on the surface as distorted
reflections of these lives. Barnabas' speed in outstripping K. is
so great that before K. can shout to him he has covered an

56. Heselhaus, "Kafkas Erzählformen," *Deutsche Vierteljahrsschrift*, p. 370.
57. Anders, *Kafka Pro und Contra*, p. 25.
58. Franz Kafka, *The Castle*, trans. Eithne Wilkins and Ernst Kaiser (New
York, 1954), p. 23. Subsequent references to this volume appear in the text.

impossible distance. Thus time again is observed through an unconscious estimation of it, and Barnabas is characterized in terms of a speed experience.

An anomaly in Kafka's approach to time (reminding one of the re-creations of the past in *America*) comes when dragged on by Barnabas, K. re-creates a scene from childhood evoked by the difficulty of keeping up (p. 38). He finds himself by an old church in a marketplace surrounded by a graveyard, in turn surrounded by a high wall. K. had failed to climb the wall until one morning in an empty marketplace, flooded by sunlight, he had succeeded. The sense of triumph of that moment returns now to succor him. In the unconscious world there is no past. If Kafka had been consistent here, he would have had the adult K. attempting to climb the wall. However, another interpretation is that this scene is a memory within a memory as in *The Trial* Kafka used the dream within the dream.

One notices throughout *The Castle* that Kafka avoids measuring time. For instance, when K. goes to see the superintendent in Chapter 5 there is no mention of how many days or hours later this visit occurred after he left Frieda and the landlady. Thus the reader is shocked to learn from Pepi at the end of the book that only four days have elapsed since Frieda left her work at the bar. It is, probably, part of Kafka's technique to reveal this only at the end where it does not distort his time values, which are not of calendar or clock. That the inner time of the mind prevails in the book is suddenly proved by Pepi's remark, which is incredible except on the level of idea. Earlier in the book to learn the day would have only oriented us to conventional time values and spoiled the effect of the dream-like atmosphere. But now that hour and day have ceased to have meaning, to be reminded of them produces in the reader the surprise that Kafka wishes to induce so that they suddenly seem much more unreal than the inner time in which the reader is immersed. The doubt that Hermann Uyttersprot has cast on Brod's arrangement of the chapters in *The Trial* extends also to *The Castle*. However, it is reasonable to assume that Chapter 20, although it may not be the last chapter, describes events taking place well after those in Chapter 5. Nevertheless, as Uyttersprot points out, because of the fragmentary and incomplete character of Kafka's work, "whatever can be said of it must be of a hypothetical nature."[59]

Telephone calls to the castle are of no avail, for the superintendent tells K. that all K.'s contacts with the castle have been illusory, "but owing to your ignorance of the circumstances you take them to be real" (p. 93). All outside contact is illusion. K. mistakenly tries to use human logic and reason in dealing with the castle and its officials; therefore, he and the officials never talk on the same level, for their reasoning is incomprehensible to the human mind. That we interpret our deities in human terms, however, is shown by Kafka when, for instance, Momus, the secretary, crumbles salt and caraway seeds on his paper.

Reality in the village is what the people make it. Thus Klamm's appearance fluctuates. He looks one way in the village and another way on leaving it. He looks different when he is awake from the way he looks when he is asleep. On one point only all the villagers agree—he wears always a black morning coat with long tails. The differences, Kafka explains, are the result of the mood of the observer—of his degree of excitement, hope, or despair (p. 231). They are the varied impressions that the supplicant holds of the features of the oracle, the confessed of his confessor, or the patient of his psychoanalyst. The people's confusion of Momus and Klamm and Barnabas' doubts about the real Klamm are also explained by Kafka's concept of reality. Likewise, in a passage deleted by Kafka, K. feels as if Barnabas is two men whom only K., not outside judgment, can keep distinct (p. 428). Barnabas, the messenger, and Barnabas, the brother and son, do not, therefore, ever really merge for the reader but remain, as for K., different, one of the castle, the other of the village. This points to the real nature of the Barnabas symbol—the man divided by having only partially attained his goal. Reality depends then on the observer, not on

59. Hermann Uyttersprot, "Zur Struktur von Kafkas 'Der Prozess,'" *Revue des Langues Vivantes* (1953), 332-76. See also Hermann Uyttersprot, "Zur Struktur von Kafkas Romanen," *Revue des Langues Vivantes* (1954), 367-83.

a set of unchanging values. Felix Weltsch sees in these "Dop-pelwesen" a comic element, "a duality which is recognized as unity and a unity which is always falling apart into duality."[60]

The castle dignitaries have the distinction of being freed from memory. This is but another of the bafflements and frustrations against which K. must contend, for each meeting with Klamm will be a new start. Although K. challenges the landlady's remark about Klamm's memory as "improbable and indemonstrable" (p. 111), we are told by Kafka that anyone whom Klamm "stops summoning he has forgotten completely, not only as far as the past is concerned, but literally for the future as well" (p. 108). K. himself has practically no past; we hear hardly anything of earlier events in his life. The other characters as well are without childhood or ancestors. True, Frieda claims a childhood acquaintance with Jeremiah with whom she played on the slope of the castle hill (p. 323), and K. accuses Frieda of having succumbed to the influence of memories, the past, in her "actual present-day life" (p. 327); but for all practical purposes there is no distant past in *The Castle*. With the exception of the story Olga tells K. or the hints of the landlady's affair with Klamm, there is little perspective in even the recent past. The larger racial past of the human species is, however, often implied, for the unconscious level of the mind is, of course, much concerned with our primitive origins. Thus one sees, for example, in the connection of the villagers and K. to the castle the bafflement of man in relation to forces of nature and in relation to deity. Implied also are basic anxieties men have always felt about their relation to other men and to gods. It is well to note, nevertheless, that it is only the officials who lack memory of a dismissed case.[61] The villagers and K. do have memory, though it is little exercised

60. Felix Weltsch, *Religiöser Humor*, p. 129.
61. Some critics understand Kafka's officials as our deities, for as Secretary Bürgel remarks, "We make no distinction between ordinary time and working-time" (p. 338). Edwin Muir sees in Kafka's world the influence of "Kierkegaard's doctrine of incommensurability of divine and human law." Values in the divine world are incomprehensible to the human mind (Edwin Muir, "Franz Kafka," in *A Franz Kafka Miscellany: Pre-Fascist Exile* (New York, 1940), p. 62).

because *The Castle* is written in the realm of dream where the past is disguised and integrated with the present.

Kafka probes deeper by placing his entire story on the unconscious level than Proust does despite his brilliant analyses of human experience on the conscious level. For Kafka past and present are bound together indistinguishably in the objects and shadows of his dream world.[62] As in a dream, all that goes on is known at once by everyone in the village; for instance, the maids enter the room to move in with all their clothes hardly after K. has spoken the words accepting the post at the school (p. 125). The landlady is aware of all that happens to K. as is everyone K. meets. This disconcerting state of affairs is further evidence of the dream atmosphere of the book, for in a dream our enemies and friends alike know with unerring certitude all the hidden embarrassments and decisions of our lives. Furthermore, the dream is burdened with anxieties in the form of the hostility, indifference, and fear of the villagers toward K.

Kafka's dream is broad enough to include all mankind and yet specific enough to apply to any particular individual.[63] As the culmination of Kafka's work, *The Castle* depicts general themes: the alienation of man, the incomprehensibility of the divine, the quest of the hero for the fulfillment of an ideal. Behind Kafka's themes lies a concept of time based on the reality of the inner world which gives rise to his technique of objectifying the dream and phantasy. Kafka's attitude toward time and reality alone makes possible his method of writing. Reality is of the mind; therefore, the dream is real and our ideas are real. In *The Castle* we find Kafka's dream world and his idea of truth.

62. The long winters in the village lend an atmosphere of darkness fitting to the dream. In fact, spring and summer seem to Pepi no longer than two days (p. 408).

63. Otto C. Friedrich writes that "Kafkas Tiefe gerade in seiner Mehrdeutigkeit liegt.... und der Fehler liegt darin, irgend eine von ihnen mit dem Anspruch der Alleingültigkeit ins Extreme zu treiben.... Der rastlose Jude, der unglückliche und isolierte Einzelne, der existentielle Denker, der Geschichtenerzähler und der Humorist" are aspects of Kafka's personality, but that no one of these aspects outweighs or contradicts another ("Der doppeldeutige Kafka," *Prisma*, No. 22 [1948], pp. 8-9).

PART IV

AMERICA

INTRODUCTION

Concerning the matter of time, the Gallic influence on the two American writers, Thomas Wolfe and William Faulkner, has been much greater than the Germanic. The juxtaposition of the Kafka and Wolfe chapters well illustrates such an assertion. K-19, the number of a Pullman car, is about the nearest Wolfe ever came to K., the hero of Kafka's novels. The only point of similarity between the two German writers and the two Americans lies in archetypal figures. Faulkner's, although there is no question of direct influence, resemble Mann's in some ways, but this is simply a chance similarity of genre and of point of view. For the background of Faulkner's interest in archetypes, one should perhaps go to Greek drama.

Nor is the Gallic influence itself essentially a profound one. For both Wolfe and Faulkner involuntary memory is often no more than a gimmick. This is particularly true of Faulkner with, for example, his almost self-conscious use of the smell of wistaria in evoking the past. Involuntary memory is less obtrusive in Wolfe's work. Nevertheless, the scene at the end of *Look Homeward, Angel* is not evoked by involuntary memory at all. It is not the past that is re-created in this scene, but a reality beyond past, present, and future, a mystical moment like one from a novel of Virginia Woolf. This scene, with the picturing of the ghost of Ben, is even more mystical in its implications than Stephen's consecration scene in *A Portrait* although it has some elements in common with Joyce's scene.

A sense of return is partially achieved by Wolfe and achieved by Faulkner, but there is no elaborate scaffolding employed nor does theory ever intrude in the narrative. Whereas with the two German writers one feels a close connection between theory of time and technique and content, and with the English writers a conscious awareness of philosophical precedents, with Wolfe and Faulkner one might say that there is little conscious speculation as to philosophy, that what is borrowed is part of the unconscious heritage to which they are heirs.

By framing the two German writers within the British and American writers, one can observe in relief the often abstract character of time in German literature in contrast with the quality of time as it is experienced and lived in English and American writing. In particular, with Wolfe and Faulkner one is aware of the flow of everyday time. Both methods have their own virtues. Whereas the quality of everyman about the symbolic character and of every experience about the symbolic situation allow one to identify more readily with the position described by the author, the depiction of the individual experience allows one not only to identify but to separate oneself from that experience. Both points of view toward reality are essential in an effective human role.

The mystical moment for Thomas Wolfe, the archetypal figure for Faulkner are their means of transcendence, but these abstractions never erase the flow of the river, the motion of the train, or the creak of wagons on the dusty roads of the deep South.

CHAPTER SEVEN

THOMAS WOLFE:

DARK TIME

"And time still passing ... passing like a leaf ... time passing, fading like a flower ... time passing like a river flowing ... time passing ... and remembered suddenly, like the forgotten hoof and wheel. ..."[1]

The train and the river are for Thomas Wolfe two basic symbols in getting across to his readers his feelings about time— time at whose mystery Wolfe never failed to marvel. The river with its ceaseless flow, its continually new combination of particles, its irrevocableness, contained for Wolfe in its essence the sadness, the loneliness, and the loss that time passing brings. The river represented, although Wolfe would not have named it in this way, a sense of Heraclitean flux. Against the river, act-ing as its foil, stands the train. For the train although carrying with it a sense of sadness and loneliness as its whistle sounds in the Virginia night, is not irrevocable. There are always tracks leading in the opposite direction and trains traveling on them, and roundhouses where trains may be reversed. Thus although Louis Rubin[2] suggests that the train was comforting to Wolfe

1. Thomas Wolfe, *The Hills Beyond* (New York, 1941), p. 348.
2. Louis D. Rubin, Jr., *Thomas Wolfe: The Weather of His Youth* (Baton Rouge, 1955), p. 39.

because on it he "kept up" with time, it would seem that on the train Wolfe was able also to counteract time. It is in this sense that James Joyce uses trains, trams, and ships as imagery in his Viconian system of return. It is evident too that the river as well as the train represents a kind of immobility, for as Wolfe himself points out the river is "eternal in its flow" and thus immutable as well as transient.

These two ideas are represented again in the often interpreted symbols, the stone, the leaf, and the door. The leaf like the river is transient; it is continually changing until it disappears into the earth as the river merges with the sea. In the stone as in the train there is a kind of immobility although it is a different kind from the circular recurrence represented by the train. It is the immobility of the earth which Wolfe never tired of comparing with man's transient existence. With the stone and the leaf stands the door which acts as a catalyst and represents the possibility of merging that which changes and that which is immutable. It was in the hope of discovering this door which stood between permanence and change that Wolfe wrote the novels of his tetralogy.

Critics have written of Wolfe's relation to philosophers and systems of philosophy, but Wolfe's only attempt to formulate his theories of art came in a short volume, *The Story of a Novel*. In the following summary of critical theories on Wolfe's work, it is necessary to keep in mind that Wolfe himself was a novelist and not a metaphysician. It is, nevertheless, helpful to see where Wolfe stands on the question of time in relation to his contemporaries.

A great deal has been written about the time concepts of Wolfe, and distinctions have been made between his idea of time and the ideas of Proust and of Joyce on time. Wolfe apparently read Proust in the original in 1925.[3] In a letter from Wolfe to Henry T. Volkening in August, 1929, we find that Wolfe still read Proust. Later letters speak of his admiration for Proust, and in two letters Wolfe admits the Proustian char-

3. Daniel L. Delakas, *Thomas Wolfe: La France et les romanciers français* (Paris, 1950), p. 118.

acter of "The Party at Jack's."[4] Wolfe has several times expressed his debt to James Joyce—in *The Story of a Novel,* in *Of Time and the River,* and in letters. Wolfe speaks of *Look Homeward, Angel* as his *"Ulysses* book,"[5] of Joyce's great talents, of *Ulysses* as containing the best writing in English.[6]

It was inevitable that Wolfe's concept of time should be influenced by the concepts of these two writers, but Wolfe took from Proust and from Joyce only that which was already congenial to him. Thus Herbert J. Muller points out that while both Proust and Wolfe depended upon sensory impressions to recall the past, Wolfe lacked the keen subjective analysis of Proust and stayed closer to the actual experience that produced his memories. Wolfe's interest was in fixity and change as they are in real life, whereas Proust "aspired to the realm of Essence or Being, where change is mere appearance."[7] Muller sees that Wolfe was less subjective than Proust, that he had a firmer grasp of "the elemental emotions." Other critics who point out a relation between Wolfe and Proust are Daniel Delakas, who discovers many ties between them,[8] Karin Pfister, who attempts to relate both Bergson and Proust to Wolfe,[9] and Marcel Brion, who sees that Proust is more precise than Wolfe although the mechanism of memory is similar for them.[10]

Joyce's influence on Wolfe is discussed by Herbert Muller, who sees the influence chiefly in terms of techniques, by Karin Pfister, who writes that both are concerned with the drama of the single fate and the epic of time, by P. E. Kilburn who devotes an entire thesis to Joyce's influence on Wolfe.[11] Marcel Brion writes that Wolfe's word choice, his belief that time remakes itself, his *monologue intérieur* are like Joyce's but

4. *The Letters of Thomas Wolfe,* ed. Elizabeth Nowell (New York, 1956), pp. 194, 631, 648.

5. *Ibid.,* p. 586.

6. Thomas Wolfe, *Of Time and the River* (New York, 1944), p. 661.

7. Herbert J. Muller, *Thomas Wolfe* (Norfolk, Connecticut, 1947), p. 75.

8. Delakas, *Thomas Wolfe,* p. 132.

9. Karin Pfister, *Zeit und Wirklichkeit bei Thomas Wolfe* (Heidelberg, 1954).

10. Marcel Brion, "Thomas Wolfe," *Revue des deux mondes,* XVI (August 15, 1952), 734.

11. P. E. Kilburn, *Ulysses in Catawba* (New York University, 1954).

unlike Joyce's, Wolfe's picture of the past was not an ordered one.[12] Nathan Rothman says that both Joyce and Wolfe ranged far back into the personal and the racial past.[13]

In addition to those who seek to establish the influence of Proust and of Joyce there are critics who find in Wolfe something of the transcendental or the essential. B. R. McElderry, Jr., sees that Wolfe's and Emerson's concepts of "flow" are alike.[14] And Louis Rubin (in *Thomas Wolfe: The Weather of His Youth*) writes a chapter on "intimations of immortality."

Probably the best discussions of the time theme in Wolfe are those of W. P. Albrecht, Karin Pfister, and Louis Rubin, Jr. Albrecht sees that Wolfe reconciled permanence and flux first through the act of literary creation and later through a cyclical concept of time.[15] According to Karin Pfister, Wolfe never really solved the problem of change and of mutability, for his heroes are constantly competing with time,[16] but Rubin thinks that Wolfe solved this dilemma through a kind of "semi-mysticism in which he was influenced by Wordsworth and by Coleridge."[17]

It is apparent that some further examination of Wolfe's sense of time is in order since views on it vary to such an extent. First, it is necessary to point out that Wolfe never consciously worked out a philosophy of time which he then employed in his novels. His references to time are haphazard and often more clichés that he uses again and again because of his partially subconscious obsession with the time idea.

Only once, in *The Story of a Novel,* did Wolfe attempt a formulation of his literary creed. Early in the book Wolfe states his debt to James Joyce's *Ulysses.* "I was strongly under the influence of writers I admired—one of the chief writers I ad-

12. Brion, "Thomas Wolfe," *Revue des deux mondes,* p. 738.

13. Nathan L. Rothman, "Thomas Wolfe and James Joyce: A Study in Literary Influence," in *A Southern Vanguard,* ed. Allen Tate (New York, 1947), p. 69.

14. B. R. McElderry, Jr., "Wolfe and Emerson on 'Flow,'" *Modern Fiction Studies,* II (May, 1956), 77-78.

15. W. P. Albrecht, "Time as Unity in Thomas Wolfe," *New Mexico Quarterly Review,* XIX (Autumn, 1949), 325.

16. Pfister, *Thomas Wolfe,* p. 51.

17. Rubin, *Thomas Wolfe,* p. 68.

mired was Mr. James Joyce with his *Ulysses*. . . . The book I
was writing was much influenced by his own book."[18] What is
often overlooked is that Joyce's *Portrait* must also have exercised a strong influence on Wolfe. In fact, in a letter to Robert
Raynolds, Wolfe thinks of calling *Of Time and the River* "The
Image of Fury in the Artist's Youth."[19] What Wolfe seemed to
have gotten from Joyce was Joyce's ability as Wolfe says in a
letter to Julian Meade "to make live again a moment in lost
time," as well as Joyce's ability to make his scenes radiate both
backwards and forwards. Wolfe feels that perhaps Joyce did
succeed in "penetrating reality" in "creating what is almost
another dimension of reality."[20] Wolfe's ability to re-create the
past is often attributed to his interest in Proust; thus it is
important to realize that it was Joyce as well who possessed this
talent for Wolfe.

Another aspect of Wolfe's interest in Joyce lay in Joyce's use
of myth, which we find Wolfe also using. In a letter to Maxwell
Perkins (December, 1930) Wolfe describes the argument of
Of Time and the River in terms of the legend of Antaeus, who
seeks for his father, Poseidon, but is overcome by Heracles. As
in *Ulysses*, the mythical background is implicit not explicit in
the book and the story is only "given shape by the legend."
"The idea of time, the lost and forgotten moments of people's
lives, the strange brown light of old time ... is over all the
book."[21]

In *The Story of a Novel* Wolfe goes on to mention the
quality of his memory which could "bring back the odors,
sounds, colors, shapes, and feel of things with concrete vivid-
ness."[22] For instance, he would be sitting in the Avenue de
l'Opéra and watching the people move past when suddenly he
would remember the railing at Atlantic City. "I could see it
instantly just the way it was, the heavy iron pipe; its raw,
galvanized look; the way the joints were fitted together."[23] The

18. Thomas Wolfe, "The Story of a Novel," *Saturday Review of Literature*
(December 14, 1935), 4.
19. *Letters*, ed. Nowell, p. 382.
20. *Ibid.*, p. 322.   21. *Ibid.*, p. 279.
22. "The Story of a Novel," *SRL* (December 21, 1935), 3.
23. *Ibid.*

exact dimensions, an entire scene would thus return to Wolfe through seeing a certain street, hearing a train whistle, or viewing muddy banks or a particular bridge. Wolfe, like Joyce, wanted to find words for this experience with memory, to write so vividly that the past would be reanimated for the reader. Proust's influence must also be seen in this passage from *The Story of a Novel,* although Wolfe never generalizes as Proust does on the metaphysics of the return of the past and although the "raw, galvanized look" of the pipe seems to contain more the flavor of Joyce than of Proust. In a letter written in August, 1930, Wolfe "owns up" to the fact that some of the "flavour" of Joyce "has crept into his book."[24]

In a later passage in *The Story of a Novel,* Wolfe says that in the embryonic form of his book there was a section entitled "Where now?" in which he recorded all the lost moments of the past, "the flicks and darts and haunting lights that flash across the mind of man." These flashes of the memory concerned more than man's immediate past, for they went back into "the farthest adyt of his childhood before conscious memory had begun."[25] Often, Wolfe continues, these flashes seem of no consequence, but they live with us longer than apparently more important events. This kind of memory brings unity to life and human experience.

This passage has in it more of Joyce than of Proust and more of Jung's theory of the collective unconscious than of Bergson. Wolfe had written in a letter to Maxwell Perkins: "My conviction is that a native has the whole consciousness of his people and nation in him; that he knows everything about it, every sound and memory of the people."[26] Wolfe's sense of a collective memory is more than a national memory as can be seen in the legendary background he planned for *Of Time and the River.* Wolfe felt at times that in him all experience existed.

A third passage of importance in *The Story of a Novel* is Wolfe's explanation of the time elements in *Of Time and the*

24. *Letters,* ed. Nowell, p. 254.
25. "The Story of a Novel," *SRL* (December 21, 1935), 15.
26. *Letters,* ed. Nowell, p. 279.

River. There were three elements: present time; past time, which showed people "as acting and as being acted upon by all the accumulated impact of man's experience"; and time immutable, "the time of rivers, mountains, oceans, and the earth; a kind of eternal and unchanging universe of time against which would be projected the transience of man's life, the bitter briefness of his day."[27] In Wolfe's definition of the past we find again a suggestion of Joyce. Wolfe's time immutable is in one of his letters applied only to the earth whereas the river and the ocean represent movement and wandering.[28]

In *The Story of a Novel* Wolfe formulates, then, three aspects of his interest in time: the power of involuntary memory to re-create the past, a sense of the collective unconscious which contains events from our national and racial past, and a sense of time immutable. The time concepts of Proust, of Joyce, and even perhaps of Wordsworth are evident in these formulations, but beyond them lies Wolfe's own fascination simply with the word *time* so that he could write: "I am haunted by a sense of time and a memory of things past, and, of course, I know I have got to try somehow to get a harness on it."[29]

The themes that have been enunciated in *The Story of a Novel* are clearly evident in *Look Homeward, Angel*. Early in the book Wolfe mentions his urge to return to the past through actual, not secondhand, experience with it. He speaks of his acute realization of the past which exists in each one of us and which needs only night or nakedness to reveal it. Each of us, he says, is the sum of many things we have not known or counted. Look behind the screen of the present, return to the darkness of the womb, to night, "and you shall see begin in Crete four thousand years ago the love that ended yesterday in Texas."[30] This passage is more nearly related to Joyce's sense of return and to his interest in recurrence than to Bergson's *durée*.

27. "The Story of a Novel," *SRL* (December 28, 1935), p. 3.
28. *Letters*, ed. Nowell, p. 280.
29. *Ibid.*, p. 323.
30. Thomas Wolfe, *Look Homeward, Angel* (New York, 1929), p. 3 Subsequent references to this volume appear in the text.

For Bergson time was like a snowball; therefore, for him two love affairs exist simultaneously but they are still *two* love affairs. Wolfe is emphasizing, on the other hand, the collective aspect of experience, the fact that perhaps the individual is less important than the whole of which he is a part. Wolfe erected this defense against his fear of the fleetingness of time at the very beginning of his work although it receives more complete expression in *Of Time and the River*.

In *Look Homeward, Angel* Eugene's experience with the train is one that gives him further ballast against the time experience, even though the train symbol is an ambiguous one for Eugene. The train for Eugene, from boyhood on, denoted freedom from mountain fastness. On the train alone he felt the security that fixity never gave him, because, for one thing, on the train there is always the possibility of return whereas time sells no round-trip tickets. And yet the whistle of the train sounding in the reaches of the night filled him with longing and with terror. "And it was this that awed him—the weird combination of fixity and change" (p. 192). The train enabled him to flee and yet it brought him back to Altamont; on it he competed with time and in a sense became temporarily the winner. Scenes in Virginia sped by him and yet he was able to transfix certain scenes. As he passed a town, a slattern standing in a doorway, both seemed suspended or frozen in time. They stood "without the essential structure of time. Fixed in no-time, the slattern vanished, fixed, without a moment of transition" (p. 192). To the viewer on the train the landscape speeds by like a moving film and yet certain scenes from this film are immutably fixed in the mind of the viewer. On the train Eugene achieved thus a detachment from time, a God-like view of the universe, the ability to choose what he wished to retain from experience. It gave to Eugene a sense of being beyond change and at the same time it gave him the security of knowing that "he *could* go home again." Yet its whistle heard in the night represented the very fleetingness that he escaped when he was on board. Eugene's insecurities in regard to time arise from this sense of not being "on board" in life; a recognition of his role in life would later give him the sense of detachment which he achieves through the substitute of the train at this point.

His need to transfix time in a suspended instant is illustrated elsewhere in the book. Two scenes are described in the square of Altamont when time is suddenly suspended. W. O. Gant, standing on his porch, is the God-like viewer in the first scene. Fagg Sluder, a policeman, the fireman, a farmer, Yancey stop simultaneously their activities. The fountain, which plays in the center of the square, is suspended. And Gant feels as if he were looking at a photograph of himself taken years earlier and as if he alone were moving toward death in this world of shadows of reality. He feels like a man who recognizes himself in a photograph—perhaps on "his elbow near Ulysses Grant before the march" (p. 269). This scene is for Gant a kind of effort to stem the tide of time, and it is also a prelude to the final scene in the book when Eugene meets the ghost of Ben in the square.

In both scenes the square lay in moonlight but whereas for Gant the square had been full of people, for Eugene it is empty. Gant's search for meaning depends on others; Eugene must seek within himself for the meaning of his role. In the final chapter of *Look Homeward, Angel* Wolfe imitates perhaps unconsciously the consecration scene of Stephen in *A Portrait*. "Do you know why you are going, or are you just taking a ride on the train?" (p. 619) Ben asks. This question makes clear Eugene's substitution of the train experience for the real experience of life. Ben knows that Eugene is *not* coming back; that this is not just a ride on the train. Like Stephen Dedalus, Eugene goes forth "to forge in the smithy of my soul the uncreated conscience of my race,"[31] and there is no more turning back home. "He was like a man who stands upon a hill above the town he has left, yet does not say 'The town is near,' but turns his eyes upon the distant soaring ranges" (p. 626). Thus Eugene finds the sense of detachment which he has sought.

Furthermore, in the square Eugene discovers, as Stephen

31. James Joyce, *A Portrait of the Artist As a Young Man* (New York, 1928), p. 299.

had in his vision of the Danes, his relation to all experience. He sees fabulous cities, Thebes, the temples of Daulian, and Phocian lands. He sees all the life and death of all time. In the square this night "all the minutes of lost time collected and stood still" (p. 623), lost shapes, lost events, lost meetings. But whereas for Gant the fountain had stood still, for Eugene it pulses "with a steady breezeless jet," and whereas for Gant, the life of Altamont had been suspended, for Eugene the square contains all of life, from Thebes to the demons of the South, standing transfixed before him. Eugene's vision is one that foretells not death, as Gant's had, but a new life, a new point of view, for the stone angel raises its arm, and in the shop the heavy tread of angels may be heard, angels that through his art Eugene will bring to life. Against the vision of the passage of millions to their death stands the rhythm of the seasons, the continual return of spring granting a surer security than the rail-bound return of the train.

In his need to reanimate the past, his need to achieve a sense of the identity of all experience, his need to transfix the moment, his need to achieve artistic detachment, Wolfe (in *Look Homeward, Angel*) is very close to Joyce. He has deduced the very essence of Joyce's experience and translated it into terms of "the artist as a young man" in the United States. Proust's moments of recall and a Wordsworthian sense of pre-existence lie perhaps in the background, but the temper of the book is more akin to Joyce's than to the reflective temperaments of Proust and of Wordsworth. Wolfe himself called *Look Homeward, Angel* "my *Ulysses* book."[32]

In *Of Time and the River* the influence of Proust is much more evident although what Wolfe learned from Joyce has not been forgotten. Wolfe's concepts of time are analyzed more fully here than in his first book. *Of Time and the River* is, as the title indicates, a kind of time epic. Wolfe's preoccupation with time still concerns, of course, its fleetingness, its grandeur, its pathos, "the immense and murmurous"[33] sound of time which

32. See p. 209, above.
33. Wolfe, *Of Time and the River*, p. 136. Subsequent references to this volume appear in the text.

rises over great railroad sheds or over huge cities. But here he is sometimes concerned with the nature of time and its properties. Passages that inquire into its nature are more frequent in this second novel than in the others.

At the opening of the book Wolfe thinks, for instance, of the relative qualities of space and time on his trip between Asheville and New York. The distance, he says, is more than seven hundred miles. "But so relative are the qualities of space and time, ... that in the brief passage of this journey one may live a life" (p. 25).

Again in the train the present fades and, as he fingers the watch that Ben had given him, the image of Ben appears and the scene changes to his twelfth birthday when he had received the watch from his brother. He wonders what time is. The watch is to keep time with. "What is this dream of time, this strange and bitter miracle of living?" (P. 52.) This scene with the watch is, of course, reminiscent of Proust. Here the watch instead of the *madeleine* recalls the past into the present and fuses them into one timeless instant.

And once again on the train present and past time fuse when he thinks of his life with his father. Suddenly the thousand images of his father become as "one terrific image." But here in contrast to the preceding scene with the watch, there is no key, no magic word with which to unlock the past. Only in his memory does time become a unit; he does not re-experience the past as he does with the watch.

It must not be forgotten that Eugene Gant and, consequently, Wolfe were persistently searching for a key that would admit them into the past. Proust's *madeleine* was only one of the keys that Wolfe tried. Through the memories and tales of his mother Eugene comes closer to the actual past than he is able to come by other means. When he meets Bascom Pentland in Boston, he thinks that his uncle will reanimate for him all the scenes and faces of old about which he wanted to know. But Bascom can not do this; he has somehow lost the key and is unable to give Eugene a feeling of the reality of his past life. This intense desire on Wolfe's part to reanimate things lost and

dead is probably closely connected with his search for a father
or an antecedent. And it is ironical that it is his mother who
most nearly fulfills his desire with her stories of the Pentland
tribe. Yet his seekings into past time almost exclusively concern
men, Ben, his father, the Joyner brothers, "The Four Lost
Men," Garfield, Arthur, Harrison, Hayes. "Who had heard the
casual and familiar tones of Chester Arthur?"[34] This familiar
and exact quality of the living was what Wolfe sought to
capture in much the same way that Proust desired to, but
Proust more nearly succeeded, for Wolfe never ceased to feel
that the past was irrevocably lost. Change was but appearance
to Proust, whereas to Wolfe, despite rationalizations, it was a
bitter fact of existence, separating him from all life.

Loneliness was another condition that often made Eugene
see time in unusual perspective. At Harvard and later in
Tours, there were periods when he would spend days or weeks
by himself without seeing a face he knew. These days were like
dreams and during them weeks seemed like a single day, and
then he would awake and find time once more in normal
perspective.

His childhood recurred frequently during these years. "A
voice half-heard, a word far-spoken, a leaf, a light that came
and passed and came again. But always when that lost world
would come back, it came at once, like a sword thrust through
the entrails, in all its panoply of past time, living, whole, and
magic as it has always been" (p. 200). This description of the
return of the past reminds one of Proust's description of recalling bygone days. It also contains perhaps some of the longing
that Wordsworth felt for lost childhood. Although Wolfe did
not aspire to the "realm of Essence," he incorporated into this
book some of the aspects of time that he held in common with
Proust.

That he had become curious about the metaphysics of time
is apparent in the excerpt from his notebook, which he included
near the end of the novel. He believes that his query about the
nature of time has been finally answered after a visit to the

34. Thomas Wolfe, *From Death to Morning* (New York, 1935), p. 121.

American Library in Paris where he reads the *Americana* and William James. In fact, William James, rather than Bergson, is probably Wolfe's source for his ideas on duration.

Here he discovers that "the time-units of both time and space are neither points nor moments, but moments in the history of a point" (pp. 670-71). The significance of the title, *Of Time and the River,* becomes clearer if we examine this statement in the light of certain passages, He speaks, for instance, of "the moving tide of time as it flows down the river" (p. 510). Again and again the river and time are connected, especially in the scenes in which he travels up the Hudson to meet Joel. Time, for Wolfe, is an unchangeable, unalterable thing, like a river, but paradoxically it always changes. "Moments in the history of a point" would apply to either time or the river. Time-units and the waves of the river are only the surface of a larger reality. James and other theorists on the metaphysics of time put the emphasis on the larger unit while the rest of us swimming or sinking in the river and time worry about the waves. Wolfe at least implies then that his book is to deal with time in both its aspects, fixity and change. The fixity of change constantly impresses Eugene, the stillness of the macrocosm and the disturbing fluctuation of the microcosm. Life, he says, is "like a river, and as fixed, unutterable in un-ceasing movement and in changeless change as the great river is, and time itself" (p. 245). The earth, sweeping past a train on which he rides, has this same quality of "unchanging changefulness," but time is "as fixed and everlasting as eternity" (p. 245). And for Abe's mother seven thousand years, "yester-day, tomorrow, and forever [are but] a moment at the heart of love and memory" (p. 492).

The idea of song as a means of invoking the past is part of Wolfe's heritage from Proust. For Wolfe often "trashy" songs like "K-K-K-Katy," he says in a letter, "are able to make me live again some night in summer twenty or twenty-five years ago and hear the people talk on their porches."[35] In Book VII, "Kronos and Rhea: The Dream of Time," Wolfe invokes the

35. *Letters,* ed. Nowell, p. 377.

past by means of music as Swann does in Proust. "Play us a tune on an unbroken spinet" (p. 853) is Wolfe's thematic sentence. And through this tune of the spinet he recalls Athens as it actually was, people in the Middle Ages, their casual words, the trains in Baltimore in 1853. The difference between Wolfe and Proust here is that Wolfe wishes to reproduce all time, for a recurrent dream while he is in France would take Eugene back to the days of Homer, while Proust was interested only in his own segment of it.

As the sexton rings the church bell in Dijon, sounds of another bell come to Eugene. He is once more ringing the college bell "and now the memory of that old bell, with all its host of long-forgotten things, swarmed back with living and intolerable pungency" (p. 896). This is like an illustration of Proust's assertion that the past is hidden in some material object. If there is a difference it is that Proust would say the college bell was still there, that he had unconsciously been carrying its sound with him, for time only served to obscure the true perspective in which things stand, whereas Wolfe meant that one bell reminded him of another although his actual experience may not have been unlike Proust's.

For as he watches the scene in Dijon the lonely sounds of his native Catawba awaken in him, and there in the square in the French village he sees the square of his own town, Altamont, hears his father slam their iron gate, feels "the magic of full June," smells turnip greens, and hears the slamming of screen doors. The life of twenty years past is thus recalled to him, but for Wolfe it tends to be *recalled* and not *recaptured*. Proust was surer of his ability to stem the flow of the river, and it is because of his uncertainty that Wolfe is continually faced with the mystery of time, "the mystery of strange, million-visaged time that haunts us with the briefness of our days" (p. 899).

Although the influence of Proust has been stressed in discussing *Of Time and the River*, the mythical implications of the headings of the books are obviously inspired by *Ulysses*. However, the parallel between the present situation and its mythical counterpart is much less carefully worked out by Wolfe than by Joyce. Thus, for instance, the book entitled "Telemachus" describes Eugene's trip with three rich young men to Blackstone and his being jailed there with the others and his release paid for by his brother, Luke. Only in a most general way can this incident be understood as Telemachus' search for the father. Close similarities between the myth and the present are impossible to find. However, the headings do indicate that Wolfe was conscious of the recurrent nature of reality and of its function in his work. *Finnegans Wake (Work in Progress)* was being published in *Transition* during the time that Wolfe was writing *Of Time and the River.* Joyce had remarked to Eugene Jolas: "Time and the river and the mountain are the real heroes of my book."[36] Joyce's influence on this second book of Wolfe's should not, therefore, be overlooked. The relationship between the river and the mountain, transience and immobility, is one that stands at the very core of the work of both men.

In *The Web and the Rock* and *You Can't Go Home Again,* Wolfe treats the subject of time much less fully than in his second novel. Nevertheless, several passages, which are worth mentioning here, further develop Wolfe's thoughts on time. Aunt Maw in *The Web and the Rock* is, of course, substituted for Eliza in the earlier books, and it is through her that George hears "lost voices in the mountains long ago."[37] But George laments Aunt Maw's callousness, for he says she cannot know "the eternity of living in a moment" (p. 24) or the swift flash of change. The old problems of fixity and change and the desire to recall lost voices continue to haunt Wolfe. Aunt Maw's words bring to George the voices of his Joyner ancestors, the smell of a pine blaze, but, somehow, like Uncle Bascom's words, they fail actually to re-create the past.

During his trip to Richmond to see a football game, Monk takes part in events that happened during the Civil War. He

36. Richard Ellmann, *James Joyce* (New York, 1959), p. 565.
37. Thomas Wolfe, *The Web and the Rock* (New York, 1939), p. 8. Subsequent references to this volume appear in the text.

hears Grant and his soldiers fighting their way into Richmond, he knows Lee is digging in at Petersburg, that Lincoln is waiting to hear the news, that Jubal Early "was swinging in his saddle at the suburbs of Washington" (p. 153). Monk and his friends did more than just imagine these events, for "they felt, they knew, they had their living hands and hearts upon the living presence of these things" (p. 183). Thus Richmond reanimates for Wolfe a past era; he sees no ghostly procession of historical events, but rather the living images of them. Like the memories of his childhood, these memories become "living, whole and magic."[38] But in Wolfe no matter how live memories become they still tend to be memories and images, not actual events. One main difference between Proust and Wolfe is that Wolfe sees that the whole past, not only the individual's past, is recoverable. In this he is close to Joyce.

However, Wolfe, like both Proust and Joyce, recognized the immobility of time, its immeasurableness, its relativity. For he describes an estuary of the sea as "motionless as time"; the fight between Firpo and Dempsey lasts a three minutes that seem like hours; men measure immeasurable time by arbitrary symbols; they even measure the timeless sea; and "every man on earth held in the little tenement of his flesh and spirit the whole ocean of human life and time" (p. 262). Then suddenly a sound, an odor, a city square brings to him the "streets of noon some dozen years ago" (p. 276), the shuffle of leather on the pavements, the shouts of children, the smell of turnip greens, the slamming of screen doors. Constantly he cries out that he may find lost eras, knowing his wish impossible of accomplishment, for man is but "that little, glittering candle-end of dateless time who tries to give a purpose to eternity" (p. 299).

Even Esther fits into his schemes of recovering the past, for in his manhood it is Esther, and not Eliza or Aunt Maw, who regales him with tales of bygone days. It is Esther who gives him "a blazing vision of lost time" (p. 367), Esther who makes "ghosts of forgotten hours" (p. 367) move about her. As she

38. Wolfe, *Of Time and the River*, p. 200.

talks all life reawakens for Monk, all the lost and secret recesses of the past are opened, and she brings her living warmth and presentness to reanimate lost faces, her father's world of the theater, her first party. "She was like time," Monk says, for she could give the feeling of distance and memory to events that had occurred only an hour before. But sometimes during her descriptions of her childhood days he would think that there was no way actually to bring back even a few seconds of lost eras. Always he is haunted by past moments, by a devouring curiosity, which makes him go to any lengths to secure a peephole through which he can view the past. For the time of each man is different; there is the time of great bells in a tower, the time of a tiny wrist watch, the time of each human being. And the "dark rich river [is] full of strange time, dark time, strange tragic time" (p. 427).

That spring in New York with Esther and the new novel he is writing, he feels that both mistress and novel make "the past as real as the present" (p. 541). He is living "the events of twenty years ago with as much intensity and as great a sense of actuality as if they had just occurred" (p. 541). There is no *now* and no *then*, for George feels a unity with the larger purposes of time and destiny. And as he looks at the green tree that stands outside his window, he feels as if it had the magic qualities that had unlocked the past. Like the *madeleine* for Proust, the green tree is the key that admits Wolfe into lost days. Wolfe comes very close to Proust here, for in this passage change is mere appearance to Wolfe; and the green tree, like the *madeleine,* unlocks memories that the author is to record in a book. But still this process of recall is not the central theme of Wolfe's tetralogy, though an important coulisse of the central theme, the recovery of past. For Wolfe never tires of repeating that each man has his own time, that there is the time of clocks, of mountains, of rivers, for time has ten thousand faces and yet is a fable, a mystery.

In the last section of *The Web and the Rock,* the hero flees to Paris. By the end of Wolfe's third book one knows that Eugene and George have become Eugene-George. For example, in Paris George feels "that he has been here before" (page 631), and he immerses himself in the "fixed and living eternity of the earth" (p. 631). Eugene-George came to stand in Wolfe's mind as a symbol, the kind of symbol that Thomas Mann's Joseph was. Mann uses Joseph as a figure who represents many, who is not sure even of his own identity, and Wolfe eventually sees his hero as representing the summation of all young men's experience and especially of the experience of the creative artist of the 1920's. For the episode in the French town of *Of Time and the River* is repeated in *The Web and the Rock.* Instead of the bell, here the laughter of a woman recalls to him a scene from his childhood in Old Catawba, the sound of a distant train, the sleeping streets, and the start of a motor. Mortal time is clock time George knows, as he lies in a German hospital and listens to a clock strike "with a solemn and final sweetness" (p. 674).

From *You Can't Go Home Again* the party at Jack's reminds one of Proust's description of the party given by the Guermantes, while George, like Proust's hero, stands broodingly in the background observing and commenting. In two letters Wolfe has mentioned that this scene is "somewhat Proustian." He writes: "its life depends upon the most thorough and comprehensive investigation of character,"[39] and yet he feels that despite its "unintentional" Proustian characteristics, it does contain a good deal of action. Wolfe here points out quite clearly a central difference between his writing and Proust's. Proust did achieve a stasis of a kind through his minute character analysis. Wolfe, on the other hand, worked to re-create the flow of his characters in action.

As George looks at a portrait of Mrs. Jack as a young girl the mystery of time passes over him. It seems to him that 1901, when the portrait was painted, was centuries ago. "Yes, he had lived and died through so many births and deaths...that... the sense of time had been wiped out."[40] These years had become a "timeless dream." For had they not been Thracian

39. *Letters*, ed. Nowell, p. 631.
40. Thomas Wolfe, *You Can't Go Home Again* (New York, 1942), p. 252.

captives together? Had she not launched the ship? And had she not "come to charm remission from the lord of Macedon?" (P. 253.) And now she had stepped out of these former selves and stood before him. The portrait here is the means of momentarily freeing George from the present. He travels far, into the days of Thrace and Macedon, and all time is for him vivid and immediate.

Thus the four novels of Wolfe's tetralogy echo the voice of time. Like the great railroad sheds, they harbor its sound. For Wolfe was secure only when he was in motion and never so sure of himself as when he was on a moving train. His books came from the huge railroad stations of his mind where "the voice of time remained aloof and imperturbed, a drowsy and eternal murmur,"[41] and where the train whistle evoked for him a million images: "old songs, old faces and forgotten memories."[42]

It is not surprising that in Wolfe's last piece, "A Western Journey," he should have resurrected past days. For as he journeyed through western plains, he saw the thundering Sioux in storm-herds, and he knew that long ago some man had stood and, looking over those same rolling plains, had envisaged the future with its thundering trains. And in Arizona he watches from a mountain a distant train, "advanceless moveless-moving through timeless time."[43]

In fact, it is fitting that Wolfe's last words concerning his "dark time" should also concern trains. For the train, like the square in Altamont, was changeless in its change. There is a danger in attempting to formulate in terms of philosophy Wolfe's theories of time, for in such an attempt the critic tends to move far away from the works themselves and from Wolfe himself. For Wolfe it was the experience with time which counted, and although this experience was often not unlike that of Joyce, of Proust, of Wordsworth or Coleridge, Wolfe never became involved in metaphysics. Such an involvement

41. *Ibid.*, p. 48.
42. Thomas Wolfe, "Boom Town," *American Mercury* (May, 1943), p. 21.
43. Thomas Wolfe, "A Western Journey," *Virginia Quarterly Review*, XV (Summer, 1939), 340.

would have perhaps brought him closer to the solution to the problem of change and transience which haunted him all his days. The title *You Can't Go Home Again* indicates not only that Wolfe was now oriented toward the future but that he had never solved the mystery of the past as Joyce, who had influenced *Look Homeward, Angel,* had found it in eternal recurrence, as Proust, whose influence is everywhere in *Of Time and the River,* had found it in involuntary memory, and as Wordsworth, whose "intimations of immortality" appear now and then in Wolfe's work had found it in a semi-mystical connection between man and nature. One sees Wolfe reaching out toward a cyclical concept of time in his last books, but it is never a driving force for him. In the last chapter of *You Can't Go Home Again,* he feels that the circle has "come full swing" (p. 741). But in the next sentence he talks of the future as if there were a linear progression in time. What offers hope for Wolfe is not a sense of cycles in *You Can't Go Home Again* but a faith in the future of America and a blind faith at the very end in "another world" beyond this one. Cyclical recurrence and involuntary memory were facets of his bulwark against time passing, but they never completely eased for him the ache of separation when "the doors are closed, and the ship is given to the darkness and the sea."[44] The last words of *You Can't Go Home Again* concern the flowing of rivers.

44. Wolfe, *Of Time and the River,* p. 912.

CHAPTER EIGHT

WILLIAM FAULKNER:

MYTH AND DURATION

Whereas Thomas Wolfe never succeeded in conquering the sense of flux of the river which caused him insecurity, William Faulkner's basic sense of time is one that enables him to stand on firmer ground. Wolfe searched in vain for something that would stem time's passing. Joyce's sense of cyclical recurrence, Proust's sense of involuntary memory, a vague mysticism—none of these actually convinced Wolfe that time could be arrested. Faulkner, on the other hand, shows from the beginning of his work an almost inherent sense of patterns in time which life has followed and which life will follow. As Olga Vickery puts it, Faulkner felt that "the communal and anonymous brotherhood of man can be re-established if each man . . . accepts responsibility for all time as well as for the particular time into which he was born."[1]

Faulkner, no more than Wolfe, formulated a metaphysics of time. But Faulkner is surer than Wolfe of an eternal recurrence in time. Faulkner's use of symbolic characters and legendary themes is more sustained that Wolfe's. Characters to whom

1. Olga Vickery, *The Novels of William Faulkner* (Baton Rouge, 1959), p. 236.

time is of individual interest only, like Quentin Compson, are
not his ideal figures. Fusion and then transcendence of past,
present, and future shape Faulkner's time pattern. He condemns those whose vision is centered on time, makes leading
figures of those who see beyond its confines.

In addition to his sense of cyclical recurrence, there is in
Faulkner a very real sense of Bergson's *durée*. One of the
difficulties in analyzing Faulkner's time sense comes from the
fact that at some points his concept of time is durational; at
others it is transcendent. This basic contradiction in Faulkner's
thinking about time is made clear in Loïc Bouvard's "Conversation with William Faulkner." "Since we had brought up Bergson, I next asked Faulkner to explain his conception of time.
'There isn't any time,' he replied. 'In fact I agree pretty much
with Bergson's theory of the fluidity of time. There is only the
present moment, in which I include both the past and the
future, and that is eternity.' "[2] Later in the same conversation
Faulkner told Bouvard: "I was ... influenced by Bergson,
obviously. And I feel very close to Proust. After I had read *À la
Recherche du Temps Perdu* I said 'This is it!'—and I wished I
had written it myself."[3]

Bergson substituted durational for nontemporal values;
whereas philosophy since Plato had eliminated duration, had
regarded time as illusion, Bergson insists that finite being
endures, may in fact be time itself. If an author is to be consistent, he chooses either the durational approach, and his
emphasis is then placed on the individual time of the characters
involved, or he chooses an approach to time in which the grand
pattern itself is more important than the individual experience
with time, like Kafka, who expresses his novels in terms of
universals. Faulkner often, however, attempts both approaches
to time within a single novel because, as his remarks to Bouvard
make evident, the distinction between the two was not a sharp
one for him. "There isn't any time" is not a remark with which

2. Loïc Bouvard, "Conversation with William Faulkner," *Modern Fiction
Studies*, V (Winter, 1959-1960), 362.
3. *Ibid.*, p. 364.

Bergson could have concurred without qualification. Jeal Pouil-lon makes a distinction between these two kinds of novels when he analyzes in his book *Temps et roman* the novel of duration and the novel of destiny. He sees Faulkner's novels in the latter group in that, unlike Proust's, Faulkner's past is not only *his* past, but the past of the world.[4]

Neither Pouillon nor other critics point out what is often a basic inconsistency in Faulkner's approach to time although Jean-Paul Sartre sees in Faulkner's time two characteristics: first, an emphasis on the past, a past ordered by the heart and, second, a sense of suspension or arrested motion in time. Sartre states that Faulkner uses the same metaphysic as Proust except that for Proust salvation lies in the recovery of the past—for Faulkner the past is never lost. Proust and Faulkner, says Sartre, have decapitated time, taken away its future. In this he sees the basis for Faulkner's despair.[5]

Peter Swiggart has answered Sartre in essays in which he claims that Faulkner's despair is shown through such characters as Quentin, who is actually only his "control and moral con-demnation."[6] In characters such as the preacher and Dilsey, who see at the basis of human experience "the first and the last" inextricably joined, lies the true reality beyond the divisions of time. The answer for Faulkner lies then in tran-scendence of time according to Swiggart.

Critics who have more or less agreed with Sartre are M. le Breton, who talks of Faulkner's pessimism and fatalistic philos-ophy of despair,[7] and J.-J. Mayoux, who states that Faulkner's works show the gloomy obstinacy of time: "c'est le même toujours changé et le changé toujours même."[8]

4. Jean Pouillon, "Temps et destinée chez Faulkner," in *Temps et roman* (Paris, 1946), pp. 238-60.

5. Jean-Paul Sartre, "Time in Faulkner: *The Sound and the Fury,*" in *William Faulkner: Two Decades of Criticism,* ed. Frederick J. Hoffman and Olga W. Vickery (East Lansing, Michigan, 1951), p. 184.

6. Peter Swiggart, "Moral and Temporal Order in *The Sound and the Fury,*" *Sewanee Review,* LXI (Spring, 1953), 232.

7. M. le Breton, "Temps et personne chez William Faulkner," *Journal de psychologie normale et pathologique,* XLIV (January-June, 1951), 344-54.

8. J.-J. Mayoux, "Le temps et la destinée chez Faulkner," in *La profondeur et le rhythme* (Cahiers du Collège Philosophique, 1948), p. 306.

However, Faulkner's time sense is sometimes both transcendent and durational. The reason, for instance, that Faulkner seems far less abstract than Kafka is that he does descend to the time of the individual. On the other hand, unlike Proust's, Faulkner's characters do partake of the mythical and universal. It is with this paradox in mind that this chapter will be developed. Faulkner's inability to resolve this conflict lies at the basis of some of his artistic failures (such as *Pylon,* a failure that Jean Pouillon has attributed to the character of witness possessed by the reporter).[9] Perrin Lowrey, for instance, has stated that the Compsons are like Paolo and Francesca—their story is individual, but they represent the punishment for adultery,[10] and Jean-Jacques Mayoux claims that there is in Faulkner a drama that unfolds in time while, on the other hand, "Nous sommes dans le monde des symboles, de l'imagination, de la représentation."[11]

Mirrors of Chartres Street, the collection of Faulkner stories from the *New Orleans Times-Picayune* (Spring, 1925), turns out to be a revealing source in this connection. In the title story, for instance, the policeman becomes Caesar "mounting his chariot among cast roses and the shouts of the rabble."[12] The irony of this contrast is rivaled by that in the title "Damon and Pythias Unlimited"—a story of two hypocrites. But despite the irony, one sees in these references an attempt by Faulkner to enlarge the scope of his reference, to move from the particular and the individual to the larger historical or mythical area. "Out of Nazareth," as the title implies, is another attempt of this sort. In this story the young man's time sense foreshadows that of Dilsey or of Lena: "He reminded one of a pregnant woman in his calm belief that nature, the earth which had spawned him,

9. Jean Pouillon, "William Faulkner, un témoin," *Les temps modernes,* II (October, 1946), 172-78.

10. Perrin Lowrey, "Concepts of Time in *The Sound and the Fury,*" in *English Institute Essays, 1952,* p. 64.

11. J.-J. Mayoux, "La création du réel chez William Faulkner," *Études anglaises,* V (February, 1952), 33.

12. William Faulkner, *Mirrors of Chartres Street* (Minneapolis, Minnesota, 1953), p. 5. Subsequent references to this volume appear in the text.

would care for him, that he was serving his appointed ends" (p. 37).

On the contrary, we find in the story "Home" a truly Proustian touch as the lilting provençal air played by the man with the saw and the bow moves Jean-Baptiste to reanimate his homeland. Around him "rose the land he called his; the wooded hills and valleys, willow and tall chestnuts in the meadows . . . , young love and nightingales among the chestnut trees. . . . He saw the cottage where he was born" (p. 24). Stirred by these memories, he determines not to become an accomplice in a crime. Also in "The Cobbler" an old dried, twisted rose renews yearly in the memory of the cobbler the girl who had deserted him for another suitor.

These two methods of dealing with time are present throughout most of Faulkner's work. Each method concerns a relationship of the present to the past. The first one abolishes a sense of past and present through symbol and myth. "For every Southern boy fourteen years old," writes Faulkner in *Intruder in the Dust*, "not once but whenever he wants it, there is the instant when it's not yet two o'clock on that July afternoon in 1863."[13] Much of Faulkner's interest in transcending time comes from an instinctive Southern preoccupation with its own history and myths. "That July afternoon in 1863" becomes immortal only when it is neither present nor past. But it is not only the South that is the subject of Faulkner's interest. On occasion moments from the racial past of man are fused by him into timeless instants that partake of no chronological succession.

The other kind of time in Faulkner includes a present and a past. It is the individual recalling of the past (often through a catalyst as in Proust); it is the actual reliving of these moments by the characters involved. But in order to implement this method there must, of course, be a present in which the past may be relived. Thus in *Soldier's Pay* (1926) through Mahon, Margaret Powers is able to reanimate the figure of her dead husband. Her identification of Mahon with her husband

13. William Faulkner, *Intruder in the Dust* (New York, 1948), p. 194.

and the completion and fulfillment through her final marriage to Mahon of her truncated first marriage is paralleled by Mahon's own laying of the ghost of his fiancée through marriage to Margaret Powers. As her name indicates, she embodies the *power* to liberate Donald. Her thoughts, however, keep returning to Dick as they always do when she is with Mahon. Thus Mahon and Margaret Powers become catalysts by which the past is invoked.

Mahon, however, achieves a kind of anonymity because he is blind and partially unconscious. He scarcely ever speaks and is revealed chiefly through others like Emmy and his father. He might be "everyman" or "every soldier." He becomes thus more easily the central figure in a legend, a legend of death in war and of the unfinished patterns which it leaves. He is a kind of archetype of the corporal in *A Fable,* one the "unknowing," the other the "unknown" soldier.

The counterpoint technique used by Faulkner in *Soldier's Pay* is effective also in preparing us to accept a sense of timelessness. We are shifted from scene to scene, shuttled from point to point in the action.

But the combination of these two time schemes in Faulkner's novel is a disturbing element. The reader is caught between a point of view which claims a definite place for present, past, and future and one which would transcend these states. We shift too rapidly from the specific to the general. It is difficult to believe in Donald Mahon both as symbol and as Donald Mahon. In some of Faulkner's novels this conflict is sometimes quite fortuitously, it appears, resolved, and these novels make up his best writing. *Soldier's Pay,* however, combines both time concepts to its detriment. The legend is too thin a cover, concealing only partially a commonplace tale.

Sartoris (1929) is scarcely more successful although the theme here is not centered around an individual but the name Sartoris. The legend is that of the role of the dominant white in the South, his establishment, his rise, and his fall. But the novel is also based on an individual sense of present and past, on a Proustian recalling of the past through a catalyst, in this book the pipe of John Sartoris which recalls for old Bayard the image of his father so that "it seemed to him that he could hear his father's breathing even."[14] Coming as this passage does at the beginning of the book, it sets a tone for the novel.

But conflicting with this sense of the individual past is the timeless region of the Sartoris legend, of man who by his courage and strength runs a railroad into the wilderness, a railroad that will one day be bought by a syndicate, a railroad that will run from Lake Michigan to the Gulf of Mexico; of his son, a banker, and of Virginia Du Pre, who danced in crinoline and hooped muslin beneath the mistletoe and holly boughs of Baltimore. It is the magic of this legend of the South which gives the book whatever strength it possesses.

If an author is to make us believe in his myth he must deprive his characters of some of their individual identity; on the other hand, if an author wishes to stress his characters as such he must to some extent abandon his myth. Thomas Mann has a deep sense of myth; Proust and Virginia Woolf have a deep sense of the importance of the individual. But with Faulkner the triviality of many of his scenes and individuals invades and contorts the mythical level. In *Sartoris* old Bayard and Aunt Jenny are satisfactory as universal figures at times, but Narcissa and young Bayard fail completely to rise above themselves. It is not that myth and the individual past may not be combined, but that they must be used in proper relation to one another. As in the *Joseph* books, the sense of myth must pervade individual time.

It is because Faulkner keeps these two conceptions of time in separate compartments in *The Sound and the Fury* that this is his first successful work. We deal with individual time in the sections of Ben, Quentin, and Jason; we deal with a timeless region in the passages about Dilsey and the preacher. It should be noted here that the characters whom Faulkner idealizes in this novel are primitives. Transcendence of time is achieved by these people alone whereas the Quentins with their rational powers of observation are defeated. Faulkner's pessimism in

14. William Faulkner, *Sartoris* (New York, 1929), p. 1.

The Sound and the Fury lies not so much in his preoccupation with the past, but in his denial of the value of civilization.

Of course, the entire novel is in itself a myth of the South: "a tale told by an idiot, full of sound and fury, signifying nothing." But within this overlying element there are separate elements of time. These have been analyzed by Perrin Lowrey:[15] the time of Ben for whom time does not exist; the time of Quentin, obsessed with the past, with time from which he would escape; the time of Jason which represents money; the time of Dilsey, who is aware of the continuum of time in an instinctive way and for whom there is no opposition between the temporal and the eternal.

In a sense the sections of Ben, Quentin, and Jason have one point in common. All three characters stand in a false relation to clock time, Ben because through his irrationality he disregards it, Quentin because in his rationality he would escape it, and Jason because he would use it. Carvell Collins[16] sees this as the tragedy which accompanies lack of love—love in its largest sense which demands both a sense of time and the ability to transcend time.

Ben's and Quentin's sections both share a sense of duration, a Bergsonian sense of time accumulating like a snowball, but Ben's memories are so sporadic that no rational development of character or plot is possible. Quentin, however, often recalls time in much the same way as Proust's hero. There are, in fact, many examples of involuntary memory. One which is particularly Proustian is the smell of wistaria[17] and its consequent evocation of past time. There are many others. But Quentin could not be Proust's hero because Quentin's motive is escape from past, present, and future. He is horrified and yet spellbound by the panorama of the past as it unfolds before him. Proust's hero, on the contrary, is fascinated by the region he explores and would become part of it. His nostalgia is translated by Faulkner into Quentin's fear and revulsion. The sense

15. Lowrey, "Time in *The Sound and the Fury*," in *Essays*, pp. 69-82.
16. Carvell Collins, "The Interior Monologues of *The Sound and the Fury*," in *English Institute Essays, 1952*, pp. 29-56.
17. William Faulkner, *The Sound and the Fury and As I Lay Dying* (New York, 1946), p. 187.

of duration is one that Quentin protests against; he would live outside of time.

Dilsey, however, has both a sense of duration and the ability to transcend this. But as a touchstone to condemn the intellectual abstractions of Quentin, Dilsey does not entirely succeed, for her clock has but *one* hand (like the clock in Temple's room). The reader must select for himself the qualities that make up the touchstone in this novel. The instinctive sense of transcendence of a Dilsey, the trained intelligence and insight of a Quentin must be combined. Faulkner does not do this for us here and perhaps does not even intend to, for this is "a tale of sound and fury signifying nothing" in terms of the title. Dilsey is able to accept and then transcend time because she is essentially not a part of the society with which Quentin has to cope. It is the characters in Faulkner's work who come to grips with this elaborate social organization who are its heroes.

Darl Bundren in *As I Lay Dying* is one of these. Darl remarks that the motion of the wagon is so soporific, so dreamlike as to be without inference of progress.[18] The book itself is couched in this sort of motion. Even violence here has the effect on the reader of violence in a dream. Darl, the philosopher and poet, Cash, the practical man, Jewel, the man of feeling are seen in relation to the flooded stream of time. The flux of the river runs throughout the book. Events run inevitably on within a pattern toward a distant end. The dreamlike quality of the action may be attributed to the muffling and deadening effect of water on motion. This sense of immersion in water correlates with the motionless progress of the mules.

We are not dealing here with individual time, but with all time as we lie dying, as the South lies dying. All of the action is seen in terms of the river which transcends time while simultaneously representing it. There is no individual here whose past becomes present and more important than the myth in which it is involved. Addie says of her affair with Whitfield:

18. Faulkner, *The Sound and the Fury and As I Lay Dying*, p. 413. Subsequent references to this volume appear in the text.

"to me there was no beginning nor ending to anything then" (p. 467).

The river is the most important time symbol in the book. Like the flooded Mississippi in *The Wild Palms*, it stands for a sense of time which carries one away from the banks which represent mechanical time. For Darl (p. 443) time actually becomes the river, a horizontal quality and not something running ahead of him. The distance between bank and bank becomes then, not an interval, but the crossing or transcendence of time itself. The task of laying Addie to rest is one that requires more than the physical crossing of a river. It is Darl's recognition of this inner level of reality which causes him to set fire to the barn. He knows that Addie may be laid to rest without the ritual of the journey to Jefferson, that, in fact, she is laid to rest once the symbolic river is crossed.

Having crossed the river and having thus transcended time, Addie is reborn and then purified in Darl's fire. She is at rest for Darl. The others, however, are still immersed in the water of time, and for the practical Cash getting Addie into the earth is more important even than seeing Dr. Peabody about his leg. It is Darl, for whom the task of burying Addie is already completed, who suggests taking Cash first to Dr. Peabody. "'Go on,' I [Cash] said. 'We'll get it done first'" (p. 511). And for Jewel, too, immersed in the flux of time, the literal carrying out of his mother's wish is of prime importance. He has even sacrificed his horse to this end, and Darl knows that "Jewel's mother is a horse."

But in the end it is Darl with his highly developed sense of reality who is sacrificed. "'Do you want me to go?'" he asks Cash. Cash's answer, though evasive, is in the affirmative, and Darl accepts the role allotted to him by his family for the ultimate good of the whole. It is Jewel's horse, but it is Darl's whole being which is given in this service of sacrifice and self-abnegation. Faulkner does not thereby condemn Darl and his point of view. Rather Darl's sacrifice is an ironic comment on the fate that awaits those who see beyond the flux of the river. This is the reason that Darl laughs. Darl is neither a Quentin nor a

Dilsey, but he embodies qualities of both. He comes closer to the corporal of *A Fable* who like him accepts his sacrificial role.

The time sense in *As I Lay Dying* is perfectly consistent, and as such it is one of the best integrated of Faulkner's works. The flux of the river is the essential medium for all but Darl, who is able to accept and to transcend it. But unlike Dilsey, he is not simply intuitive in his relation to reality. Thus he is more satisfactory and more significant because he is able to direct his actions to an end, the welfare of those he loves. Dilsey could only observe, not alter, the dilemma of the Compsons.

But *Sanctuary*, unlike *As I Lay Dying*, has no central figure such as Darl. In *Sanctuary*, the individual time of the characters involved becomes more important than the myth they are to represent. There is no river to absorb and merge the sharp differences in personality. Thus it is difficult to believe that Temple, despite her name, can represent the desecrated South, for Temple Drake, as we see her in the novel, is simply Temple Drake. Her time is clock time; in representing her, Faulkner makes only perfunctory attempts at transcending time. The myth, one feels, is scarcely more than scaffolding, a purely intellectual structure imposed on a sensational story.

Miss Reba's clock, which hangs in Temple's room, like Dilsey's, has but one hand, halfway between ten and eleven. This is contrasted briefly with Temple's own watch that "keeps" time.[19] But the image is not a sustained one. Neither Miss Reba nor Temple is a Dilsey. There are moments when Temple's time sense appears confused, as in the section where she thinks that if it is half-past-ten then "this is not me. Then I am at school" (p. 182). She rises with the intention of dressing, watches the clock face, then draws the bolt on the door and returns to bed. But as she eats, her thoughts return to her father, her brothers, to the girls eating supper at school. Thus her own individual time breaks in on the sense of timelessness effected by the clock.

For Horace Benbow there are moments in the novel when

19. William Faulkner, *Sanctuary* (New York, 1932), p. 189. Subsequent references to this volume appear in the text.

time stands still, when his house appears "marooned in space by the ebb of all time" (p. 267). Essentially, however, these are interpolations. Thus the myth loses force because it is not supported by a sense of timelessness. The characters in *Sanctuary* are individuals in their own right, and it is difficult to transpose them into more far-reaching roles. One may illustrate this graphically by observing what would happen to Kafka's K. had the author given him eyes that looked like "two phlegm-clots." Faulkner has difficulty in creating "everyman" because time keeps intruding into his attempts to transcend it. There is no river in this novel to submerge a sense of clock time and no character who transcends clock time.

However, Faulkner's next novel, *Light in August*, partially obviates these difficulties. In *Light in August* various times are exemplified by Lena, Hightower, and Joe Christmas. The first chapters concerning Lena are a tour de force. The nearly motionless wagon, Lena's acceptance of her fate and her intuitive knowledge of time combine to give this part of the book a unity that the later pages do not achieve. Here it is the wagon, instead of the river, which is the objective correlative for time and which submerges individual time. Its "slow and terrific" motion transcends the story of which it is a part, and Lena's time sense is seen in terms of this motion.

In contrast, the Reverend Hightower, who "lives dissociated from mechanical time,"[20] possesses a sense of time which is distorted by an event that happened twenty years before he was born. At his death he knows finally that he has not lived, that he has not been able to let himself live or die. Only when he leaves his body "it can be now Now." This attitude toward the past, on the mythical level an attitude that typifies the South, is, Faulkner shows us, futile and decadent. It represents the ivory tower, the "high tower" of isolation from reality, and it leads to despair, destruction, and waste.

Joe Christmas, however, has both Lena's intuitive acceptance of time and the ability to reason about it. Like Darl he is

20. William Faulkner, *Light in August* (New York, 1950), p. 320. Subsequent references to this volume appear in the text.

sacrificed to society partially because his sense of time is more real than that of the society of which he is a part. The chapter introducing him begins with the line: "Memory believes before knowing remembers" (p. 104). He had no need of a watch (p. 149). Later the motionless progress that has been used to characterize Lena's journey is used in connection with Christmas. "He entered the street which he was to run for fifteen years" (p. 195). The thousands of streets which he travels become as one street. But the motion involved is not a sustained motion as is the motion of Lena's wagon. Christmas is more conscious of the past as such. He experiences at times a Proustian recall of the past as, for instance, when he eats the field peas in the dark of Miss Bundren's kitchen. His jaw stops, memory clicks, and he *sees, hears* McEachern. Christmas *thinks* about time: for thirty years he has lived inside it and then after the murder he feels that he is outside of it as if he were outside a fence (p. 290). Time loses its orderliness. As he flees, he flees time also. But on approaching Mottstown (page 296) he re-enters the paved street, thirty years long, which for the last seven days he has escaped. This street is circular, he discovers. Actually he has never been outside this circle although for seven days he has had no pavement. During these seven days he has traveled farther than ever before. Christmas realizes that in "cutting across time" (as Darl "cuts across" the river) one transcends time, but that in so doing one must also accept what one has done and can never undo, for it is this that forms the circle or the river that encloses us. The street image appears again at the end when Christmas runs from the jail to Hightower's house and in Stevens' words his whole past keeps pace with him "stride for stride" (p. 393). If the stride of Christmas could have been sustained throughout, it would have been a powerful objective correlative for Faulkner's message in the book.

The realization that comes to Christmas as he cuts across the circle of time is, however, one that goes with him to his death. From it comes a sense of purpose which is realized in his final acceptance of his role of passivity when with the loaded and unfired pistol in his hand he "let them shoot him to death" (p. 394). Faulkner sees Christmas as the victim of the mixture of black and white, as the South is the victim of this mixture. Christmas knows that he cannot escape time (the realities of his black and white blood), but that he can "cut across" it, transcend it, through "a blind faith in something read in a printed book" (p. 393). He thus becomes a symbol of the larger love for mankind which Darl, too, has realized. In sacrificing himself through the brutality of Percy Grimm, he is triumphant and "rises soaring into their memories forever and ever" (p. 407).

Because society accepts the Lenas, because they do not struggle with insanity or death, does not mean that Faulkner wishes them to represent humanity. Lena rides out of the last page of the book in the same vegetable state that she entered it. Ironically enough she will prevail. Christmas, however, progresses in the book from one who is concerned chiefly with time to one who recognizes that the highest role in life is the transcendence of time. He is able to use this realization for an end and to deny "the black jungle where life has already ceased before the heart stops" (p. 393). Only in a conscious recognition of this transcendence is Christmas able to lead others to a knowledge of transcendence, to a denial of the primitive black jungle where violence and brutality supersede love and justice. Through Christmas' sacrifice Percy Grimm becomes the representative of the jungle, whereas Christmas with his black blood comes to represent the highest achievement of man.

Darl and Joe Christmas prefigure the corporal, who is the culmination of the sacrificial figure in Faulkner's novels. Darl's circle of influence is only that of his family, Christmas' circle is Jefferson, the corporal's is the world.

Two characteristics of Faulkner's best work seem to have emerged thus far: (1) the relation of the myth to the story must be carefully proportioned, that is, the myth must pervade and supersede time as such; (2) the central character must possess a realization of his ability to transcend time, and he must know that truth is an inner affair. *Light in August* needs a central image like the river in *As I Lay Dying* to submerge the time sense of the individual, but Christmas as a figure in a myth is in many ways more forceful than Darl.

But in *Pylon,* which followed *Light in August,* the myth is only a feeble attempt to elevate the tone of the story. The myth of those who live dangerously and for the sake of danger is superseded by the much larger element of individual action. When the reporter is with the pilot, the jumper, and the woman, time appears to be clock time. Apart from them, he does not think about time "since the one moment out of all the future which he could see where his body would need to coincide with time or dial would not occur for almost twelve hours yet."[21] The myth that should be that of the pilot is told in terms of the clock whereas the reporter, who is no part of the myth, possesses a sense of timelessness.

As a central figure the pilot is not satisfactory, for he lives, as the reporter tells us, for the six and a half minutes each day when he covers twenty-five miles. The reporter, however, does know that time may be transcended, but he is outside the story, *un temoin,* and his knowledge leads to no end.

Faulkner avoids this dilemma to some degree in *Absalom, Absalom!* by making Quentin's past essentially the past of the people he tells about. Thomas Sutpen in his death does not transcend time as Christmas does; there is no "light in August." There is no image like the river, for Sutpen's Hundred decays rather than persists. This is because Sutpen's chief interest is in his own individual time, in the establishment of *his* progeny and *his* plantation. He does not come to the realization that this can be done only in the relinquishing of his individual identity.

However, Quentin attempts to sustain a sense of timelessness against the individual time of Sutpen. It is through Quentin that we see Sutpen as a figure in a myth. As a Southerner himself Quentin is heir of the heritage of which Sutpen is a part. Quentin is, in Faulkner's words, a ghost because he was born and bred in the South. However, one cannot ignore the fact that, through the use of Quentin, Faulkner removes the

21. William Faulkner, *Pylon* (New York, 1935), p. 201.

story one step from the reader. Thus Quentin's sense of timelessness has less effect than Darl's who is a part of the Bundren
family. Faulkner says of Quentin: "he was not a being, an
entity, he was a common-wealth. He was a barracks filled with
stubborn back-looking ghosts."[22] As such he stands necessarily
apart from the main flow of the novel. Like the reporter, he is
un temoin to some degree even though he "breathed the same
air in which the church bells rang out that Sunday morning in
1833" (p. 31).

Miss Rosa Coldfield, through whom Quentin learns most
of his tale, is also narrator but less of a witness than Quentin.
What Quentin remembers he remembers through his blood, his
heritage, for what happens in the book has occurred before
Quentin was born. He has "absorbed it already without medium
of speech somehow from having been born and living beside
it" (p. 212). But most of what Miss Rosa tells she has herself
lived. The wistaria evokes the past for her. "That is the substance of remembering—sense, sight, smell: the muscles with
which we see and hear and feel—not mind, not thought" (p.
143). Thus Miss Rosa's time sense is chiefly durational and
individual in the sense of the time of Proust's hero. When we
reach Thomas Sutpen at the core of the story, we have passed
through two screening devices: the individual time of Miss
Rosa and the time of the mythmaker Quentin.

Quentin creates about Sutpen a sense of timelessness.
Through Miss Rosa, Quentin tells us that when Sutpen put
the ring on her finger it was "as if he had turned all time back
twenty years and stopped it, froze it" (p. 165). Grandfather
Compson, another of the narrators, tells Quentin who tells us
that when Sutpen came from the mountains as a child, his trip
had no definite beginning or ending (p. 224); it was a per-
pendicular descent through temperature and climate. Thus
Quentin turns Sutpen into a timeless figure.

But Sutpen goes to defeat at the end, a defeat that could
have been transcended had he been able to see himself in a

22. William Faulkner, *Absalom, Absalom!* (New York, 1951), p. 12. Subsequent references to this volume appear in the text.

larger role than as founder of a single dynasty. It is Quentin who sees as he tells the tale to Shreve that this is a story of the whole South. As hero, Sutpen does not rank with Christmas or Darl because of his limited vision of his role. Through the narrator device Faulkner loses some of the effect of the myth. Although the synthesis of time and timelessness must be made, the particular way in which it is done in *Absalom, Absalom!* gives the novel a sense of duality.

Paradoxically more unity is achieved by the juxtaposition of two discrete plots in *The Wild Palms*. In this book Faulkner abandons the reporter technique. The contrapuntal method used in this novel makes it one of the most interesting of Faulkner's works, but with the exception of W. R. Moses[23] critics have for the most part neglected to recognize the unity of the book. There are many curious parallels: for instance, the convict saves the life of the woman but returns to penal labor; Harry Wilbourne, on the other hand, is the cause of the death of Charlotte and becomes a convict, sentenced to hard labor. For the convict, time on the river is fluid and is in sharp contrast with time in his prison camp—exact and demarcated. Harry Wilbourne finds time in eclipse through the flooding in of love that like the river carries him on for a while until he too is returned to clock time as a convict. The convict and the wave hang "suspended simultaneously and unprogressing in pure time";[24] Wilbourne at the cabin provided by McCord feels that he is in "a sunny and timeless void into which individual days had vanished" (p. 114).

It is impossible to discuss the myth without taking both parts of the novel into consideration. The "old man" that surges over its banks is the "wild palms," thrashing in typhoon or hurricane. Both represent violent and elemental forces of nature which are in conflict with man. The abortive thrashing of the palms and the rushing waters of birth actually parallel the actions in the story. The myth is the myth of all mankind

23. W. R. Moses, "*The Unity of The Wild Palms*," *Modern Fiction Studies*, II (Autumn, 1956), 125-31.
24. William Faulkner, *The Wild Palms* (New York, 1939), p. 170. Subsequent references to this volume appear in the text.

in conflict with forces of nature. The rushing waters of the river are a device, as in *As I Lay Dying,* to sustain the mood of timelessness. Faulkner does not succeed in sustaining this mood as well when he turns to the uncontrolled passion of Charlotte and Wilbourne, and this is perhaps the reason that this part of the novel is generally considered inferior.

Both the convict and Wilbourne (who are together the central character) find that they have transcended time, and each has a sense of purpose: Wilbourne, who chooses at the end to live in order to justify and become custodian of the love he has known, and the convict, who completes Wilbourne's actions in becoming custodian of the woman and deliverer of the child. Both characters are necessary to bring to fruition the action of the story. The sacrificial nature of the role of the central character leads to imprisonment as Darl's had led him to a different kind of imprisonment. In combating these forces of nature Wilbourne and the convict show us that love in its highest sense is the only means. This is a disinterested love that asks nothing for itself.

This knowledge is chiefly conscious with Wilbourne when he rejects death at the end; with the convict it is chiefly intuitive. Wilbourne has to learn it; the convict acts without knowing why he acts as he does. Both a conscious and an intuitive sense of reality working together are perhaps necessary to bring about salvation: on the physical level, the salvation embodied in the birth of the child, on the spiritual level, the salvation in the rebirth of Wilbourne when he learns that love transcends passion. There is a duality then in this book too. Since Wilbourne and the convict are both one figure and two at the same time, the intuitive and conscious approaches to reality do not merge as they do in Darl or Christmas. By himself Wilbourne fails as does the convict by himself; one is too ignorant to give meaning to his action, the other too conscious of his role. Faulkner avoids this duality in the figure of Sam Fathers in "The Bear."

"The Bear," like *The Wild Palms,* is the myth of man in conflict with the elemental forces of nature. The forest here stands, as the river may, as the timeless background to the legend. Through his style Faulkner shows us the nature of man's inner life which flows on beneath the superficial shadows of everyday existence. These shadows are seen to be superficial when the development of man's inner life takes precedence over his actions. The bear and the boy are absolved of mortality, and this becomes a tale of "memory from the long time before it even became his memory."[25]

In pursuing his goal, the boy abandons the mechanical aids of civilization, his compass and his watch. He learns that skill alone without humility and pride is not enough when Sam Fathers leads him to watch the little mongrel dog attack the bear. Neither Sam Fathers nor the boy shoots the bear because Sam knows and the boy is learning that "what the heart holds to becomes truth" (p. 297).

It is this recognition of an inner reality which has come to Darl, to Joe Christmas, and to Harry Wilbourne which composes the essence of Faulkner's heroes. For the boy it took fourteen years; for Sam Fathers seventy; and for the Negro race, "It will be long" (p. 297). This knowledge that what transcends time is what is essential is not then instinctive. It must be learned. The distinction here is not between white and black since McCaslin and Sam both know that truth is an inner affair, nor is it between the primitive and the civilized man. It is because, according to Faulkner, the Negro race will endure that they will become custodians of this knowledge that at present is in the hands of only a few. The Dilseys, the Lenas, with their instinctive understanding of their transcendence of time, will be translated into those more powerful figures like Darl, Christmas, and the corporal, who through their conscious knowledge of this power are able to employ it for larger ends. It is Sam's voice that speaks at the end when the "boy" encounters the snake, whereas it is Boon Hogganbeck, who has not learned that truth is an inner affair, who hammers frantically at his gun, a mechanical invention that

25. William Faulkner, *Go Down, Moses* (New York, 1942), p. 207. Subsequent references to this volume appear in the text.

like the boy's watch has no relation to the reality that lies within man.

The sense that the boy possesses of this particular hunt and of its past history, his sense that he has "already inherited" the bear, is secondary in this story to the larger conception of the hunt. The hunt for the bear and its eventual death and the history of the McCaslin tribe are the history of the South and its conflicts. The white man, equipped with weapons, enters the domain of the wild, the Negro. Possession means control, and for years "civilized" man shoots and traps, possessing and controlling and enslaving. Only one force, the bear, symbolic of the black race itself, remains beyond the power of force. Man is wary of this brute, lets him run his own way, trapping only those of lesser power, until the bear encroaches on the rights of man, killing the foal. Reasoning that the bear has now broken an unwritten code gives man the right to possess and kill. In a kind of glorified lynching, the death of the bear is brought about, both nature and man are destroyed, the South is laid waste. "Don't you see?" he cried. "Don't you see? This whole land, the whole South is cursed, and all of us who derive from it, whom it ever suckled, white and black both, lie under the same curse?" (P. 278.)

"The Bear" exemplifies the doctrine of original sin, of inherited evil, and the death and destruction dealt alike to the hunter and the hunted are the results of man's original folly, born of his pride and desire for possession. Even the forest at the end is about to be destroyed by a lumber camp. Lion, Sam, and Old Ben become symbols in the drama that unfolds, and their reality lies in their essence rather than in their existence. Sam Fathers' existence is subordinated in the end to the fact that, as his name indicates, he is the Father, the guiding principle behind the hunt. It is Sam who has found Lion, the instrument of this principle. The bear itself is more than mortal bear. The boy, who stands apart from the hunt, who does not shoot even when he is so close to the bear that he sees a tick fastened to it, observes the truth that embodies Faulkner's idea of truth. He sees that the challenge and the chase belong to a different realm, an abstract realm in which any challenge becomes larger than its actual statement. On his last visit to the camp he hunts for the graves of Sam Fathers and of Lion and finds the grave of Lion still marked by the huge paw of the bear. Now he knows that there is no death, that they are now free to pursue "the long challenge and the long chase, no heart to be driven and outraged, no flesh to be mauled and bled" (p. 329). This is Faulkner's solution to the plight of the South and of man, a recognition that truth is something more than physical possession.

In this fable of everyman, Sam Fathers plays a double role. Inextricably bound to his human state, to his existence, he follows the hunt, provides the means for concluding it, and experiences a kind of relief when the end appears in sight. At the same time Sam can also see beyond the hunt, advises the boy to abandon his gun, and himself does not shoot when the chance occurs. He thus plays the role of intermediary between the physical and the metaphysical, the existence and the essence, and it is he who points the way to the boy's understanding that truth may supersede the experience from which it springs.

From Sam Fathers we see that Faulkner does not feel that sacrifice in terms of brutality or imprisonment is essential. This kind of sacrifice seen in other novels of Faulkner is simply a temporary condition, for in Hightower's words man cannot accept pleasure so his religion drives him to the crucifixion of himself and others.

One can see then in Faulkner's novels a development that leads to *A Fable*. Lucas Beauchamp in *Intruder in the Dust* and Nancy in *Requiem for a Nun* are further attempts at creating the sacrificial figure who possesses a sense of transcendence of time. Lucas is not successful as such a figure because of his limited recognition of the inner nature of truth. Faulkner in this novel crowds all his action into one timeless instant: an instant of waiting for a momentous event. The action itself is almost comic relief compared with the intensity of this instant. Nancy is perhaps more successful than Lucas, but her sacrifice is a futile gesture, for Temple is too irresponsible to be worthy of it. Unlike Joe Christmas, Nancy does not become a symbol. Both novels possess a strong sense of the specific time of the South, which detracts from the timelessness of the myth.

The figure of the corporal in *A Fable* is then the result of a line of development starting with Darl Bundren. In this development we can see the influence of the New Testament on Faulkner's work. It is as if he were rewriting this story in terms of the South, the story of the man who seeks salvation for others through his own personal sacrifice and who thus transcends time and becomes a symbol. It is in this figure that Faulkner sees hope for the South and for mankind.

It is interesting to speculate too on the influence of Joyce on Faulkner's archetypal figures. By 1929 Faulkner had read *Dubliners* and *A Portrait;* he read *Ulysses* a year later. He has stated that he is heir to Joyce in the methods employed in *The Sound and the Fury.*[26] It can, therefore, be suggested that the corporal may be a descendent of Leopold Bloom or of HCE in that he represents, as both of them represent in some of their aspects, the Christ figure.

As myth *A Fable* is successful. The sense of timelessness is sustained in the early chapters by the shuffling of the days of the week. As the book works toward the climax, time in the chapter headings becomes chronological, but the style continues to create a timeless continuum. There is no sense of the individual past here. The division commander seems to have "been intended by fate itself to be the perfect soldier: pastless, unhampered, and complete."[27] The groom upon coming to America (in what is generally considered an interpolation) is a new man "without past, without griefs, without recollections" (p. 151). (Actually the story of the groom and the horse complements the main plot in much the same way as the two plots in *The Wild Palms* complement each other.) The story of the groom and the horse is a legend, the legend of "Adam and

26. Richard Ellmann, *James Joyce* (New York, 1959), p. 308.
27. William Faulkner, *A Fable* (New York, 1954), p. 21. Subsequent references to this volume appear in the text.

Lilith and Paris and Helen and Pyramus and Thisbe" (p. 153). It is the legend of love between two living creatures. Beyond this tale is seen contrapuntally the larger love of the corporal for all mankind. *A Fable* is essentially the fable of the "meteor-course of love and sacrifice" (p. 161), of the groom in a lesser sense, of the corporal in the larger sense.

A Proustian sense of duration appears only once—in the recalling by the division commander of his boyhood through the "chirring" of the cicada (p. 37). Essentially, however, with this exception a sense of timelessness is achieved by Faulkner. We have again here the timeless primitive in Marya, whose face "had no age at all; it had all ages or none" (p. 214). The division commander feels as if his speech to the old general had been part of him since the moment he knew he would go to officers' school. It was "part of the equipment with which he would follow and serve his destiny with his life" (p. 231). As a myth *A Fable* is not cluttered with the individual times of its characters and its events. Its background, World War I, is not essential to its character as myth. Any war could have set the scene for what Faulkner has to say. The central character, the corporal, is in full possession of the knowledge of his role in relation to past and future, and he permits his sacrifice in the realization that through it he transcends time.

The old general seeks to prevent the sacrifice because he knows that a symbol such as the one the corporal would create transcends civil power of which he is custodian. As custodian of the power of love, however, the corporal frees man from his blind subjection to civil power. The old general is the Father of the Old Testament, the law giver, from whom man is freed by the corporal, the new god, so that he may know the chief reality is an inner one. The corporal cannot read, but neither is he completely intuitive in his understanding of time. Like Darl he knows that ideas and feelings transcend time, and his sacrifice is an attempt to transmit this awareness to others. Until man abandons his watch and his compass, he is lost. In losing himself, however, in his forest, he will find himself. Faulkner's message is essentially the message of the New

Testament which is best transmitted to the reader in those novels like *A Fable* in which a sense of myth absorbs and transcends any sense of individual time.

Because Faulkner's figures are not always big enough to live up to their roles, figures such as those in *Sanctuary* or *Pylon*, critics have often turned with relief to such novels as *The Hamlet, The Town*, and *The Mansion* where Faulkner makes little attempt to invest his characters with anything but their individual significance. The final novel, *The Reivers*, also represents a line of development in which the archetypal, central figures and the transcendence of time are less significant than the particular activity described. The time of these novels is chiefly linear even though Flem Snopes may be seen as a figure in a legend of greed, dishonesty, and opportunism in the eternal "reconstruction" of the South and the boy in *The Reivers* the avatar of all plundered innocence. These books indicate, however, Faulkner's essential pessimism about the time process itself and demonstrate the reason for his need to transcend time through symbol and myth. Faulkner's dependence on linear time in some of his novels points to a despair more profound than that evoked by the thought, "You can't go home again." But these books have the virtue of avoiding the duality of subjectivity and essence which is disturbing in novels like *Sanctuary*.

PART V
RETURN
TO FRANCE

CHAPTER NINE

JEAN-PAUL SARTRE:

FLIGHT

INTO THE FUTURE

1

Sartre has written of Faulkner, "I like his art, but I do not believe in his metaphysics."[1] A metaphysics of time with no progression into the future, a "Fui. Non sum" attitude, is for Sartre a decapitation of time. The very nature of consciousness is according to him a progression into the future. He rejects the deprivation by both Faulkner and Proust of time's "dimension of deeds and freedom."[2] Faulkner's heroes face backwards, he claims.

Part of Faulkner's art in his novels comes directly from his concept of time. For example, Faulkner's "undiscoverable" men, whom Sartre admires, who exist beyond their consciousness of existing, exist thus for Faulkner because of their "pastness," their inherent awareness of their roles in terms of history, not of the future. It is the universal, extra-temporal, or abstract

1. Jean-Paul Sartre, *Literary and Philosophical Essays*, trans. Annette Michelson (New York, 1955), p. 87.
2. *Ibid.*, p. 84.

quality that Bayard Sartoris, Joe Christmas, and the corporal possess that gives them their silentness, their darkness. Faulkner is consistent in his "decapitation" of time, nor can he be claimed by existentialists as one who reveals to us only concrete, subjective existence. The future rests for Faulkner often in terms of the symbol, of the role that Dilsey or Joe Christmas plays, not in individual plans or decisions. What Sartre admires in Faulkner's use of time is, as Pierre de Boisdeffre writes, the way he makes temporality the substance of consciousness and of things.[3] And yet Faulkner's temporality is one based on the past.

Sartre's own conception of time marks a sharp departure from the Bergsonian-Proustian metaphysics of time seen thus far as basic to much of the fiction which has been discussed. In *Being and Nothingness* Sartre affirms that a consciousness of *durée*, of the flowing of time, only discovers itself to him when he wants to see it.[4] Sartre's philosophy of time also marks a departure, as does Bergsonism, from the Hegelian abstraction, from the Platonic theory of ideas which are in line with such symbolic representations as Faulkner's characters in *A Fable*, Kafka's K., or Mann's Faustus. Writing of Kafka in the essay "Aminadab," Sartre suggests that for Kafka "a transcendental reality certainly existed" but that since it is beyond our reach it gives us "a sharper feeling of man's abandonment in the realm of the human."[5] Sartre sees Kafka as only a stage on the way and says that M. Blanchot "delivers us from him." Is a technique based on a transcendent reality one from which we need deliverance? Its purposes and ends are only different from Sartrian technique, not better or worse. Identification with the symbolic character is possible in a different way from identification with concrete representation. And both identification and a sense of separateness are necessary and possible in the confrontation of either type of character. Kafka's K. represents a wider spectrum of qualities than Sartre's Antoine Roquentin.

3. Pierre de Boisdeffre, *Metamorphose de la littérature* (Paris, 1951), II, 210.

4. Jean-Paul Sartre, *Being and Nothingness*, trans. Hazel E. Barnes (New York, 1956), p. 169.

5. Sartre, *Essays* p. 59.

(It is difficult to agree with Iris Murdoch that Sartre intends to offer us in Roquentin "an image of the human situation in general.")[6] Everyman, Bunyan's Christian, Milton's Adam, Kafka's K. because of their general character do not preclude the individual identity of the reader while at the same time they include that identity. Camus' Meursault or Sartre's Delarue encourage both identification and an objective view of their positions, for they are individuals and yet individuals who proclaim their own identities.

Sartre's own ideas of time as outlined in *Being and Nothingness* contribute directly to the techniques and character development employed in his novels. In his chapter on temporality Sartre, as Jeanne Delhomme puts it, transforms the Bergsonian thesis of activity and priority of consciousness so that consciousness becomes a negative dimension of being.[7] Delhomme sees Bergson as a metaphysician, Sartre as an ontologist. Time for Bergson is the condition of creative liberty whereas for Sartre liberty is a negation and consequently a negation of time. Sartre sees consciousness not as the essence of the spirit but as an original flaw of being.

Sartre shows us that the past gets its meaning from the present and the present from the future. There are two kinds of being, the For-itself and the In-itself. The temporality of the human consciousness, or of the For-itself, is the present. Everything is present, even the past "as a present impression in the body."[8] "The present is really the For-itself in its flight out of the past into the future."[9] Sartre believes that we gain nothing by conceding being to the past, for the past is never "isolated in its pastness."[10] "The past can haunt the present, but it cannot *be* the present; it is the present which *is* its past."[11]

For Sartre it is the future that defines each moment of

6. Iris Murdoch, *Sartre: Romantic Rationalist* (New Haven, Connecticut, 1959), p. 11.

7. Jeanne Delhomme, "Le problème de l'intériorité: Bergson et J.-P. Sartre," *Revue internationale de philosophie*, No. 48 (1959), p. 201.

8. Sartre, *Being and Nothingness*, p. 108.

9. Wilfred Desan, *The Tragic Finale* (Cambridge, Massachusetts, 1954), p. 39.

10. Sartre, *Being and Nothingness*, p. 110.

11. *Ibid.*, p. 113.

consciousness. The conscious being plans and waits for the future, which is "the continual possibilization of possibles."[12] The image of "gnawing," which was also Bergson's, is used by Sartre differently to indicate the action of the For-itself, in its freedom, on the future. Thus there is progress in time as a result of the freedom of the For-itself, which determines that which can be and that which cannot be.

It is evident that these ideas are directly related to Sartre's techniques as a novelist. In *What Is Literature?* Sartre talks of a new dimension of temporality for the writer, the Present. The aim of art must be to "restore to the event its brutal freshness, its ambiguity, its unforeseeability."[13] This quality of the irreversibility of time, he says, belongs to our age alone. The technical problem will be solved by giving up the omniscient narrator, by "suppressing the intermediaries between the reader and... the viewpoints of our characters."[14] For this reason Sartre abandoned the stream-of-consciousness technique he had used in *Nausea* for a technique of multiplicity, "an orchestration of consciousness," employed in his later novels. Pierre de Boisdeffre in an excellent analysis of Sartre's later style suggests the contradiction implicit in the aims of the multiple technique. If the author must not come between the reader and the subjectivity of the characters, who is to direct the camera? A brutal realism excludes the author entirely and all art on the part of the novelist.[15] Sartre explains, however, that the artist must mask his choices by aesthetic tricks so that the story will *appear* to retain "the innocence of the virgin forest."[16] Even the reader must forget himself as an onlooker. Still, as Maurice Blanchot sees, writing is the experience of experience and as such makes renewal of original experience impossible.[17]

12. *Ibid.*, p. 129.
13. Jean-Paul Sartre, *What Is Literature?* trans. Bernard Frechtman (London, 1950), p. 167.
14. *Ibid.*, p. 229.
15. Boisdeffre, *Metamorphose*, p. 213.
16. Sartre, *What Is Literature?* p. 229.
17. Maurice Blanchot, "Les romans de Sartre," *L'Arche*, X (October, 1945), 121-34.

2

In the novels of Sartre his philosophy of time can be seen to have a directive influence. The undated entries at the beginning of *Nausea* indicate an initial dependency in Roquentin on the mechanics of time, for without the assurance of the regular recurrence of the tram he would feel lost. The diary that follows is just such a means of marking out time. But it becomes clear that far from being cured from fear, as he thinks, by his confidence in clock time, one of Roquentin's problems centers around his innocence about the nature of time.

Time, like other physical referents, must in Sartrian thinking be delivered from its name. Roquentin characterizes time as "wide, soft instants, spreading at the edge, like an oil stain."[18] This is the time of purple suspenders and broken chair seats. Thus he pictures time as an object, perceptible to the senses. Time is a mode of existence, and an oil stain indicates Sartre's particular kind of time in this novel—greasy, almost stagnant, slightly odorous. One critic sees time in this novel as having the consistency of soft dough.[19]

Music, which is to show Roquentin the real nature of time, a present always plunging into the future, is introduced as a theme early in the novel. Music jabs at time, tears at it, inserts its own rhythm. Within it lies the possibility of deliverance from clock time; it is not as with Thomas Mann another means of measuring time. Music's internality will crush time's shell and allow its hearer a possibility of fulfillment. *Our* time will be replaced by another. The richness of a moment filled with music comes from the fact that so many notes have died that this note might be born. This is in sharp contrast to Bergson's parallel between music and time in which he sees each previous note still existing in the present one as the past persists in the present. The voice of the Negress which recurs throughout the novel defines the very nature of the time

18. Jean-Paul Sartre, *Nausea*, trans. Lloyd Alexander (Norfolk, Connecticut, 1959), p. 33.

19. Louis Bolle, *Les lettres et l'absolu, Valéry-Sartre-Proust* (Genève, 1959), p. 126.

experience for Sartre. Unlike the Vinteuil sonata that for Proust revives the past in the present, this song of the Negress stresses contemporaneity, drawing the listener into its presentness. Even the words of the lyric, "Some of these days/ You'll miss me, honey," fit in with the Sartrian rationale, for they point not to the past "retrouvé" but to the future, to a decision in the present which will shape a future. It is difficult to feel that this musical theme is not used with an irony directed at Proust. Sartre in the terms of one critic is "a poor man's Proust."[20] The Negress' song says to Roquentin: if you neglect me now, you will later be sorry. Vinteuil's sonata says to Swann: if you are neglected now, you can be reassured for the past is never lost. Although Sartre found interesting the effect of the work of music in Proust and the relation between artistic creation and the recapturing of lost time, he alters their significance by rejecting Proust's veneration and nostalgia for the past itself and by suggesting that the past is dead and may not be relived in the present, even though it may "haunt" the present.

The nature of time for Sartre is made graphically clear through Roquentin's meditations on an old woman whom he sees from his window. He knows she will turn right on the Boulevard Victor-Noir, but he watches her crawl along, fascinated by the process of the present turning into the future. He cannot be sure whether he sees her motions or foresees them. This is the very core of existence laid bare. Furthermore, the passage comments on the movement of time. Its realizations are slow, take an eternity, for we know and at the same time do not know the future. The old woman could have turned left. But her motions are more meaningful evaluations of time than the movement of the hands of the clock, for whereas the clock is utterly predictable, it omits the human element—the decision to walk fast or slow, the decision to turn right or left.

In fact, the entire novel could be seen as an attempt to

20. Henry A. Grubbs, "Sartre's Recapturing of Lost Time," *Modern Language Notes,* LXXIII (November, 1958), 522.

define or pin down the nature of time. In a sense it is the story of Roquentin's education in the subject of time. His initial innocence about time as seen in his dependence on clock time at the beginning begins to be dispelled as, for instance, he meditates on time and the oil stain or as he watches the old woman. Then the relation of the past to the present begins to occupy his thoughts. Two years ago he had been able to conjure up the past. Now he is unable to do this, for he feels his past is fragmented and scattered like dead leaves. Calm descends when he no longer feels the passing of time. Robert Champigny writes that whereas the bourgeois of Bouville recognize themselves in their photographs, Roquentin does not see himself in his picture of the past.[21] He learns that things are what they appear to be and that behind them is nothing. It is after this realization that he decides to abandon his biography of M. de Rollebon. An attempt of this sort, to re-create the past, is meaningless, for it assumes that the past can be made to live again. He calls the past bourgeois, "a landlord's luxury," for when you wish to understand something, you confront it alone and without help. It is this growing sense of nothingness behind things and events, the sense of an inert past, which marks Roquentin's maturation. The necessity of recurrence, of the return of the tram or of the man from Rouen, is no longer a necessity for Roquentin. He recognizes that a sense of adventure is something we add to events and that it comes from the fact that time is irreversible. We simply think we see time passing. Actually adventure is adventure only when it is dead.

The train for which Roquentin waits at the end is a symbol of the moving present which will carry him into the future. In the meantime as he waits, he experiences an almost Joycean epiphany in his recognition that through an artistic expression that aims not at describing what *has existed* but at what is above existence, a work of pure imagination, he can perhaps be saved as the Jewish composer of the song and the Negress

21. Robert Champigny, "Sens de *La Nausée*," *PMLA*, LXX (March, 1955), 39.

singer are saved. In Bouville he leaves behind only rain.

Seen sociologically Proust's work looks back with nostalgia to the nineteenth century; Sartre's on the contrary, is a philosophy of the future in which the past is abandoned, obliterated to make room for seemingly impossible, new creations. For Sartre the gesture in the past must have vanished so that other gestures can be born.

Although Sartre was later to object to the "monologue intérieur," which he employs in *Nausea,* as a rhetorical process that comes between the consciousness of the reader and the character, because thoughts are not equivalent to words,[22] *Nausea* does succeed to some degree in enabling the reader to merge with the central character and in giving a sense of the presentness of events and of the onrushing future. Sartre himself called *Nausea* not a novel but a "journal intime." It is perhaps the fact that it *is* a journal, that it is Roquentin's transcription of his own thoughts into his own words, that presents less of a barrier to the reader than the ordinary employment of this technique. Champigny sees that through this technique "the present is interiorized and takes on an aesthetic aspect as if it were dreamed. . . ."[23] By contrast the first person narrative used, for example, in the short story "The Wall" lacks interiority, although the style of "The Wall" and of "Erostratus" may be seen as closely linked to that of *Nausea.*

Furthermore, Fredric Jameson has pointed out how Sartre's use of punctuation reflects his theory of time, his theory of its continuity and its divisibility, its expansion and its contraction. Time is "the way we live the world," and Sartre's style is founded on this theory. His dialogue, Jameson says, sounds as if it were lifted from someone's mind.[24]

Not only is the present interiorized by Sartre's style in this novel but it is objectified at the same time. The frequent staccato rhythm, the clipped sentences, remind one of Flaubert's precise style, of his clinical detachment. There is less sense of

22. Boisdeffre, *Metamorphose,* p. 210.
23. Champigny, "Sens de *La Nausée,*" *PMLA,* p. 39.
24. Fredric Jameson, *Sartre: The Origins of a Style* (New Haven, Connecticut, 1961), Chapter 3.

flow than in the usual stream-of-consciousness method as seen, for example, in Mrs. Woolf's *The Waves*. Roquentin writes: "I knew him: he was in the library the evening I was so frightened. I think he was afraid too. I thought: how far away all that is."[25] These sequences give less the effect of mind time than of a scientific commentary on experience. Although the reader is within Roquentin's mind, he is there not first-hand but as a result of the consideration of Roquentin upon his experiences. Thus an objective point of view combines with a subjective one to give us an indication of the nature of experience in which we continually see the present not only in terms of our feelings but in terms of our judgments on those feelings. The same combination of the objective and the subjective is found in Flaubert, who could write of Emma Bovary with scientific detachment while at the same time proclaiming: "Madame Bovary, c'est moi."

The Flaubertian parallels cannot be fully explored here, but it should be noted that the simultaneous reading of *Eugénie Grandet* by Roquentin and the conversing of the husband and wife in the Brasserie Vézélin recall the technique in Flaubert's famous scene at the agricultural show, granted an interesting difference in purpose, and that Bouville with its Watchdog Club and its Boy Scouts is a twentieth-century Yonville fashioned by the progeny of M. Homais. But chiefly it is the abrupt rendering of experience which Sartre and Flaubert have in common—the "jerkiness" Sartre speaks of in connection with the rhythm of time. "Rollebon is dead" echoes the words of Flaubert at the death of Charles Bovary's first wife. Both styles imply the nothingness behind being, a stripping of experience to its barest essentials, a denial of essence.

But whereas Flaubert's target may have been in part the general romantic attitude as embodied by Emma Bovary, Sartre may satirize more specifically, as some critics have suggested, the concept of time and reality of Proust. Rémy G. Saisselin shows that whereas Bouville is present and possesses only

25. Sartre, *Nausea*, p. 216.

a false past, Combray is full of past time.[26] Instead of the romantic echoes associated with Combray, Bouville echoes, as does Bovary, that which is bovine. *Bouvier* (cowherd), *bouvillon* (steer), *bouc* (goat) all come to mind as well as the Latin *bos, bovis*. Set against Combray with its pink hawthornes, its lilacs, and its Corot-like landscapes, Bouville represents a reality beyond which a transcendence is impossible. There is also the French word *boue* meaning mud. The mockery implied in Sartre's use of the musical phrase has already been mentioned. In general, there is a transcendence in Proust, an existence beyond the object or person which characterizes Proust's approach to reality; with Sartre we are arrested by the thing itself, for there is nothing beyond it, nothing behind it.

Sartre's derogatory attitude toward Proust is, of course, well known. However, it is impossible not to feel that although he rejects Proust and his emphasis on a transcendent reality, on a past persisting in the present, Proust appears, as Robert Cohn puts it, as a "revenant father ghost"[27] especially in *Nausea* the conclusion of which echoes at the same time that it derides the conclusion of *Swann's Way* where there is ironically no real catharsis as there is in *Nausea*.

The return of Anny near the end of *Nausea* is not for Sartre the same kind of return which Roquentin has experienced in the return of the man from Rouen at the beginning or the same kind of return which we find in Joyce's or Mann's novels. For Roquentin has learned that experience cannot be reduplicated. Had Sartre believed in an eternal recurrence the novel would have ended happily with Anny's reappearance. But since there is for Sartre no essence of experience which can continue into the present, the meeting with Anny is a new meeting and not a return. It is a meeting in which Roquentin discovers that there are no perfect moments, that both he and Anny have "changed together and in the same way." Both move into their

26. Rémy G. Saisselin, "Bouville où l'anti-Combray," *French Review,* XXXIII (January, 1960), 234.

27. Robert Greer Cohn, "Sartre vs. Proust," *Partisan Review,* XXVIII (November, 1961), 635.

separate futures as does the Self-Taught Man, who in the final pages achieves his own particular destiny. It is Roquentin alone, however, who is saved through his recognition of his error in wishing to revive the Marquis de Rollebon. Reoriented through the music toward the future, toward the moving train that will carry him to Paris, he sees that he can succeed only by accepting the past as a *fait accompli*, that the desire to revive the past is a desire to change it, but that it is the future, not the past, that may be changed or decided. Unlike Camus' Meursault, who experiences joy in a passive acceptance of his role in society as a condemned murderer, Roquentin experiences joy in his knowledge of his active ability to determine his future, even though this determination is "simply a sketch of a solution."[28]

3

Sartre's technique in his next novel, *The Age of Reason* (1945), differs from that in *Nausea* although the aim is similar—the capturing of true temporality. The use of the third-person narrative is, at first glance, more or less conventional. The order is chronological, involving a kind of counterpoint or interplay among the main characters. But examining the style more closely we can see how Sartre attempts to render here an effect of "multi-dimensionality" more possible of achievement in the third person than in the first person narrative of *Nausea*.

Sartre's own comment on time in this novel, "time passed with abrupt and fateful jerks,"[29] characterizes his style. Since conversions, or moments of change, are the only real moments in our lives, according to Sartre, we progress through time in a series of leaps, everything in between each stop becoming insignificant. Not only the sentence structure, as Jameson has shown,[30] but the structure of episodes in the novel reflect this theory. Each episode is in itself an entity, a moment of decision, a "projet." The opening scene between Mathieu and

28. Murdoch, *Sartre: Romantic Realist*, p. 12.
29. Jean-Paul Sartre, *The Age of Reason*, trans. Eric Sutton (New York, 1959), p. 50.
30. See Jameson, *Sartre*, pp. 49 ff.

Marcelle gives us Mathieu's decision for freedom. Then a scene between Boris and Lola shows us Boris' attempt to make a similar decision. But Boris' freedom is a mockery, for passion picks him up by the neck "like a rabbit." At the same time he succeeds in maintaining a certain degree of detachment with Lola. Perhaps he has chosen an older woman for the very reason he suggests for her choice of him—that he is too young, thus avoiding the dangers of involvement. A third scene between Mathieu and Sarah likewise assumes a completeness and yet is tied to Chapter 1 by its irony in the light of Mathieu's "projet" to take the responsibility for his own existence. His first move has been to seek help from another and from one whose humility makes him want to hurt her. Each of these scenes contains the wholeness of a short story; at the same time each contributes to the organic unity of the novel. They illustrate Sartre's feeling about time as "a unity which multiplies itself"[31] and as such contribute to the sense of "multi-dimensionality" in the novel.

Another means of creating this sense is the polyphony of states of consciousness and events found in Sartre's style. The thoughts of the characters are brought out at crucial moments of conflict or decision like that of Mathieu after his visit to Sarah. These passages stress the inner flow of consciousness and thereby achieve continuity whereas a series of events recorded by Sartre often gives one a sense of time's divisibility. Sartre had characterized in *Nausea* two different kinds of moments: those that may be reversible and those when the links have been tightened.[32] Adventure or events, he says, occur when time seems to be irreversible. A state of consciousness, however, embodies the reversibility of time. The interplay of these two subject matters in his novels creates the same sort of tension between continuity and divisibility that Jameson points out in the sentence structure.

Furthermore, the inner being of the characters is brought forward at points in the novel when the future seems dead.

31. *Ibid.*, p. 45.
32. Sartre, *Nausea*, p. 80.

Thus in Chapter 3 the problem of Marcelle's pregnancy leads Mathieu to turn to the past, to a day in his childhood when he had played at ceasing to exist and to another day when he had smashed a three-thousand-year-old vase. States of consciousness may indicate for Sartre time's continuity; at the same time they are inserted by Sartre when despair for the future overtakes a character, for through them the fresh future of each day may be arrested in static introspection.

These theories become especially clear in the climactic scenes of both Mathieu and Daniel near the end of the novel. After Mathieu's rejection by Ivich, he feels that no one now inhabits his body. Mathieu's thoughts here indicate a stasis in which the man's future that once challenged him is dead. In this passage we feel that Mathieu loses touch with reality. Not until he makes the decision to steal the money from Lola does the world of cars, people, and shop windows return.

The emphasis in the climactic scene involving Daniel is different, however. Mathieu negates his freedom; Daniel finds his. Despairing of a future, Daniel confronts the razor in a scene in which we see into his mind. Unlike Mathieu's loss of touch with reality, this scene indicates a close engagement with reality as the images show. For instance, "The flame runs along the fuse"[33] shows symbolically the progression of time, the present moving into the future, a future that seems at the moment to lead to an explosion, to death or disfigurement. But Daniel's inner experience is coherent whereas Mathieu's had not been. Daniel never loses sight of the razor; thus he is enabled to reject it and its power and to run from it. The fuse then sputters and goes out, but a future is gained for Daniel as he learns that "there is a way." At the same moment as Daniel runs from the scene, the emphasis on inner reality is abandoned for a narrative of events. Real movement into the future returns. Interplay of states of consciousness and events seems to indicate then a concerted effort to combine both time's irreversibility and its reversibility at the level of experience. In *What Is Literature?* Sartre wrote of a style that

33. Sartre, *The Age of Reason*, p. 303.

would permit him "to render the multi-dimensionality of the event" (p. 229). He hoped to go beyond Joyce's subjective realism to a new realism, that of temporality. Temporality involves both events and states of consciousness. Both are reflected in all three volumes of *The Roads to Freedom,* and this discussion has attempted to show at what moments and why Sartre turns to the inner man.

In contrast to other writers of interior monologue, Sartre often uses quotation marks when his characters' thoughts are given. This enables him to stand apart from the character and enables the reader to see the character not through Sartre, but immediately. Of Kafka, Sartre has written that he "sees the fantastic *from the outside,* as a spectacle."[34] Sartre's heroes like Kafka's are seen from the outside and thereby lend us their point of view. This is what Sartre means by a new realism of temporality which allows the reader complete access to the character. The difficulty in the way of the success of Sartre's style is, of course, the pronoun *he* which implies an *I* observing the *he.* Sartre's aim, to mask the choices of the author,[35] is unlikely to be realized. Perhaps "un journal intime" is after all the closest approach to this ideal.

The subject matter of *The Age of Reason* plays on the same theory of time's reversibility and irreversibility found behind the style. Although the main theme of the book is that of freedom, Sartre's view of freedom is closely connected with his concept of the past. The smashing of the three-thousand-year-old vase enables Mathieu as a boy to achieve freedom from the past, "from the world, without ties or kin or origins."[36] Such an act underlies the meaning of the entire novel. What Sartre and Mathieu want is an act, "a free, considered act" that will "stand at the beginning of a new existence"[37] to which they can pledge their entire lives. This is what Roquentin has perhaps found at the end of *Nausea* in the book he will write. But this act must not be tied to the past as the vase or as Proust's

34. Sartre, *Essays,* p. 65.
35. Sartre, *What Is Literature?* p. 229.
36. Sartre, *The Age of Reason,* pp. 52-53.
37. *Ibid.,* p. 54.

madeleine. As Louis Bolle puts it, the memories in Sartre's novels do not ever take on body; they are signs, not reality.[38] The past is dead; M. de Rollebon cannot be revived. The problem is to engage oneself in the present, which Mathieu has never been able to do. He feels still unborn. But the unborn child within Marcelle is an ironic commentary on Mathieu's plight. For Marcelle, unable to free herself from a past act, experiencing morning sickness, the word *Freedom* has only sardonic overtones. Unborn, like the child he has created, Mathieu too faces possible abortion, abortion signifying death of the future. Over the whole book hangs Mathieu's commitment to Marcelle and his frantic attempts to find money for the abortion, creating an irony in connection with his utterances about freedom which can be seen only in the light of the present in which he is trapped. It is Daniel who achieves freedom, not by aborting himself (i.e., castrating himself), but by committing himself to Marcelle and to the future of that which is unborn. This is a new existence but an unauthentic one. It is Daniel who lives what Mathieu preaches, but he does so by denying his identity.

Mathieu's despair grows. His childhood resolution "I will be free" is continually being retouched by the present. In Sartre the past is never seen as an entity in itself—only in relation to its future. Thus the characters seem to come together by chance in the present; like Kafka's characters they have no childhoods of any extent. There is no history of their past relations with each other. We pick them up seemingly *in medias res.* Although Proust and Faulkner may have decapitated one head of time, its future, Sartre may have decapitated another head, its past. Time is reversible for him only at moments when the future is dead.

At the end of the novel Mathieu still has not found his act of commitment. He is nothing and will not change. Tried and proved rules of conduct, "disillusioned epicureanism, smiling tolerance, resignation, flat seriousness, stoicism,"[39] all have sup-

38. Bolle, *Valéry-Sartre-Proust,* p. 126.
39. Sartre, *The Age of Reason,* p. 342.

ported him in his failure. The book is the tragedy of the death of the future of Mathieu's youth, for "the age of reason" he attains at the end represents the failure of his dream. The title of the book is a phrase uttered first by Mathieu's "sensible" lawyer brother, Jacques, who tells Mathieu that he should have attained this age. But for Mathieu the age of reason is the age of resignation, of resignation to nothingness. However, he is to be granted a reprieve.

4

The Reprieve describes a period during which as Robert Campbell points out the past is contaminated by the future. It is an imaginary future filled with nightmares and hallucinations, which envelops everything, smothers everything, even the past that becomes detached like an organ exterior to the body.[40] The book reflects a theory of time quite different from Bergson's. No episode has being until the last instant that gives the event its determining character. For Bergson, every note of a composition contains all the other notes; for Sartre, the future or the final note affects and determines those that precede it. Thus until the reprieve, brought about by the decision at Munich, is announced, no judgment of the epoch is possible. The whole book rests on the final instant in which Daladier pronounces the judgment: "The God-damned fools!"

It is not that Sartre denies the past or its significance or the reversibility of some moments. He feels rather that writers like Proust in attempting to reanimate or recapture the past in the present have distorted it. The past is in a constant state of re-evaluation by the present, and the meaning of the past varies in relation to future *projets*. Thus in *The Reprieve* Sartre examines only the present moment. The characters seem thrown together or apart by chance, not causality. Even if a memory is reborn, it is reborn in the present. And in the present we find being as well as nothingness behind or beyond being.

The Reprieve illustrates more fully the theories of style

40. Robert Campbell, *Jean-Paul Sartre où une littérature philosophique* (Paris, 1947), pp. 70-71.

discussed in the section on *The Age of Reason*, the interplay of continuity and divisibility. Beneath each date, a shell of reality, which heads each chapter runs a mélange of events. There is less interpenetration of events than in *The Age of Reason*. Some are related after others or interrupt one another with no transi- tions whatsoever. There is no apparent order or meaning to the arrangement although all episodes are tied together by their contemporaneity. This is raw temporality through which Sartre attempts to rid his book of a sense of the manipulating author. Aldous Huxley's technique of multiplicity seems stylized and self-conscious by comparison.

For example, on Saturday, September 24, we begin at Crévilly with the waking of Daddy Croulard, turn to Hitler, to Chamberlain, to Daniel, then return to Daddy Croulard, who is to paste the mobilization posters on the walls; Ivich moans faintly in her sleep. These people are related only in that they all exist on this date, but they exist in different milieu, play different roles. Each is subject, however, in his own way to the mobilization orders. The evaluation of the past is for each a separate act.

Nor is the story seen through the mind of one character. In the passage discussed above only two of the characters know each other personally. This multiple effect gives a sense of confusion and allows the reader to feel omnipresent and yet unable to sort out what he is observing. However, in spite of Sartre's attempt to negate his own role, we are aware of an author, an author who, for example, inserts the names of Hitler or Chamberlain as a kind of threat, an ominous warning to the ant-like societies they control. It is the author who pauses on one scene and then runs very rapidly through a number of scenes. It is Sartre who believes that time proceeds by jerks. Champigny suggests that although the world of *Nausea* had been almost Parmenidean, that of *The Roads to Freedom* is Heraclitean.[41] The interior monologue used in *Nausea* leads to a sense of rest, of stasis, for when we turn to the inner man we

41. Robert Champigny, *Stages on Sartre's Way, 1938-52*, (Bloomington, Indiana, 1959), p. 43.

put the emphasis on the unity of time. On the contrary, the blind conjunction of events reported in *The Reprieve* emphasizes the infinite number of positions achieved by the arrow in its jerky progression toward its target.

Furthermore, we are aware of the author in the figure of Mathieu, who in his search for a free act has an affinity with Sartre. Although the age of reason collapses for Mathieu in this novel, his childhood resolution to be free remains warm. His commitment is not achieved, but there is a reprieve granted. It is possible to see emerging here in Mathieu, through the efforts of Sartre to present raw temporality, a figure who can stand for the general figure of the Western European trapped by the threats that hovered over Europe in the 1930's, trapped by the future and by consequence longing for a freedom that his times have denied him. There is perhaps a transcendence in Sartre's work which he never intended. Mathieu's life parallels that of Western culture of which he is a part. His childhood dream of freedom, like that fostered by World War I, has not been realized but replaced by "the age of reason," a false façade of maturity adopted by an entire society in the twenties and thirties, a resignation to a *status quo*. The reprieves granted this society by the appeasements of Hitler are at the expense of the rape of helpless countries to which an age of reason closed its eyes, an age of Daladier's "God-damned fools!"

5

In the third volume of *The Roads to Freedom*, *Troubled Sleep*, Western culture does not die as Mathieu does, but there is "death in the soul" ("la mort dans l'âme") as there is death in Mathieu's finally achieved act of commitment. "He fired: he was cleansed, he was all-powerful, he was free."[42] This is a decision for the future, for life through death. Not all France, not all the West laid down its arms. Part 1 of this novel leads us from the futile laughter of the men at the moment of sur-

42. Jean-Paul Sartre, *Troubled Sleep*, trans. Gerard Hopkins (New York, 1961), p. 200.

render, at the mock armistice, as they hang their heads "against the wall of Absurdity and the wall of Fate" to Mathieu's commitment to freedom, a commitment which was that of his culture as a whole. It is the freedom of the boy in Faulkner's "The Bear" who by losing himself finds himself.

Pinette, the young subway employee, whom Mathieu follows through his own decision to join those who are holding out, reaches his fulfillment. His birth and death meet and he is wholly himself. For Mathieu it at first seems that Pinette will die for nothing. Then Sartre projects Mathieu into a future without Pinette, a future in which he thinks back upon the "tender youth who had been killed June 18, 1940."[43] It is this projection that enables Mathieu to make his own decision, for he feels utterly alone in this imagined future. Roquentin had recognized that in a sense we know the future; Mathieu in this scene knows the future by distinguishing between two futures and thereby choosing to die the same death as Pinette.

Part 2 of the novel turns to Brunet, who represents the communist future of Europe as Sartre may have seen it at this time. Critics suggest that Sartre has not finished volume four of *The Roads to Freedom* because there seems now nowhere for the future to go.

Brunet's time sense differs from Mathieu's because he has made his decision; Mathieu had not made his until near the end of his life. Brunet is able, as Mathieu had not been able, to resist the distortion of time brought about by his imprisonment. Mathieu, imprisoned in a different way in *The Age of Reason,* had succumbed to that distortion. Brunet resents the fact that the prison experience filches time from him. Normal referents are meaningless and events that seem to go fast actually fill up long periods of time. Subjectivity of this sort he terms "a sticky sap."[44] For Brunet, made whole by his commitment to communism, imprisonment is simply a shell within which he functions. For Mathieu the fact of Marcelle's pregnancy imprisons his whole being.

43. *Ibid.*, p. 157.
44. *Ibid.*, p. 251.

Brunet's time sense becomes especially clear in the scene in which he climbs a hillock in the prison yard. Below he views the men playing, ironically, prisoner's base. A scene from his earlier life revives in which he had seen children in a town playing at the same game. Unlike Mathieu in the episode in *The Age of Reason* when he remembers his childhood, Brunet cannot remember "where that was." Mathieu had been unable to remake the past in the present. Brunet, on the contrary, ponders on his future, on his reason for working with the communist cell while he is in prison. He will not, like the men he watches, play at imprisonment while he is imprisoned. Instead he is able to reject the sterile past for his work as a communist, for the future which he sees born in each instant.

An escape into the past is an escape from reality. And only once does Brunet succumb to it when he hears the first train rolling again in the night. In spite of himself the past revives and he imagines a sleeping car of the era of his childhood. His rude awakening to six bats clinging to his prison ceiling soon dispels his fantasy, however.

A train symbol is used in this novel at the end as it was at the end of *Nausea* but in a different way. On the train into Germany Brunet feels that the inner man is paralyzed. He is going nowhere; no future is possible. "He was in a great ash can; somebody was kicking about inside it."[45] Sartre thus demonstrates that real movement, like time, is in terms of the inner man, not in terms of the train. All progress is suspended— only darkness and black birds remain, birds that will pick at the dead printer's body. Time stops although the train proceeds by jerks. Even Brunet's commitment to his party does not nullify the fact that complete immobility is possible on the train of life.

The two episodes of a proposed volume four printed under the title "Drôle d'amitié" do little to alleviate this immobility. "Time runs, the rain runs, time and the rain are the same."[46]

45. *Ibid.*, p. 330.
46. Jean-Paul Sartre, "Drôle d'amitié," *Les temps modernes,* V (November, 1949), 769-806; (December, 1949), 1009-1039.

But Brunet remains alone and immobile for he has recognized that the party has made a fool of him. During an attempt to escape, his friend Vicarios is wounded, but Brunet stays by him knowing that when Vicarios dies it is to him that death has come as Mathieu had recognized with Pinette. However, the title, "the absurdity of friendship," suggests the absurdity of both Mathieu's and Brunet's final decisions. The streaming of the rain indicates the same empty motion as that of the train, and yet like the train, which returns, the rain enables life to return perhaps foretelling a renewal and rebirth that thus far Sartre has not implemented.

Sartre's abandonment of dates or hours as a framework for Part 2 of *Troubled Sleep* makes the jerks that Sartre has seen as an underlying characteristic of time less evident. Part 2 is less episodic and more continuous in its effect. This is partly the result of the change in time values caused by the deprivation of exterior freedom that throws the characters into an interior world where the emphasis is on an inner continuum. We turn to states of consciousness freed from the twenty-four clock hours by virtue of the death of the future for the prisoners. The despair or immobility experienced by Brunet in the final pages of *Troubled Sleep* can only be reflected in a time experience where all progress into the future is arrested. Clock time in the other novels and in Part 1, then, although only a scaffolding for Sartre is significant in that through it the possibilization of the possible is realized. In *Nausea* Roquentin's diary did not get underway until a symbolic procession of hours and days could be erected to support the superstructure of Roquentin's spiritual catharsis. One can see in Sartre's novels a use of time's compressibility and its expansions, its divisibility and its unity beyond and yet related to the mechanical progress of the clock.

Furthermore, one notices in Sartre a tendency to deal with comparatively short periods of time in his novels. In fact, *The Age of Reason* conforms to the Aristotelian unity of time with its twenty-four hours of action. "If I pack six months into a

single page," Sartre wrote, "the reader jumps out of the book."[47]
The longest time period covered by Sartre in his four novels is
that of the probable five weeks in *Nausea*. On the contrary, a
brief period of time is never excessively expanded by Sartre.
Even the episodes within the novel as a whole reflect as little
as possible the intervention of the author in the matter of time.
The interview with Anny although marking an important turning point for Roquentin is given only a little more space than,
for instance, the visit to the museum. All this is in keeping with
Sartre's desire to prevent his books from pointing to the author,
"to hurl the reader into the midst of a universe where there are
no witnesses."[48]

And where there is—and we must return to this point in
conclusion—no past in the sense of memories and deeds in-
fluencing and dragging down the present. Sartre wants his
books to "remain in the air all by themselves."[49]

The "return to France," then, brings us to a radically
different concept of time. Although for Sartre the past may not
be reanimated nor does it persist, he like some of his predeces-
sors saw that life must be understood in its relation to death.
As the streaming of the rain in "Drôle d'amitié" may suggest
a rebirth, so also it is not chance that the resurrection theme,
the resurrection of HCE, of Mrs. Ramsay, of Ben Gant, of the
corporal, of Joseph, is a frequent one, for death is a part of
life and through acceptance of death man is transformed. The
fear of non-being may be faced through the knowledge that
Leopold Bloom acquires that one is neither first nor last in a
series extending to infinity. Each individual wave must break
on the shore, but it will be drawn again into the sea and new
waves formed. This is true both within the individual life and
within life itself. Combray may be revisited; the fountain
pulses forever in the square of Altamont; that July afternoon
in 1863 is part of every Southern youth; the steward Montkaw
forever hurries across the courtyard; castles and trials are part
of the existence of every man. Having faced non-being,

47. Sartre, *What Is Literature?* p. 229.
48. *Ibid.*, p. 169.
49. *Ibid.*

Virginia Woolf could say with Clarissa Dalloway, "I shall come back." And on the train, oppressed by the mechanical click of the wheels, Brunet, like Eugene Gant, finds that complete inner immobility is possible.

BIBLIOGRAPHY

The purpose of the bibliography is to give a thorough and reliable source of reference for works on the question of time and reality in the contemporary fiction covered in this book. Some of the books and articles that appear here have not been used in the footnotes.

BOOKS

Albérès, R.-M. *Jean-Paul Sartre.* Paris, 1953.
Alker, Ernest. *Franz Grillparzer, Ein Kampf um Leben und Kunst.* Marburg, 1930.
Anders, Günther. *Kafka Pro und Contra.* München, 1951.
Aristotle. *The Works of Aristotle,* ed. W. D. Ross. Oxford, 1930.
Atkins, John. *Aldous Huxley.* London, 1950.
Auerbach, Erich. *Mimesis: The Representation of Reality in Western Literature,* trans. Willard R. Trask. Princeton, New Jersey, 1953.
Autret, Jean. *L'Influence de Ruskin sur la vie, les idées et l'oeuvre de Marcel Proust.* Genève, 1955.
Baumann, Gerhart. *Franz Grillparzer.* Wien, 1954.
Beach, Joseph W. *American Fiction.* New York, 1941.
Beissner, Friedrich. *Der Erzähler Franz Kafka, ein Vortrag.* Stuttgart, 1952.
Bennett, Joan. *Virginia Woolf.* New York, 1945.
Bense, Max. *Die Theorie Kafka.* Berlin, 1952.
Bergson, Henri. *Creative Evolution.* trans. Arthur Mitchell. New York, 1944.

——. *Matter and Memory*, trans. Nancy M. Paul and W. Scott Palmer, London, n.d.

——. *Time and Free Will*, trans. F. L. Pogson. London, 1928.

Blackall, Eric. *Adalbert Stifter*. Cambridge, 1948.

Blackstone, Bernard. *Virginia Woolf: A Commentary*. New York, 1949.

Boden, Gerard. *Franz Kafka: Aspects de son oeuvre*. Alger, 1946.

Boisdeffre, Pierre de. *Metamorphose de la littérature*. 2 vols. Paris, 1951.

Bolle, Louis. *Les lettres et l'absolu, Valéry-Sartre-Proust*. Genève, 1959.

Bowra, Cecil M. *The Heritage of Symbolism*. London, 1943.

Bradley, F. H. *Appearance and Reality*. London, 1925.

——. *The Principles of Logic*. London, 1928.

Brée, Germaine. *Marcel Proust and Deliverance from Time*. London, 1956.

Brod, Max. *Franz Kafka, eine Biographie*. Berlin, 1954.

——. *Franz Kafkas Glauben und Lehre*. Winterthur, 1948.

——. *Verzweiflung und Erlösung im Werk Franz Kafkas*. Frankfurt am Main, 1959.

Brooke, Jocelyn. *Aldous Huxley*. Bibliographical Series of Supplements to *British Book News*. London, 1954.

Buddeberg, Else. *Heidegger und die Dichtung*. Stuttgart, 1953.

Campbell, Harry M., and Foster, Ruel E. *William Faulkner: A Critical Appraisal*. Norman, Oklahoma, 1951.

Campbell, Joseph, and Robinson, Henry Morton. *A Skeleton Key to "Finnegans Wake."* New York, 1944.

Campbell, Robert. *Jean-Paul Sartre où une littérature philosophique*. Paris, 1947.

Camus, Albert. *Le Myth de Sisyphe*. Paris, 1942.

Chambers, R. L. *The Novels of Virginia Woolf*. London, 1947.

Champigny, Robert. *Stages on Sartre's Way, 1938-52*. Bloomington, Indiana, 1959.

Chastaing, Maxime. *La philosophie de Virginia Woolf*. Paris, 1951.

Collins, Carvell. "The Interior Monologues of *The Sound and the Fury*," in *English Institute Essays, 1952*. Pp. 29-56.

Crémieux, Benjamin, *XXe siecle*. Paris, 1924.

Czoniczer, Elisabeth. *Quelques antécédents de "À la recherche du temps perdu."* Genève, 1957.

Daiches, David. *New Literary Values*. London, 1936.

——. *The Novel and the Modern World*. Chicago, 1939.

——. *Virginia Woolf*. Norfolk, Connecticut, 1942.

De Billy, Robert. *Marcel Proust lettres et conversations*. Paris, 1930.

Delakas, Daniel L. *Thomas Wolfe: La France et les romanciers français*. Paris, 1950.

Delattre, Floris. *Bergson et Proust: Accords et dissonances*. Paris, 1948.

——. *Le roman psychologique de Virginia Woolf*. Paris, 1932.

Desan, Wilfred. *The Tragic Finale*. Cambridge, Massachusetts, 1954.

Deutsch, Babette. *Poetry in Our Time*. New York, 1952.

Deutsche Literatur im zwanzigsten Jahrhundert, ed. Hermann Friedmann and Otto Mann. Heidelberg, 1954.

Dreyfus, Robert. *Souvenirs sur Marcel Proust*. Paris, 1926.

Dumesnil, René. *Gustave Flaubert*. Paris, 1932.

Dunne, J. W. *An Experiment with Time*. New York, 1927.

Edel, Leon. *The Psychological Novel*. New York, 1955.

Eichner, Hans. *Thomas Mann*. München, 1953.

Ellmann, Richard. *James Joyce*. New York, 1959.

Eloesser, Arthur. *Thomas Mann sein Leben und sein Werk*. Berlin, 1925.

Emrich, Wilhelm. *Franz Kafka*. Bonn, 1958.

Faesi, Robert. *Thomas Mann*. Zürich, 1955.

Farrell, James T. *The League of Frightened Philistines*. New York, 1945.

Faulkner, William. *Absalom, Absalom!* New York, 1951.

——. *A Fable*. New York, 1954.

——. *Go Down, Moses*. New York, 1942.

——. *Intruder in the Dust*. New York, 1948.

——. *Light in August*. New York, 1950.

——. *Mirrors of Chartres Street*. Minneapolis, Minnesota, 1953.

——. *Pylon*. New York, 1935.

——. *Sanctuary*. New York, 1932.

——. *Sartoris*. New York, 1929.

——. *The Sound and the Fury and As I Lay Dying*. New York, 1946.

——. *The Wild Palms*. New York, 1939.

Flaubert, Gustave. *Bouvard and Pécuchet*, introduction by Lionel Trilling, trans. T. W. Earp and G. W. Stonier. Norfolk, Connecticut, 1954.

——. *The Temptation of St. Anthony*, trans. Lafcadio Hearn. New York, 1910.

Frank, Joseph. "Spatial Form in Modern Literature," in *Critiques and Essays on Modern Fiction*, ed. John Aldridge. New York, 1952.

A Franz Kafka Miscellany: Pre-Fascist Exile. New York, 1940.

Franz Kafka Today, ed. Angel Flores and Homer Swander. Madison, Wisconsin, 1958.

Gilbert, Stuart. *James Joyce's "Ulysses."* New York, 1952.

Gray, Ronald. *Kafka's Castle.* Cambridge, 1956.

Grillparzer, Franz. *Grillparzers Werke in sechs Bänden,* ed. Eduard Castle. Wien, 1924.

——. *Tagebücher und literarische Skizzenhefte.* Wien, 1924.

Gruber, Ruth. *Virginia Woolf: A Study.* Leipzig, 1935.

Hafley, James. *The Glass Roof.* Berkeley and Los Angeles, California, 1954.

Hamburger, Käte. *Thomas Manns Roman "Joseph und seine Brüder."* Stockholm, 1945.

Hatfield, Henry. *Thomas Mann.* Norfolk, Connecticut, 1951.

Heidegger, Martin. *Sein und Zeit.* Tübingen, 1953.

Heller, Erich. *The Disinherited Mind.* Cambridge, 1952.

——. *The Ironic German.* Boston, 1958.

Hoffman, Frederick J. *Freudianism and the Literary Mind.* Baton Rouge, Louisiana, 1957.

Holtby, Winifred. *Virginia Woolf.* London, 1932.

Homer. *The Odyssey,* trans. E. V. Rieu. Harmondsworth, England, 1946.

Hubben, William. *Four Prophets of Our Destiny.* New York, 1952.

Hulme, T. E. *Speculations.* New York, 1924.

Humphrey, Robert. *Stream of Consciousness in the Modern Novel.* Berkeley, California, 1954.

Huxley, Aldous. *After Many a Summer Dies the Swan.* New York, 1939.

——. *Ape and Essence.* New York, 1948.

——. *Arabia Infelix and Other Poems.* New York, 1929.

——. *Collected Essays.* New York, 1959.

——. *The Devils of Loudun.* New York, 1952.

——. *Do What You Will.* London, 1949.

——. *Eyeless in Gaza.* New York, 1936.

——. *The Genius and the Goddess.* London, 1955.

——. *Limbo,* New York, n.d.

——. *Little Mexican.* London, 1948.

——. *The Perennial Philosophy.* New York, 1945.

——. *Point Counterpoint.* New York, 1947.

——. *Proper Studies.* New York, 1928.

——. *Those Barren Leaves.* New York, 1925.

——. *Time Must Have a Stop.* New York, 1944.

Hyman, Stanley Edgar. "Maude Bodkin and Psychological Criticism," in *Art and Psychoanalysis,* ed. William Phillips. New York, 1957. Pp. 473-501.

Isaacs, J. *An Assessment of Twentieth-Century Literature.* London, 1951.

Jäckel, Kurt. *Bergson und Proust.* Breslau, 1934.

Jacob, Gerhard. *Thomas Mann und Nietzsche, Zum Problem der Décadence.* University of Liepzig, Inaugural Dissertation, 1926.

James Joyce: Two Decades of Criticism, ed. Seon Givens. New York, 1948.

Jameson, Fredric. *Sartre: The Origins of a Style.* New Haven, Connecticut, 1961.

Janouch, Gustav. *Conversations with Kafka,* trans. Goronwy Rees. New York, 1953.

Jauss, Hans Robert. *Zeit und Erinnerung in Marcel Prousts "À la recherche du temps perdu."* Heidelberg, 1955.

Johnson, Edgar. *Charles Dickens: His Tragedy and Triumph,* 2 vols. New York, 1952.

Joyce, James. *Dubliners.* New York, 1926.

———. *Finnegans Wake.* New York, 1955.

———. *A Portrait of the Artist As a Young Man.* New York, 1928.

———. *Stephen Hero,* ed. Theodore Spencer. New York, 1944.

———. *Ulysses.* New York, The Modern Library, 1934.

Kafka, Franz. *America,* trans. Edwin and Willa Muir. London, 1938.

———. *Briefe, 1902-1924.* New York, Schocken Books, 1959.

———. *The Castle,* trans. Eithne Wilkins and Ernst Kaiser. New York, 1954.

———. *The Diaries of Franz Kafka, 1910-1913,* ed. Max Brod, trans. Joseph Kresh. New York, 1948.

———. *The Diaries of Franz Kafka, 1914-1923,* ed. Max Brod, trans. Martin Greenberg and Hannah Arendt. New York, 1949.

———. *The Great Wall of China: Stories and Reflections,* trans. Willa and Edwin Muir. New York, 1946.

———. *Letters to Milena,* ed. Willy Haas, trans. Tania and James Stern. London, 1953.

———. *The Penal Colony: Stories and Short Pieces,* trans. Willa and Edwin Muir. New York, 1948.

———. *The Trial,* trans. Willa and Edwin Muir. New York, 1957.

The Kafka Problem, ed. Angel Flores. New York, 1946.

Kain, Richard M. *Fabulous Voyager.* New York, 1959.

Kenner, Hugh. *Dublin's Joyce.* Bloomington, Indiana, 1956.

———. *The Invisible Poet: T. S. Eliot.* New York, 1959.

Kierkegaard, S. *Repetition,* trans. Walter Lowrie. Princeton, 1946.

Kilburn, P. E. *Ulysses in Catawba.* New York University, 1954.

Kolb, Philip. *La Correspondance de Marcel Proust*. Urbana, Illinois, 1949.

Lesser, Jonas. *Thomas Mann in der Epoche seiner Vollendung.* München, 1952.

Lewis, Wyndham. *Time and Western Man*. New York, 1928.

Lowrey, Perrin. "Concepts of Time in *The Sound and the Fury*," in *English Institute Essays, 1952*. Pp. 57-82.

McCole, C. John. *Lucifer at Large*. London, 1937.

Magalaner, Marvin, and Kain, Richard. *Joyce the Man, the Work, the Reputation*. New York, 1956.

Magny, Claude-Edmonde. "A Double Note on T. S. Eliot and James Joyce," in *T. S. Eliot: A Symposium*, ed. Richard March and Tambimuttu. London, 1948. Pp. 208-17.

——. "Faulkner où l'inversion théologique," in *L'âge du roman américain*. Paris, 1948. Pp. 196-243.

Mann, Thomas. *The Beloved Returns (Lotte in Weimar)*, trans. H. T. Lowe-Porter. New York, 1940.

——. *Betrachtung eines unpolitischen*. Frankfurt am Main, 1956.

——. *The Black Swan*, trans. Willard R. Trask. New York, 1954.

——. *Buddenbrooks*, trans. H. T. Lowe-Porter. 2 vols. New York, 1935.

——. *Confessions of Felix Krull*, trans. Denver Lindley. New York, 1955.

——. *Doctor Faustus*, trans. H. T. Lowe-Porter. New York, 1948.

——. *Die Entstehung des Doktor Faustus*. Amsterdam, 1949.

——. *Essays of Three Decades*, trans. H. T. Lowe-Porter. New York, 1947.

——. *The Holy Sinner*, trans. H. T. Lowe-Porter. New York, 1951.

——. *Joseph and His Brothers*, trans. H. T. Lowe-Porter. New York, 1938.

——. *Joseph in Egypt*, trans. H. T. Lowe-Porter. New York, 1938.

——. *Joseph the Provider*, trans. H. T. Lowe-Porter. New York, 1944.

——. *Last Essays*, trans. Richard and Clara Winston, Tania and James Stern. New York, 1959.

——. *The Magic Mountain*, trans. H. T. Lowe-Porter. New York, 1953.

——. *Royal Highness*, trans. A. Cecil Curtis. New York, 1916.

——. *A Sketch of My Life*, trans. H. T. Lowe-Porter. Paris, 1930.

——. *Stories of Three Decades*, trans. H. T. Lowe-Porter. New York, 1941.

——. *The Tables of the Law*, trans. H. T. Lowe-Porter. New York, 1945.

——. *The Theme of the Joseph Novels*. Washington, 1942.

——. *Three Essays*, trans. H. T. Lowe-Porter. London, 1932.

——. *The Transposed Heads*, trans. H. T. Lowe-Porter. New York, 1941.

——. *Young Joseph*, trans. H. T. Lowe-Porter. New York, 1935.

Marill-Albérès, René. *Jean-Paul Sartre: Philosopher without Faith.* New York, 1961.

Maurois, André. "Aldous Huxley," in *Prophets and Poets*. New York, 1935.

——. *Proust: Portrait of a Genius*, trans. Gerard Hopkins. New York, 1950.

May, Rollo. "Contributions of Existential Therapy," in *Existence*, ed. Rollo May, Ernest Angel, Henri F. Ellenberger. New York, 1958. Pp. 37-91.

Mayer, Hans. *Thomas Mann*. Berlin, 1950.

Mayoux, J.-J. "Le temps et la destinée chez Faulkner," in *La profondeur et le rhythme*. Cahiers du Collège Philosophique, 1948. Pp. 303-31.

Mendilow, A. A. *Time and the Novel*. London, 1952.

Meyerhoff, Hans. *Time in Literature*. Berkeley and Los Angeles, California, 1955.

More, Paul Elmer. "Nietzsche," in *Shelburne Essays*. 8th series. Boston, 1913. Pp. 147-90.

——. "Victorian Literature: The Philosophy of Change," in *Shelburne Essays*. 7th series. Boston, 1910. Pp. 245-69.

Muir, Edwin. *Transition*. New York, 1926.

Müller, Günther. *Die Bedeutung der Zeit in der Erzählkunst*. Bonn, 1947.

——. "Erzählzeit und Erzählte Zeit." *Festschrift Paul Kluckhohn und Hermann Schneider gewidmet zu ihrem 60. Geburtstag*. Tübingen, 1948.

Muller, Herbert J. *Thomas Wolfe*. Norfolk, Connecticut, 1947.

Muller, Maurice. *De Descartes à Marcel Proust*. Neuchâtel, 1947.

Murdoch, Iris. *Sartre: Romantic Rationalist*. New Haven, Connecticut, 1959.

Németh, André, *Kafka ou le mystère juif*, trans. Victor Hintz. Paris, 1947.

Painter, George. *Proust: The Early Years*. Boston, 1959.

Peacock, R. *Das Leitmotiv bei Thomas Mann*. Bern, 1934.

Pfister, Karin. *Zeit und Wirklichkeit bei Thomas Wolfe*. Heidelberg, 1954.

Philippe, Charles-Louis. *Bubu of Montparnasse*, trans. Laurence Vail. Paris, 1932.

Pierre-Quint, Léon. *Comment parut "Du côté de chez Swann."* Paris, 1930.

Pippett, Aileen. *The Moth and the Star.* Boston, 1955.

Pouillon, Jean. "Temps et destinée chez Faulkner," in *Temps et roman.* Paris, 1946. Pp. 238-60.

Poulet, Georges. *Studies in Human Time,* trans. Elliott Coleman. Baltimore, 1956.

Proust, Marcel. *À un ami.* Paris, 1948.

——. *Les cahiers Marcel Proust.* Paris, 1928-1932. Vols. IV-VI.

——. *The Captive,* trans. C. K. Scott Moncrieff. New York, 1929.

——. *Cities of the Plain,* trans. C. K. Scott Moncrieff. New York, 1927.

——. *Correspondance générale.* 6 vols. Paris, 1930-1936.

——. *The Guermantes Way,* trans. C. K. Scott Moncrieff. New York, 1925.

——. *Lettres à une amie.* Manchester, 1942.

——. *Swann's Way,* trans. C. K. Scott Moncrieff. New York, 1928.

——. *The Sweet Cheat Gone,* trans. C. K. Scott Moncrieff. New York, 1930.

——. *The Past Recaptured,* trans. F. A. Blossom, New York, 1932.

——. *Within a Budding Grove,* trans. C. K. Scott Moncrieff. New York, 1924.

Rehm, Walther. *Nachsommer zur Deutung von Stifters Dichtung.* Bern, 1951.

Reiss, H. S. *Franz Kafka Eine Betrachtung seines Werkes.* Heidelberg, 1952.

Rochefort, Robert. *Kafka oder die unzerstörbare Hoffnung,* trans. Hubert Greifeneder. Wien, 1955.

Rothman, Nathan L. "Thomas Wolfe and James Joyce: A Study in Literary Influence," in *A Southern Vanguard,* ed. Allen Tate. New York, 1947. Pp. 52-77.

Royce, Josiah. *The Conception of God.* New York, 1898.

——. *The Conception of Immortality.* Boston, 1900.

Rubin, Louis D., Jr. *Thomas Wolfe: The Weather of His Youth.* Baton Rouge, 1955.

Russell, Bertrand. *A Critical Exposition of the Philosophy of Leibniz.* London, 1900.

——. *Our Knowledge of the External World.* London, 1914.

——. *The Philosophy of Bergson.* London, 1914.

St. Augustine. *Confessions,* trans. E. B. Pusey. London, 1946.

Salvan, Jacques. *To Be And Not To Be.* Detroit, 1962.

Santayana, George. *Realms of Essence in the Works of George Santayana.* New York, 1937.

——. *Scepticism and Animal Faith in the Works of George Santayana.* New York, 1937.

Sartre, Jean-Paul. *The Age of Reason,* trans. Eric Sutton. New York, 1959.

——. *Being and Nothingness,* trans. Hazel E. Barnes. New York, 1956.

——. *Intimacy and Other Stories,* trans. Lloyd Alexander. London, 1950.

——. *Literary and Philosophical Essays,* trans. Annette Michelson. New York, 1955.

——. *Nausea,* trans. Lloyd Alexander. Norfolk, Connecticut, 1959.

——. *The Psychology of Imagination.* New York, 1950.

——. *The Reprieve,* trans. Eric Sutton. New York, 1947.

——. *Troubled Sleep,* trans. Gerard Hopkins. New York, 1961.

——. *What Is Literature?,* trans. Bernard Frechtman. London, 1950.

Savage, D. S. "Aldous Huxley and the Dissociation of Personality," *Critiques and Essays on Modern Fiction,* ed. John W. Aldridge. New York, 1952. Pp. 340-61.

Simon, Pierre-Henri. *L'homme en procès.* Neuchâtel, 1950.

Slochower, Harry. *Thomas Mann's Joseph Story.* New York, 1938.

——. *Three Ways of Modern Man.* New York, 1937.

Smidt, Kristian. *James Joyce and the Cultic Use of Fiction.* Oslo, 1955.

——. *Poetry and Belief in the Work of T. S. Eliot.* Oslo, 1949.

The Song of God: Bhagavad-Gita, trans. Swami Prabhavananda and Christopher Isherwood. New York, 1954.

Staiger, Emil. *Adalbert Stifter als Dichter der Ehrfurcht.* Ostern, 1943.

——. *Die Zeit als Einbildungskraft des Dichters.* Zürich, 1953.

The Stature of Thomas Mann, ed. Charles Neider. New York, 1947.

Sterne, Laurence. *Tristram Shandy.* New York, 1950.

Strong, L. A. G. *The Sacred River.* London, 1949.

Symons, Arthur. *The Symbolist Movement in Literature.* London, 1908.

Thieberger, Richard. *Der Begriff der Zeit bei Thomas Mann.* Baden-Baden, 1952.

Thody, Philip. *Jean-Paul Sartre.* London, 1960.

Thomas, R. Hinton. *Thomas Mann.* Oxford, 1956.

Tindall, William York. *James Joyce.* New York, 1950.

Troy, William. "Virginia Woolf: The Novel of Sensibility," in *Literary Opinion in America,* ed. M. D. Zabel. New York, 1937. Pp. 340-58.

Ussher, Arland. *Journey through Dread.* New York, 1955.

Vickery, Olga. *The Novels of William Faulkner.* Baton Rouge, 1959.

Ward, A. C. *The Nineteen-Twenties.* London, 1930.

Weigand, Hermann. *Thomas Mann's Novel "Der Zauberberg."* New York, 1933.

Weltsch, Felix. *Religiöser Humor bei Franz Kafka.* Winterthur, 1948.

Wiget, Erik, *Virginia Woolf und die Konzeption der Zeit in ihren Werken.* Zürich, 1949.

William Faulkner: Two Decades of Criticism, ed. Frederick J. Hoffman and Olga W. Vickery. East Lansing, Michigan, 1951.

Winterstein, Alfred. *Adalbert Stifter.* Wien, 1946.

Wolfe, Thomas. *From Death to Morning.* New York, 1935.

——. *The Hills Beyond.* New York, 1941.

——. *The Letters of Thomas Wolfe,* ed. Elizabeth Nowell, New York, 1956.

——. *Look Homeward, Angel.* New York, 1929.

——. *Of Time and the River.* New York, 1944.

——. *The Web and the Rock.* New York, 1939.

——. *You Can't Go Home Again.* New York, 1942.

Wolff, Hans M. *Thomas Mann.* Bern, 1957.

Woolf, Virginia. *Between the Acts.* New York, 1941.

——. *The Captain's Death Bed.* New York, 1950.

——. *The Common Reader.* London, 1925.

——. *The Common Reader. Second Series.* London, 1932.

——. *Granite and Rainbow.* London, 1958.

——. *A Haunted House and Other Short Stories.* New York, 1944.

——. *Jacob's Room.* New York, 1923.

——. *The Moment and Other Essays.* New York, 1948.

——. *Mrs. Dalloway.* New York, 1925.

——. *Night and Day.* New York, 1920.

——. *Orlando.* New York, 1928.

——. *A Room of One's Own.* New York, 1929.

——. *To the Lighthouse.* London, 1932.

——. *The Waves.* New York, 1931.

——. *A Writer's Diary.* New York, 1954.

——. *The Years.* New York, 1937.

PERIODICALS

Aitken, D. J. F. "Dramatic Archetypes in Joyce's *Exiles,*" *Modern Fiction Studies,* IV (Spring, 1958), 42-52.

Albrecht, W. P. "Time as Unity in Thomas Wolfe," *New Mexico Quarterly Review,* XIX (Autumn, 1949), 320-29.

Anders, Guenther. "Kafka: Ritual without Religion," *Commentary*, VIII (December, 1949), 560-69.

Angelloz, J. F. "Le 'Journal Quotidien' de Kafka et les 'Cahiers de Malte Laurids Briggs' de Rilke," *Mercure de France*, No. 1062 (February 1, 1952), 340-42.

Arland, Marcel. "Essais critiques," *La nouvelle revue française* LI (July 1, 1938), 129-33.

Astre, Georges-Albert. "Joyce et la durée," *L'âge nouveau*, No. 45 (January, 1950), 29-38.

Bandler, Bernard. "Joyce's *Exiles*," *Hound and Horn*, VI (January-March, 1933), 266-85.

Beebe, Maurice. "James Joyce: Barnacle Goose and Lapwing," *PMLA*, LXXI (June, 1956), 302-20.

Bianquis, Geneviève. "Le temps dans l'oeuvre de Thomas Mann," *Journal de psychologie normale et pathologique*, XLIV (January-June, 1951), 356-70.

Bishop, John Peale. "Finnegans Wake," *Southern Review*, V (1940), 439-52.

———. "The Sorrows of Thomas Wolfe," *Kenyon Review*, I (Winter, 1939), 3-17.

Blanchot, Maurice. "Les romans de Sartre," *L'Arche*, X, (October, 1945), 121-34.

Bouvard, Loïc. "Conversation with William Faulkner," *Modern Fiction Studies*, V (Winter, 1959-1960), 361-64.

Breton, M. le. "Temps et personne chez William Faulkner," *Journal de psychologie normale et pathologique*, XLIV (January-June, 1951), 344-54.

Brion, Marcel. "Thomas Wolfe," *Revue des deux mondes*, XVI (August 15, 1952), 731-40.

Brod, Max. "Über Franz Kafka," *Die literarische Welt*, II (June 4, 1926), 1.

Brown, E. K. "Thomas Wolfe: Realist and Symbolist," *University of Toronto Quarterly*, X (January, 1941), 153-66.

Brown, Stuart M., Jr. "The Atheistic Existentialism of Jean-Paul Sartre," *Philosophical Review*, LVII (March, 1948), 158-66.

Burnham, James. "Observations on Kafka," *Partisan Review*, XIV (March-April, 1947), 186-95.

Champigny, Robert. "Sens de *La Nausée*," *PMLA*, LXX (March, 1955), 37-46.

Cohn, Robert Greer. "Sartre vs. Proust," *Partisan Review*, XXVIII (November, 1961), 633-45.

Cuénot, Claude. "Littérature et philosophie chez J.-P. Sartre," *Renaissances*, XXI (May, 1946), 49-61.

Delattre, Floris. "La durée bergsonienne dans le roman de Virginia Woolf," *Revue Anglo-Américaine*, IX (December, 1931), 97-108.

Delhomme, Jeanne. "Le problème de l'intériorité: Bergson et J.-P. Sartre," *Revue internationale de philosophie*, No. 48 (1959), 201-19.

Doubrovsky, Serge. "Sartre and Camus: A Study in Incarceration," *Yale French Studies*, No. 25, pp. 85-92.

Fishman, Solomon. "Virginia Woolf of the Novel," *Sewanee Review*, LI (1943), 321-40.

Fitzmorris, Thomas J. "Vico Adamant and Some Pillars of Salt," *Catholic World*, CLVI (February, 1943), 568-77.

Fleming, Rudd. "Dramatic Involution: Tate, Husserl, and Joyce," *Sewanee Review*, LX (Summer, 1952), 445-64.

Friedman, Norman. "The Waters of Annihilation: Double Vision in *To the Lighthouse*," *English Literary History*, XXII (March, 1955), 61-79.

Friedrich, Otto C. "Der doppeldeutige Kafka," *Prisma*, No. 22 (1948), 8-9.

Fritz, Helen M. "Joyce and Existentialism," *James Joyce Review*, II (Spring-Summer, 1958), 13-21.

Frohock, W. M. "Thomas Wolfe: Of Time and Neurosis," *Southwest Review*, XXXIII (1948), 349-60.

Gamble, Isabel. "The Secret Sharer in 'Mrs. Dalloway,' " *Accent*, XVI (Autumn, 1956), 235-51.

Girard, René, "Existentialism and Criticism," *Yale French Studies*, XVI (Winter, 1955-1956), 45-52.

Graham, John. "Time in the Novels of Virginia Woolf," *University of Toronto Quarterly*, XVIII (January, 1949), 186-201.

Grubbs, Henry A. "Sartre's Recapturing of Lost Time," *Modern Language Notes*, LXXIII (November, 1958), 515-22.

Gürster, Eugen. "Das Weltbild Franz Kafkas," *Hochland*, XLIV (April, 1952), 326-37.

Guyot, Charly. "Notes sur Henri Bergson et les lettres françaises," *Revue internationale de philosophie*, No. 48 (1959), 249-71.

Haas, Willy. "Meine Meinung," *Literarische Welt*, II (June 4, 1926), 1-2.

Hartley, Lodowick. "Of Time and Mrs. Woolf," *Sewanee Review*, XLVII (April-June, 1939), 235-41.

Havard-Williams, Peter and Margaret. "Mystical Experience in Virginia Woolf's *The Waves*," *Essays in Criticism*, IV (January, 1954), 71-84.

Heselhaus, Clemens. "Kafkas Erzählformen," *Deutsche Vierteljahrs-*

schrift für Literaturwissenschaft und Geistesgeschichte, XXVI (1952), 353-76.

Higginson, Fred H. "Homer: Vico: Joyce," *Kansas Magazine* (1956), 83-88.

Hubben, William. "Kafka's Apocalyptic Message," *Christian Century*, LXIV (October 1, 1947), 1171-73.

Humphrey, Robert. "The Form and Function of Stream of Consciousness in William Faulkner's 'The Sound and the Fury,'" *University of Kansas City Review*, XIX (Autumn, 1952), 34-40.

Hyppolite, Jean. "Du Bergsonisme à l'existentialisme," *Mercure de France*, No. 1031 (July, 1949), 403-16.

Jackson, Elizabeth R. "The Genesis of Involuntary Memory in Proust's Early Works," *PMLA*, LXXVI (December, 1961), 586-94.

Joad, C. E. M. "Philosophy and Aldous Huxley," *The Realist* (July 1, 1929), 99-114.

Kahler, Erich. "Thomas Mann's 'Doctor Faustus,'" *Commentary*, VII (April, 1949), 348-57.

——. "Untergang und Übergang der epischen Kunstform," *Die Neue Rundschau*, LXIV (1953), 1-44.

Kahn, Ernst. "Sartre the Philosopher and Writer," *Contemporary Review*, CXCVI (November, 1959), 243-45.

Kaufmann, Fritz. "Thomas Mann und Nietzsche," *Monatschefte für deutschen Unterricht*, XXXVI (November, 1944), 345-50.

Kelly, John. "Franz Kafka's 'Trial' and the Theology of Crisis," *Southern Review*, V (Spring, 1940), 748-66.

Kirkwood, M. M. "The Thought of Aldous Huxley," *University of Toronto Quarterly*, VI (January, 1937), 189-98.

Klein, A. M. "A Shout in the Street," *New Directions*, XIII (1951), 327-45.

Kohler, Dayton. "Time and the Modern Novel," *College English*, X (October, 1948), 15-24.

Kumar, Shiv K. "Bergson and Stephen Dedalus' Aesthetic Theory," *Journal of Aesthetics and Art Criticism*, XVI (September, 1957), 124-27.

——. "Memory in Virginia Woolf and Bergson," *University of Kansas City Review*, XXVI (Spring, 1960), 235-39.

——. "Space-Time Polarity in *Finnegans Wake*," *Modern Philology*, LIV (May, 1957), 230-33.

Leavis, F. R. "Eliot's Later Poetry," *Scrutiny*, XI (Summer, 1942), 60-71.

Lemaître, Henri. "Proust et Ruskin," *Pyrénnées*, No. 16 (January-February, 1944), 311-97.

Lerner, Max. "Franz Kafka and the Human Voyage," *Saturday Review of Literature*, XXIV (June 7, 1941), 3-4, 16-17.

Levin, Richard, and Shattuck, Charles. "First Flight to Ithaca," *Accent*, IV (Winter, 1944), 75-99.

Luke, F. D. "Kafka's 'Die Verwandlung,'" *Modern Language Review*, LXVI (April, 1951), 232-45.

McElderry, B. R., Jr. "Wolfe and Emerson on 'Flow,'" *Modern Fiction Studies*, II (May, 1956), 77-78.

Magalaner, Marvin. "James Joyce and the Myth of Man," *Arizona Quarterly*, IV (Winter, 1948), 300-9.

——. "The Myth of Man: Joyce's *Finnegans Wake*," *University of Kansas City Review*, XVI (Summer, 1950), 265-77.

Mann, Thomas. "The Years of My Life," *Harper's Magazine*, CCI (1950), 250-64.

Martz, Louis L. "The Wheel and the Point," *Sewanee Review*, LV (January-March, 1947), 126-47.

Mayoux, J.-J. "La création du réel chez William Faulkner," *Études anglaises*, V (February, 1952), 25-39.

——. "Le roman de l'espace et du temps Virginia Woolf," *Revue Anglo-Américaine*, VII (April, 1930), 312-26.

Moses, W. R. "The Unity of *The Wild Palms*," *Modern Fiction Studies*, II (Autumn, 1956), 125-31.

——. "Where History Crosses Myth: Another Reading of 'The Bear,'" *Accent*, XIII (Winter, 1953), 21-33.

Muir, Edwin. "A Note on Franz Kafka," *Bookman*, LXII (November, 1930), 235-41.

Müller, Günther. "Über das Zeitgerust des Erzählens," *Vierteljahrsschrift für Literaturwissenschaft und Geistesgeschichte*, XXIV (1950), 1-31.

——. "Zeiterlebnis und Zeitgerust in der Dichtung," *Studium Generale*, VIII (November, 1955), 594-601.

O'Brien, Justin. "La mémoire involontaire avant Marcel Proust," *Revue de littérature comparée*, XIX (1936), 19-36.

Paul, David. "Time and the Novelist," *Partisan Review*, XXI (November-December, 1954), 636-49.

Petitjean, Armand M. "Joyce and Mythology: Mythology and Joyce," *Transition*, No. 23 (July, 1935), 133-42.

Phillips, William, "The Great Wall of Criticism," *Commentary*, III (June, 1947), 594-96.

Politzer, Heinz. "Message of the King," *Commentary*, VIII (July, 1949), 93-98.

——. "Problematik und Probleme der Kafka-Forschung," *Monatschefte*, XLII (October, 1950), 273-80.

Pouillon, Jean. "William Faulkner, un témoin," *Les temps modernes*, II (October, 1946), 172-78.

Pritchett, V. S. "Time Frozen," *Partisan Review*, XXI (September-October, 1954), 557-61.

Proust, Robert. "Marcel Proust intime," *La nouvelle revue française*, XXIII (January, 1923), 25.

Rahv, Philip. "The Death of Ivan Ilyich and Joseph K.," *Southern Review*, V (Summer, 1939), 174-85.

——. "Franz Kafka: The Hero as Lonely Man," *Kenyon Review*, I (Winter, 1939), 60-74.

Rehm, Walther. "Wirklichkeitsdemut und Dingmystik," *Logos*, XIX (1930), 297-358.

Reichmann, Peter. "Franz Kafka and New Trends in Europe," *Canadian Bookman*, XXI (June-July, 1939), 17-19.

Reiss, H. S. "Franz Kafka's Conception of Humour," *Modern Language Review*, LXIV (October, 1949), 534-42.

Rice, Philip Blair. "The Merging Parallels: Mann's 'Dr. Faustus,'" *Kenyon Review*, XI (Spring, 1949), 199-217.

Roberts, John Hawley. "Towards Virginia Woolf," *Virginia Quarterly Review*, X (1934), 587-602.

——. "'Vision and Design' in Virginia Woolf," *PMLA*, LXI (September, 1946), 835-47.

Rubin, Louis. "Thomas Wolfe in Time and Place," *Hopkins Review*, VI (Winter, 1953), 117-32.

Saisselin, Rémy G. "Bouville où l'anti-Combray," *French Review*, XXXIII (January, 1960), 232-38.

Sartre, Jean-Paul. "Drôle d'amitié," *Les temps modernes*, V (November, 1949), 769-806; V (December, 1949), 1009-39.

Savage, D. S. "Franz Kafka: Faith and Vocation," *Sewanee Review*, LIV (Spring, 1946), 222-40.

Slochower, Harry. "Freud and Marx in Contemporary Literature," *Sewanee Review*, XLIX (April-June, 1941), 316-24.

——. "Goethe the Nourisher," *The New Republic*, XIII (October 14, 1940), 532.

——. "The Limitations of Franz Kafka," *American Scholar* (Summer, 1946), 291-97.

——. "Mann's Latest Novels," *Accent*, IV (Summer, 1943), 3-8.

——. "A Psychology of Myth," *Quarterly Review of Literature*, II (Fall, 1944), 74-77.

——. "Thomas Mann and Universal Culture," *Southern Review*, IV (April, 1939), 726-44.

Spann, Meno. "Die Beiden Zettel Kafkas," *Monatschefte*, LXVII (November, 1955), 321-28.

Spiegelberg, Herbert. "French Existentialism: Its Social Philosophies," *Kenyon Review,* XVI (Summer, 1954), 446-62.

Steinberg, Erwin. "A Book with Molly in It," *James Joyce Review,* II (Spring-Summer, 1958), 55-61.

Stern, Alfred. "Sartre and French Existentialism," *The Personalist,* XXIX (January, 1948), 17-31.

Swiggart, Peter. "Moral and Temporal Order in *The Sound and the Fury*," *Sewanee Review,* LXI (Spring, 1953), 221-37.

Thomas, Douglas M. "Memory-Narrative in *Absalom, Absalom!*" *Faulkner Studies,* II (Summer, 1953), 19-22.

Tindall, William York. "James Joyce and the Hermetic Tradition," *Journal of the History of Ideas,* XV (January, 1954), 23-39.

———. "Many-Leveled Fiction: Virginia Woolf to Ross Lockridge," *College English,* X (November, 1948), 65-71.

———. "The Symbolic Novel," *A. D.,* III, (Winter, 1952), 56-68.

Todd, Olivier. "Jean-Paul Sartre on His Autobiography," *The Listener,* LVII (June 6, 1957), 915-16.

Troy, William. "Notes on *Finnegans Wake*," *Partisan Review,* VI (Summer, 1939), 97-110.

Uyttersprot, Hermann. "Zur Struktur von Kafkas 'Der Prozess,'" *Revue des Langues Vivantes* (1953), 332-76.

———. "Zur Struktur von Kafkas Romanen," *Revue des Langues Vivantes* (1954), 367-83.

Vial, Fernand. "Le symbolisme bergsonien de temps dans l'oeuvre de Proust," *PMLA,* LV (December, 1940), 1191-1212.

Wagner, Geoffrey. "Wyndham Lewis and James Joyce: A Study in Controversy," *South Atlantic Quarterly,* LVI (January, 1957), 57-66.

Warren, Austin. "Kosmos Kafka," *Southern Review,* VII (Autumn, 1941), 350-65.

Weltsch, Felix. "Franz Kafkas Metarealismus," *Die literarische Welt,* II (June 4, 1926), 4.

Will, Frederic. "Sartre and the Question of Character in Literature," *PMLA,* LXXVI (September, 1961), 455-60.

Wilson, Edmund. "H. C. Earwicker and Family," *New Republic,* XCIX (June 28, 1939), 203-6.

Wilson, J. S. "Time and Virginia Woolf," *Virginia Quarterly Review,* XVIII (Spring, 1942), 267-76.

Wolfe, Thomas. "Boom Town," *American Mercury* (May, 1943), pp. 21-39.

———. "The Story of a Novel," *Saturday Review of Literature* (December 14, 1935), 3-44; (December 21, 1935), 3-44; (December 28, 1935), 3-44.

———. "A Western Journey," *Virginia Quarterly Review*, XV (Summer, 1939), 335-57.

Wright, Nathalia. "Mrs. Dalloway: A Study in Composition," *College English*, V (April, 1944), 351-58.

Zink, Karl E. "The Imagery of Stasis in Faulkner's Prose," *PMLA*, LXXI (June, 1956), 285-301.

Zorn, Marilyn. "The Pageant in *Between the Acts*," *Modern Fiction Studies*, II (February, 1956), 31-35.

INDEX